Agriculture and
Community Change
in the U.S.

Rural Studies Series

†Available in paperback.

Agriculture and Community Change in the U.S.
The Congressional Research Reports

edited by Louis E. Swanson

Westview Press / **Boulder and London**

Rural Studies Series, Sponsored by the Rural Sociological Society

This Westview softcover edition is printed on acid-free paper and bound in softcovers that carry the highest rating of the National Association of State Textbook Administrators. in consultation with the Association of American Publishers and the Book Manufacturers' Institute.

Published in 1988 in the United States of America by Westview Press, Inc., 5500 Central Avenue, Boulder. Colorado 80301. and in the United Kingdom by Westview Press. Inc.. 13 Brunswick Centre, London WC1N 1AF. England

Library of Congress Cataloging-in-Publication Data
Agriculture and community change in the U.S.
  (Rural Studies Series)
  1. United States—Rural conditions—Longitudinal
studies. 2. Agricultural and state—United States—
Longitudinal studies. 3. Agricultural innovations—
United States—Longitudinal studies. I. Swanson.
Louis E. II. Series.
HN59.2.A37 1988   307.7′2′0973   87-25245
ISBN 0-8133-7452-9

Printed and bound in the United States of America

10   9   8   7   6   5   4   3   2   1

Dedicated to the memory of my brother
and two very close friends:

Charles Louis Swanson II

Charles Chase Pratt

Charles Swanson Perry

Contents

About the Editor
and Contributors

Frederick H. Buttel is Professor of Rural Sociology in the Department of Rural Sociology at Cornell University. He is currently working on the implications of biotechnology for genetic resource conservation. His long term interests are in the sociology of agriculture and rural development.

David L. Chicoine is Professor of Agricultural Economics and Chair of the Department of Agricultural Economics and Rural Sociology at the University of Illinois. His research interests include a focus upon taxation and support for community services in rural areas.

Cornelia Butler Flora is Professor of Sociology in the Department of Sociology, Anthropology, and Social Work at Kansas State University. Her accomplishments include being President of the Rural Sociological Society (1988-89). She is especially interested in international development, including Farming Systems Research and women in development issues, as well as comparative domestic and international community change.

Jan L. Flora is Professor of Sociology in the Department of Sociology, Anthropology, and Social Work at Kansas State University. As a rural sociologist his work specializes in agrarian structures and community and rural change in the United States and developing countries.

Mark A. **Flotow** at the time of this research was a research
assistant in the Department of Agricultural Economics and Rural
Sociology at the University of Illinois. Presently, he is the
Illinois state demographer and works in Springfield, Illinois.

Mark Lancelle at the time of this research was Assistant
Professor of Rural Sociology at Cornell University. Currently, he
is working as a carpenter in a construction cooperative in the
Ithaca, New York, area.

David R. Lee is Associate Professor of Agricultural Economics
at Cornell University. His research interests include a close
examination of the relationships between New York state
agriculture and the world food economy.

Dean MacCannell is Professor of Community Studies and
Sociology at the University of California, Davis. His research on
irrigation public policy, the 180 acres limitation issue, and the
consequences for rural community development in the Central
Valley of California has been nationally acclaimed.

Michael J. Phillips was the project director for the Office of
Technology Assessment's report on *Technology, Public Policy,
and the Changing Structure of American Agriculture.*

Jerry R. Skees is Associate Professor of Agriculture Economics
at the University of Kentucky. His public policy research
includes work on farm and rural development policy and on
federal crop insurance policy.

Louis E. Swanson is Associate Professor of Sociology at the
University of Kentucky. His research has focused upon the
sociology of agriculture and agricultural and rural development
policy.

John C. van Es is Professor of Rural Sociology in the
Department of Agricultural Economics and Rural Sociology at
the University of Illinois. His present research interests are in
agricultural resource conservation and rural economic
development.

Foreword

American agriculture and rural communities are undergoing significant change and stress. Much of the recent change has been attributed to the financial crisis caused mainly by declining international markets for American agricultural products. However, underlying these financial difficulties are strong technological and structural forces which will cause further changes and adjustments in American agriculture and rural communities for the remainder of this century.

Congress, concerned about the nature of these adjustments, requested the Office of Technology Assessment (OTA) to analyze the underlying technological, structural, and political forces which impact American agriculture and to determine the probable future direction of the industry. Once the analysis was completed, a report entitled **Technology, Public Policy, and the Changing Structure of American Agriculture** was transmitted to Congress. In the course of conducting this study, OTA formed many technical working groups and commissioned numerous analytical papers. One such group was the rural communities work group. And the papers generated by this group are the subject of this book.

An early recognition by all of us involved in the study was that the impacts of technological and structural change in agriculture do not end with the individuals who live and work on farms. A variety of other consequences are to be expected in those rural communities that have direct and indirect linkages to farms and farmers. As with individual farmers, some communities are likely to benefit from change, while others are likely to be affected adversely.

Those rural communities that benefit from changes in agricultural technology and structure may do so in several ways. For example, as farming becomes more concentrated, some communities will emerge as areawide centers for the provision of new, high-value technical services and products. Likewise, some communities will emerge as centers for high-volume food packaging, processing, and distribution. In both cases, the economic base of these communities is likely to expand. However, centralization of services, marketing, and processing will be like a zero-sum game: the market or trade centers will benefit at the expense of other communities. Many of the communities that are bypassed will decline as a result of the process of centralization.

A landmark study that addressed the relationship between increased concentration in agriculture and community welfare was conducted by Walter Goldschmidt in 1944. Goldschmidt found a series of negative social effects associated with large-scale agriculture in the central valley of California. His research was based on a matched-pair comparison of a community of relatively large farms (Arvin) and a community of relatively small farms (Dinuba). He found higher median family income, lower poverty, better schools, more retail trade and stronger institutions associated with the set of small farms surrounding Dinuba. Although numerous methodological and theoretical criticisms have been made about this study, the thesis of this study continues to frame the discussion of structure and community relationships. A major question posed about the study is whether the findings can be generalized for the country as a whole.

The structure of agriculture and the characteristics of rural communities vary greatly across the United States, owing to major differences in soils, climate, population density, pattern of land use, economic and social history, availability of water, topography, availability of labor, and the level of education of the population. Therefore, it could be expected that changes in agricultural structure would vary in different parts of the country and that the impacts of structural change on rural communities may vary in different regions. To test this hypothesis, OTA commissioned papers analyzing five regions of the United States: the Northeast, South, Midwest, the Great Plains and the West; and the CATF (those counties with the most industrialized agriculture in four southern and western states — California, Arizona, Texas, and Florida).

This book contains the papers commissioned for each of the five regions. They are authored by highly regarded rural sociologists and agricultural economists. The papers clearly indicate that the relationship between the structure of agriculture and characteristics of rural communities do vary greatly in the United States. Some regions, such as the CATF, clearly show an inverse relationship. That is, as scale continues to increase beyond a size that can be worked and managed by a family, the quality of community life begins to deteriorate. On the other hand, in regions like the Northeast the results indicate that structural change in agriculture is not likely to have a great impact on rural communities.

These very valuable papers show that it is difficult to generalize across regions of the United States about the impacts of changing agricultural technology and structure on rural communities. As a consequence, policies designed to prevent or ameliorate adverse impacts or promote beneficial impacts will run the risk of being inappropriate unless they are crafted with consideration for regional differences.

It was my distinct pleasure to have worked closely with the authors of these papers. This collection of papers represents the first analytical approach to understanding the relationships of technological and structural change to rural communities on a national basis. It is my hope that these papers will encourage research by others to provide more information to a society which must eventually decide the fate of rural communities in America.

Michael J. Phillips

1
Farm and Community Change: A Brief Introduction to the Regional Studies

Louis E. Swanson

The prevailing hypothesis in the farm and community change literature has been that a rural community's well-being is a function of its farming hinterland. The converse of this assumption, that nonfarm socioeconomic factors associated with community rural well-being might influence farm well-being, has only recently received wide-spread attention. The traditional *unicausal* assumption that farm structure shapes rural community well-being is grounded in times past when most areas of rural America were characterized by a majority of owner-operators, whether family farmers or small town entrepreneurs. It was this class of rural people, and their agrarian and individualist value system that shaped America's populist ideology. This political tradition asserts various forms of agrarian fundamentalism, including the primacy of the family farm over rural communities, as the economic, social, and moral backbone of not only rural areas, but of the nation.

Before World War II there is considerable evidence that this unicausal assumption was not far from reality. Merrington (1978:151) argues that the preindustrial "agrarian economy established the historical limits of town development," for all types of preindustrial modes of production. Braudel (1973) adds that while agricultural trade centers were the focus of economic activities and social functions, nonetheless they were dependent upon local trade often based upon the barter of goods and services. Consequently, rural communities nestled in regions characterized by preindustrial production tended to be self-contained production-consumption units, with the primary unit being the farm family. Their persistence depended upon material

conditions created locally. The quality of these material
conditions rested upon the local human and natural resources.

In the Northeast, Midwest, and South the shift from a
yeoman family farm structure toward a commercial family farm
structure involved several significant social structural
transformations. Rather than producing for their own use and
limited local consumption, commercial family farms were
socially and technically organized for specialized commodity
production. This reorganization contributed to a realignment in
the relationship among people in farming, especially among
family members. The relationship between farmers and the local
trade center also changed. Farmers found that new local financial and trade institutions such as the bank and granary had
greater leverage over their livelihood. Those farmers who were
unable to finance their debts for whatever reason moved from a
family farm status toward tenancy or hired labor—whether in
the farm or nonfarm sector (Mooney, 1983).

The transformation to a dependency upon commercial agricultural trade introduced in some cases new and in all cases
greater class divisions than had characterized the noncommercial
period. An ancillary phenomenon of importance to the future
relationship between the farming hinterland and the rural trade
center was a steady subordination of farm and community relations to expanding nonfarm employment.

This latter phenomenon represents the gradual decoupling of
the well-being of rural communities from the fortunes of the
farming hinterland. Certainly in those regions of the nation
where farming is the primary economic base for the rural
economy the characteristics of the farming hinterland will be
the principal influence upon community well-being. But, the
tendency nationally is for rural economies to shed this type of
economic dependency for another type, one in which manufacturing, government, and service employment structures are
dominant.

These fundamental shifts in the economic structure of most
rural economies, as emphasized above, did not occur by accident
but were closely associated with the development of regional
and national market infrastructures. As the industrial and
agricultural output increased so too did the expansion of roads,
canals, and railroads. As underdeveloped, and in some cases
nonexistent, internal home markets developed, there simultaneously emerged a spatial and market hierarchy of trade centers
within regions. This spatial reorganization of rural areas greatly

influenced the abilities of trade centers to survive the modernization process. Position within the emerging trade network as well as the size of the trade center have proven to be critical factors in determining community survivability—factors that for the most part are outside the control of a trade center's inhabitants.

Of course, many areas of the South, Southwest, and West historically have been dominated by very large agricultural operations, including the old slave plantations, haciendas, and capitalist (industrial) farms. In these areas rural communities were also highly influenced by the relations of production of their agricultural hinterland, and as Goldschmidt's and MacCannell's work confirm, with highly adverse consequences.

Today, it is not possible to describe an archetypical American rural community, or even a typical rural region, given the economic diversification experienced by most rural communities during the past century. As Warren (1973) has described, horizontal linkages within local society have given way to vertical linkages with the larger society. Most rural communities have experienced a sharp decline in their dependence upon farming. It now is evident that the viability of the rural community's nonfarm economy may account for the persistence of smaller commercial family farms, as these farm families increasingly rely upon off-farm employment. Indeed, the great majority of rural people are not principally employed in farming. In 1984, national rural employment was distributed as follows: manufacturing, 39.5 percent; service and trade, 16.5 percent; government, 13 percent; farming (including hired labor), 9.1 percent; and mining, 5.7 percent (Henry, Drabenstott, and Gibson, 1986). At the beginning of this great change in rural community organization it would have been hard to comprehend an employment structure where more people would be employed by various levels of government, primarily public school employees, than in farming.

The Farm and Community Literature

There are numerous studies that examine the supposed impact of farm change on trade centers. Most of these studies propose that as farm structure becomes more concentrated rural communities will experience a decline in their economic and social well-being. Goss (1978:II.39) has succinctly summarized these assumptions:

The root cause of the decline in smaller places has been with technological change and farm size expansion and their immediate consequences of labor displacement, farm out-migration and a decrease in the density of people on the land . . . A decrease in the number of farms and density of farm people reduces the aggregate demand for [economic and social] functions, and consequently the need for nonfarm persons responsible for supplying such goods and services.

However, there are few empirical studies that examine how declining farm numbers and people and the changing farm workplace influence trade center change within the context of other regional economic and social change. While Goss implicitly seems to be assuming that agricultural technological change is responsible for these adverse effects for community well-being--the notion that the *mechanization of agriculture* has caused farm concentration—in another paper with Rodefeld (Goss and Rodefeld, 1978), he proposes that technological changes, at best, have only an indirect influence upon community change. Instead, Goss and Rodefeld believe that the influence of technological change is mediated through particular types of farm structure. Another viewpoint would be that technology, rather than an antecedent and autonomous cause of farm con-centration, reflects farmers' efforts to adopt the powers of technology in order to improve their position, or, at worst, not lose ground, in a highly competitive farm market. [The influence of technology is developed with some detail in Chapter 6 by Skees and Swanson.]

Ecological studies of the impact of farm change on nonme-tropolitan counties report that counties with a preponderance of small-scale family farms have usually experienced population loss as farms have become more concentrated (Frisbie and Poston, 1977). Between 1960 and 1970, these predominantly agricultural counties were more likely to have outmigration. Similar ecological analyses of community population change also identify an inverse relationship with increased farm concentra-tion. Munoz and Flinn (1977) examined both incorporated and unincorporated places in Ohio for the period 1930 to 1970, using county-level agricultural data. They found that increases in average farm size and value of farm land, and decline in farm residents were associated with community population decline. They also noted that increased part-time farming was positively associated with place population change, indicating that as part-time farming becomes more prevalent in a county, smaller places are less likely to decline in population. Their findings also suggest that during this period, in those counties where farming coexists with other economic activities, the farm population is more likely to be stable.

Very few studies of the relationship between the farm sector and the community focus upon direct indicators of the economic viability and quality of life of the community. Instead, most studies use change in population size as a surrogate for community well-being. These studies assume that those places experiencing an increase in population size are more viable than those places losing population. This assumption, may not always hold true, and as the nonmetropolitan turn-around of the 1970s demonstrated, may be quite misleading. Among the few studies that do focus on economic viability and social well-being, Goldschmidt's (1978) 1944 case study of two California farming communities is the acclaimed center-piece.

Goldschmidt selected Arvin and Dinuba according to what he believed were similar ecological characteristics. He pointed out that both towns were satellites of large metropolitan centers, relied upon agricultural production, and were dependent upon irrigation systems. Arvin's hinterland tended to produce row crops like cotton, while Dinuba's grew tree crops and vegetables. The major difference between these two farming centers were the structure of the farms in their hinterlands. Arvin was dominated by a few large, industrial-type farms characterized by absentee ownership and a dependence upon hired labor. Dinuba primarily consisted of family farms and larger-than-family farms (though Goldschmidt referred to all of these as "family" farms). Goldschmidt's dependent variables were economic indicators of retail vitality and social indicators of quality of life. He reported an astonishing array of differences between Arvin and Dinuba, and attributed these variations to the different farm structures in their hinterlands. Goldschmidt concluded that because Dinuba, with its relative dependence upon a family farm hinterland, had demonstrated more economic and social vitality than Arvin, with its industrial farm hinterland, that the differences were due to farm structure. By implication, Goldschmidt proposed that as farms become more concentrated and assume an industrial workplace structure, the quality of economic and social well-being within the community will decline.

The Goldschmidt study has been loosely replicated in recent years. Petterson (1977), reports that the major differences between Arvin and Dinuba continue to persist. Fujimoto (1977) expanded Goldschmidt's study to an ecological analysis of 130 places in eight counties within the San Joaquin Valley. Again, Goldschmidt's findings were confirmed. Places dominated by large-scale agriculture had fewer economic and social amenities.

Rodefeld (1974) examined how increased farm scale and workplace differentiation influenced the character of Wisconsin farm people and the ways they participate in local society. He found some support for Goldschmidt's general hypothesis that the rationalization of the farm labor process eventually leads to undesirable community characteristics. Rodefeld's findings included significant differences among three status groups: owner-managers, hired managers, and hired laborers. Owner-managers (i.e., traditional family farmers) were more likely to have high rates of participation in community organizations, whereas hired laborers generally did not participate in community organizations.

Flora, Brown, and Conboy (1977) also attempted to roughly test Goldschmidt's basic theses. However, their results provide evidence that the Goldschmidt hypothesis is not generalizable to all regions. They report two general findings. First, while counties with a higher concentration of industrial-type farms were positively related to overall county wealth, there was a negative association between the amount of wealth created and the equity of income distribution. Therefore, the more a county's farm structure had an industrial character, the higher the proportion of hired farm laborers as a proportion of all persons employed in agriculture. These results suggest that a large number of low-wage hired laborers were dependent upon a small number of large farming operations. However, their second finding was less consistent. They report that as the ratio of hired farm labor increased relative to the number of owner-operators, county and per capita income also rose. While there may be numerous methodological problems such as ecological fallacy that might account for this finding, it is doubtful that the general relationship would be changed. This study clearly presents an anomalous case for the Goldschmidt theses.

Another study of farm and population change which is not totally consistent with the Goldschmidt thesis is Swanson's

(1982) study of Pennsylvania for the period 1930-1960. Swanson identified 520 rural trade centers and their farming hinterlands in the thirty counties having the largest proportion of their labor force employed in agriculture in 1930. The empirical results suggest that declining farm numbers was not significantly associated with trade center population change during the thirty year period. However, as the average farm scale, measured in total acres harvested, increased, trade center population increased. Swanson attributed this apparently contradictory finding to the small average increase in acres harvested per farm of about 16 acres. Family farms could have mechanized their operations, thus extending their labor, which would mean that increased farm scale was not necessarily associated with changes in farm structure. In other words, while the total number of farms declined and farm scale increased slightly, the hinterlands of these trade centers continued to be dominated by family farms.

The most interesting finding of Swanson's study was that regional economic changes were the primary factors influencing trade center population change and farm change. His study suggested that changes in trade center population and farm structure were influenced by changes in regional nonfarm economy. This observation offers some support for the hypothesis that as a regional economy becomes more developed, its economic and social institutions will have a greater influence on community change than will changes in the farming hinterland. Furthermore, because the introduction of these nonfarm economic activities provide off-farm employment opportunities for the farm population, smaller farms that might otherwise go out of production can continue to operate if one or more members of these farms works off the farm. The availability of part-time farming as an option to leaving farming provides a means for family farm persistence even during a period of rapid farm concentration nationally. This does not mean that the decision to enter part-time farming is a happy one, but it might be seen as a better option than going out of production.

Similarly, Harris and Gilbert (1982) also report findings inconsistent with the Goldschmidt hypothesis. These researchers attempted to test whether this assumption held for nonmetropolitan Michigan counties, utilizing rural income as the dependent variable. Indeed, they found that the converse of the hypothesis was the case. That is, they found that the total effect of large scale farming and rural income were positively associated, thus indicating that has farm scale of a county increased so too did the measure of rural income.

Green's (1985) study of Missouri nonmetropolitan counties between 1934 and 1978 also presents important exceptions to the general Goldschmidt study. This research supports the Gold-schmidt hypothesis to the extent that the size of the population in rural Missouri is influenced by changes in farm numbers, but change in farm scale is not of importance. Green (1985) suggests that Goldschmidt's hypothesis, at least for Missouri, can be amended such that farm numbers, rather than farm size, is the primary intervening variable. Green (1985:272) concludes that "the relationship [between farming and community well-being] tends to be different among various farm production systems."

Reif (1986) examined nonmetropolitan counties in the United States. Her findings did offer limited support for the Goldschmidt hypothesis. Reif reports that counties with larger family farm agriculture were more likely to have better employment levels and higher income levels. This is consistent with Goldschmidt to the degree that the farms surrounding Dinuba, California were better characterized by larger-than-family farms than small scale family farms as is often assumed (see Skees and Swanson in Chapter 6). On the other hand, counties characterized more by corporate style farms tended to have either no relationship or a negative relationship with employment and income.

Perhaps these findings can be summarized as follows. In areas where there are few off-farm opportunities and family farming is the dominant source of community economic well-being, a decline in farm numbers and an increase in farm size will contribute to a decline in indicators of community well-being. But, in areas where there has been an increase in the nonfarm economic activity, the changing characteristics of the regional economy will exert an even stronger influence on the persistence of former farm trade centers. This would suggest that trade centers will transfer their economic and social dependency from their farming hinterlands to the regional economy as the expansion of internal markets increases their dependency on vertical ties with the larger society.

On the other hand, areas where industrial-type farm structures are dominant, such as in Arvin and among the four states that MacCannell examined for Chapter 2, there will be depressed standards of living. This is because industrial agriculture's numerically dominant class is unskilled hired workers who historically have been at the bottom of the U.S.'s labor force and therefore among the most exploited.

This leaves unanswered the fundamental question of whether movement from family farming toward industrial agriculture means a decline in community well-being. The Flora and Flora study (Chapter 3) reports modest findings that for agriculturally dependent communities this may indeed be the case. However, Van Es, et al (Chapter 4) did not find any evidence to support this hypothesis, underscoring the regional and subregional variation in the ways farms and communities may influence one another.

Moreover, Goldschmidt's model study now seems to be more limited in the degree to which it can be generalized to other regions, especially those that do not have a history of industrial farming. In the last decade Rural Sociologists have raised questions associated with Goldschmidt's regional controls as well as aspects of history and farm structure (Flora, et al, 1977; Goss 1979; Swanson, 1982). Furthermore, while follow-up studies (Fujimoto, 1977; Petterson, 1977) propose no substantive changes in Goldschmidt's original hypothesis, two empirical studies outside of California suggest substantial modifications, and, serve to limit its generalizability (Gilbert and Harris, 1982; Flora, et al.,1977; Swanson, 1982).

More recently, Goldschmidt's study has been questioned. Hayes and Olmstead (1984) argue that many factors other than differences in farm size contributed to Arvin's low quality of life. They propose that "rather than being closely matched communities, the two towns had developed within significantly different economic, demographic, and geographic settings" (Hayes and Olmstead, 1984:430). While Hayes and Olmstead do not counter Goldschmidt's most important conclusion that large farms accounted for differences in community characteristics, their findings do question both the immediate findings for the 1944 study and its generalizability to other regions of the country.

The five regional studies comprising this book, while not initially setting out to reassess the unicausal assumption of farm structure determining community well-being, nonetheless have produced a more complex and yet useful understanding of this historical relationship and how it has changed. Among the five, MacCannell's completely supports the Golschmidt study findings, the Flora and Flora and the Skees and Swanson studies report mixed results, while the Van Es et. al. and Buttel et. al. studies provide no support. Together, these studies suggest considerable regional variation for how farms and communities are presently associated with one another.

The Five Regional Studies

Probably the first inconsistency that a reader will note is the absence of a common definition of region. This inconsistency was something of a conundrum for the work group at first, but in true academic fashion was quickly ignored for reasons of expediency and in recognition of regional diversity. In fact, the five regions can fit three general regional definitions. First, the Northeast and South are historical regional distinctions that existed prior to the Civil War and are widely accepted. Second, the Midwest and Plains regions are actually identified according to the dominant agricultural commodity each produces; these are corn and wheat, respectively. The third region is not a geographical region at all. Rather, it is a collection of four states (California, Arizona, Texas, and Florida) within each of which the dominant form of agricultural production is industrial instead of family.

Consequently, while all of the reports utilize the county as the empirical unit of analysis, each has its own unique set of working hypotheses, modes of analysis, and theoretical perspective. In fact, each study stands by itself as a separate report with independent conclusions. While the absence of a consistent definition of region and methodological framework can impede comparability, I believe the reader will find that what little comparability is sacrificed is more than made up for by the detail of the analysis each report offers.

The order of presentation is as arbitrary as the definition of region. The first report is MacCannell's study of the industrial states since it most nearly reflects Walter Goldschmidt's original study of Arvin and Dinuba. The remaining four move from west to east, beginning with the Plains and Midwest, moving on to the Northeast, and finally ending with the South.

These studies collectively suggest important qualifications to traditional assumptions. Most importantly, the relationship between farm scale and rural community well-being may be neither linear or unicausal. This is because most regional nonfarm economies are of great importance in mediating the influence of farm change upon community well-being. As a regional economy expands, the well-being of a community may become more dependent upon the nonfarm economy than upon the farming hinterland. Moreover, regional characteristics may influence transformations in farm characteristics. For example, the increase in part-time farming may be due in part to the expansion of rural nonfarm employment opportunities. Finally, these studies underscore the need for social scientists and policy makers not to treat farming as a homogeneous group of production units, nor to fall into the lazy theoretical traps of technological determinism.

Summary Observations

These reports suggest that the conventional wisdom on farm and community change, emblematic of the Goldschmidt study and most similar studies, can be overstated and even misleading where non-industrial farming hinterlands are concerned. Instead, the reports demonstrate that the way in which farm structure is likely to be associated with community well-being depends upon a complex assortment of factors, including the relative dependency of the local economy upon farming, the array of farm structures and agricultural commodities produced within the immediate hinterland, the mix of nonfarm enterprises, and the relative position of the community within its regional hierarchy of places. At a national and international level both farm structure and community well-being are shaped by national fiscal and financial policy and by international market conditions.

Certainly, late 1970s and 1980s provide ample examples of these types of influences. The financial policy of controlling inflation contributed to the sharp decapitalization of all farm assets while the expanding national debt and huge international trade deficit coupled with a high dollar made U.S. manufactured products such as textiles less competitive in international markets. These local and macro factors certainly do not exhaust the list of factors. Moreover, individual community characteristics may have as much or more influence upon farm structure than farm structure has on community well-being under certain circumstances.

Rural America's class structure has undergone a remarkable transformation since the late 1930s. Small petty commodity producers and retailers, once the dominant class, have given way to rural labor markets characterized by wage-labor and salaried jobs in manufacturing, service companies, and government. While agrarianism as a value system has remained resilient within current populist ideology, including the primacy of the family farm over rural communities, its class base of small owner-operators has been greatly reduced. Most areas of late Twentieth Century rural America more resemble the backwaters of the national economy than shining examples of individual entrepreneurship. Recognition of this great transformation is a first step toward a reassessment of our assumptions about the political economy of rural areas and of agricultural production. This reassessment will need to be sensitive to regional and local economic diversity as well as avoid underestimating the influence of national and international economic and political systems. Finally, as these five regional studies either implicitly or explicitly state, any new national rural development policy to assist rural communities must be independent of farm policy while at the same time articulating the few advantages rural areas may have in improving their economic and social well-being.

REFERENCES

Braudel, Fernand
    1973 *Capitalism and Material Life, 1400-1800*. London:
          New Left Books.
Flora, Jan, Ivan Brown, and J. L. Conboy
    1977 "Impact of the type of agriculture on class structure
          and social well-being in the Great Plains." Paper
          presented at the annual meeting of the Rural
          Sociological Society, Madison, Wisconsin.
Frisbie, Parker and Dudley Poston
    1977 *Sustenance Organization and Population Redistribu-
          tion in Nonmetropolitan America*. Beverly Hills,
          California: Sage Publications.
Fugimoto, Isao
    1977 "The communities of the San Joaquin Valley," in
          U.S. Congress, Senate, Priorities in Agricultural
          Research of the U.S. Department of Agriculture—
          Appendix. Subcommittee on the Judiciary, 95th Con-

gress, 2nd Session, Prt 2, pp. 1374-1396.

Goldschmidt, Walter
1978 *As You Sow.* Montclair, N.J.: Allanheld, Osmun and Company.

Goss, Kevin F.
1978 "Agricultural change and rural community change." Unpublished paper, Pennsylvania State University.
1979 "Goldschmidt. *As You Sow.*" *Rural Sociology* 44(4): 802-805.

Goss, Kevin, and Richard D. Rodefeld
1978 "Consequences of mechanization in U.S. agriculture, 1935-1975." Paper presented at the annual meetings of the Rural Sociological Society at San Francisco, August.

Green, Gary P.
1985 "Large-scale farming and the quality of life in rural communities: Further specification of the Goldschmidt hypothesis." *Rural Sociology* 50(2):262-274.

Harris, Craig K. and Jess Gilbert
1982 "Large scale farming and rural income and Goldschmidt's agrarian thesis." *Rural Sociology* 47(3): 449-458.

Hayes, Michael N. and Alan L. Olmstead
1984 "Farm size and community quality: Arvin and Dinuba revisited." *American Journal of Agricultural Economics* 66(4):430-436.

Henry, Mark and Mark Drabenstott, Lynn Gibson
1986 "A changing rural America." *Economic Review* July/August:23-41.

Merrington, John
1978 "Town and country in the transistion to capitalism." *New Left Review* 82:736-761.

Mooney, Patrick
1983 "Toward a class analysis of Midwestern agriculture." *Rural Sociology* 48(4):563-584.

Munoz, Robert and William Flinn
1979 "Factors related to small town growth and decline in Ohio, 1930-1970." Paper presented at the annual meeting of the Rural Sociological Society at Burlington, Vermont, August.

Petterson, Steve
1977 The Family Farm: A California Small Farm Viabilty Project. Technology Task Force Report, Appendix A,

November.

Reif, Linda L.

1986   Farm structure, industry structure and socioeco-
        nomic conditions: A longitudinal study in economy
        and society. Unpublished doctoral dissertation,
        Department of Sociology and Anthropology, North
        Carolina State University, Raleigh.

Rodefeld, Richard D.

1974   The changing organizational and occupational struc-
        ture of farming and the implications for farm work
        force individuals, families, and communities.
        Unpublished doctoral dissertation. Department of
        Rural Sociology, University of Wisconsin, Madison.

Swanson, Louis E., Jr.

1982   Farm and trade center transition in an industrial
        society: Pennsylvania, 1930-1960. Unpublished doc-
        toral dissertation, Department of Agricultural Eco-
        nomics and Rural Sociology. Pennsylvania State Uni-
        versity, University Park.

Warren, Roland

1973   *The Community in America.* Third Edition. New York:
        Rand McNally and Company.

2
Industrial Agriculture and Rural Community Degredation

Dean MacCannell

This is a report on social conditions in rural communities of four Sunbelt states: California, Arizona, Texas and Florida. There are *two* main findings: (1) an advanced industrial type of agriculture is now fully established on a regional base in the U.S. Sunbelt, and (2) there is evidence for substantial deterioration of human communities and living conditions associated with the new form of agriculture. These findings will require careful consideration as they challenge widely held assumptions about the generalized beneficial effects of economic development. The people of the U.S. must prepare themselves to consider either structural or community development solutions to the problems described here. Specifically, it may be necessary to enact legislation that will have the effect of reducing the size of the nations' largest farms. Alternatively, we will have to create costly new social and environmental programs to repair the damage to human life and the environment which is endemic to the unrestrained industrialization of agriculture.

The Method Of Study

This study uses macrosocial accounting (MSA) methods for data collection and analyses which are similar in many respects to research methods used in agricultural economics. The difference between MSA and economic approaches is the level of analysis and the types of models which are made. Economic analysis of agricultural systems focuses on the integration of business enterprises in markets, and it models costs and benefits of different policies and practices at the level of the firm. As its name implies, the goal of MSA is to describe regional social structure. In the present study, the relationship between agricultural variables and rural community conditions is examined to determine the social costs and benefits of differences in agricultural productivity and efficiency.

The Sample

The counties were selected for this study by the following procedures. First, 43 counties in Arizona, California, Florida and Texas that ranked in the top 100 counties in agricultural sales nationwide were selected for inclusion based on their dominant position in the U.S. agricultural system. Second, an additional 83 counties were selected based on the ratio of agricultural sales to population, that is, every county beyond the original 43 with agricultural sales of $2000 a year or more per capita were included. These counties are both dominated by agriculture and mainly rural in character. Their selection permits the analysis of the relationship of farm structure to rural community conditions in a relatively pure state, i.e., not greatly affected by the influence of nearby major cities, although some urban data (e.g., Fresno, California, and Brownsville, Texas) is included in the analysis even under this restrictive criterion. These criteria originally produced a sample of 124 counties. Twenty-six Texas cattle and grain counties were eventually excluded from the final analysis. These counties appeared to have made the $2000 per capita sales cutoff mainly on the basis of very low population size, and it was not clear that they exhibited an industrial agriculture pattern. The final sample of 98 counties was selected as the basis for the descriptive statements and regression analysis of the relationship of industrial farm structure and rural community conditions in this report.

Theory

Certain theoretical problems appear in socioeconomic analysis of communities and regions that are undergoing rapid development. These problems are exacerbated when development occurs on an already substantial base of industrialization and modernization, that is, when development assumes advanced-industrial, hypermodern, or "post-industrial" forms. Econometric and common sense models for interpreting the social meaning of increase and decrease in economic activity and efficiency no longer apply. There is no better illustration of this than the central subject matter of this report: the social correlates of the transformation of Sunbelt agriculture into an industrial or a post-industrial type. What appears to have happened is a complete disconnection between the economic "players," the large agribusiness enterprises in the region, and any social base in the communities: it is in exactly those areas where farming is the most modern, rational and economically profitable that the worst general social conditions are found.

During the 1970s there was an increase in the number of Sunbelt farms in the highest gross sales category and a corresponding decrease in the number of farms in the lowest gross sales categories. The rapidity and extent of concentration is reflected in the fact that average sales per farm increased at a rate three times that of total sales for all farms. (See Tables 1A and 1B.) The new industrial farms are qualitatively different from even the largest family-owned and -operated farms of forty years ago, not merely in terms of size in sales or acres, but also in terms of total assets and off-farm labor requirements, the repositioning of the farm in larger multi-venture organizations, and increasing dependence on ever newer technologies including genetically altered plants and animals, electronic equipment, and synthetic fertilizers, herbicides and pesticides.

Prior to the emergence on a regional base of multi-million dollar, high-tech farming enterprises, the fate of the rural community was tied directly to the agricultural economy. Where the family-operated farms remain the most prevalent form, and where there continues to be a large and viable rural middle class, improvements in production efficiency and farm profits translate into improvements in general social well-being at both the community and regional levels. Under these conditions of positive linkage between agricultural production and community well-being there can

Table 1-A: Comparing Farm Values for 1969 and 1978:
All Counties in California, Arizona, Florida, and Texas

Attribute	1969 (n = 389)		1978 (n = 746)		Percent Change 1969–1978
Number of Farms	332,878	(856)	290,977	(746)	−9.88
Sales Categories					
$ 100K plus			31,983	(82)	N.A.
$ 40–90K			29,693	(76)	N.A.
$ 40K plus	34,028	(88)	61,676	(158)	81.25
$ 20–39K	27,672	(71)	28,536	(73)	3.12
$ 10–19K	34,973	(90)	34,856	(90)	−0.33
$ 5–9K	43,733	(112)	42,960	(110)	−1.77
$ 2.5–5K	46,947	(121)	45,679	(117)	−2.70
Less than $2.5K	145,476	(374)	76,903	(197)	−47.14
Total sales per county	$20,947.43	(1K)	$22,374.34	(1K)	6.81
Average sales per farm (1980 dollars)	$26,293		$30,687		16.71
Acreage Categories					
2000 or more acres	14,826	(38)	14,869	(38)	0.29
1000 to 1999 acres	16,969	(44)	16,468	(42)	−2.95
500 to 999 acres	32,419	(83)	27,772	(71)	−14.33
180 to 449 acres	70,513	(181)	56,773	(146)	−19.49
50 to 179 acres	96,974	(249)	81,939	(210)	−15.50
10 to 49 acres	69,878	(180)	62,002	(159)	−11.27
Less than 10 acres	31,319	(81)	31,154	(80)	−0.53
Average acreage per farm	1,939		1,957		0.93
Type of Ownership					
Family	166,911	(429)	176,448	(452)	5.71
Partnership	25,283	(65)	26,443	(68)	4.59
Corporate	5,209	(13)	9,529	(24)	82.93
Other	1,866	(5)	1,287	(3)	−31.03

* First value is the sum for all counties; the mean value per county is in parentheses.
  N.A. = Not applicable.

Table 1-B: Comparing Farm Variables for 1969 and 1978:*
Agricultural Counties in California, Arizona, Florida, and Texas

Attribute	1969 (n = 98)		1978 (n = 98)		Percent Change 1969–1978
Number of Farms	97,557	(995)	84,951	(867)	−12.92
Sales Categories					
$ 100K plus			16,184	(165)	N.A.
$ 40–90K			13,703	(140)	N.A.
$ 40K plus	16,298	(166)	29,887	(305)	83.38
$ 20–39K	13,082	(133)	11,048	(113)	−15.55
$ 10–19K	14,473	(148)	10,522	(107)	−27.30
$ 5–9K	14,240	(145)	9,942	(101)	−30.18
$ 2.5–5K	11,696	(119)	8,766	(89)	−25.05
Less than $2.5K	27,768	(283)	14,705	(150)	−47.04
Acreage Categories					
2000 or more acres	5,418	(55)	5,744	(59)	6.02
1000 to 1999 acres	6,420	(66)	6,647	(68)	3.54
500 to 999 acres	11,792	(120)	9,839	(100)	−16.56
180 to 449 acres	18,968	(194)	14,926	(152)	−21.31
50 to 179 acres	21,507	(219)	18,303	(187)	−14.90
10 to 49 acres	24,757	(253)	21,047	(215)	−14.99
Less than 10 acres	8,702	(89)	8,445	(86)	−2.95
Average acreage per farm	2,074		2,192		5.69
Type of Ownership					
Family	60,503	(617)	55,639	(568)	−8.04
Partnership	10,015	(7)	10,019	(102)	0.04
Corporate	2,096	(21)	4,048	(41)	93.13
Other	648	(7)	459	(5)	−29.17

* First value is the sum of the counties, the mean value per county is in parenthesis.
  N.A. = Not applicable.

be high levels of agreement between economists, rural sociologists, planners and government officials. There is an alignment of social and economic values in the entire system which simplifies the formation of policy and theory. This system has broken down in California and other parts of the Sunbelt where there is regional dominance by super-sized farms and a large agricultural laboring class working for minimum wages.

The industrialization of Sunbelt agriculture has resulted in technological marvels for the farm owners: land planes guided by lasers, tomato harvesters with closed-circuit television color-grading equipment, genetically constructed bacterial frost protection, etc. But this innovative technology has brought deprivation and poverty to the workers. A tract-by-tract analysis of rural social conditions in the nations' most productive agricultural areas, reveals poverty rates from 5 to 40 percentage points higher than other rural areas of the U.S. with poverty levels reaching almost as high as 50 percent of the population in the wealthiest industrial agricultural areas (See CATF Appendix A Tables 1-4 at the end of this book). The owners of the largest farms in the region live in mansions with private airplane and helicopter landing facilities, swimming pools, and research laboratories. The agricultural workers live in cramped and squalid houses. Less than one percent of the population of the United States lives in housing without plumbing, or in crowded conditions with more than 1.5 persons per room. These conditions affect up to 20 percent of the housing stock in the industrial agricultural areas. It is no longer possible to speak of a values alignment between agricultural business interests and the rural community, or between agricultural business interests in the Sun Belt and the rest of the nation.

In the place of what once appeared as a correspondence of social and economic values operating throughout the rural sector of American society, there is now a system which resembles more a "zero-sum game" in which the economic interests of industrial-scale growers are pitted first against their workers and then against the growers in other regions of the U.S. and the world. After World War II, the largest farm operators in the Sunbelt were able to exploit their natural, historical and political advantages by combining government support programs, irrigation systems built at public expense, new technologies, and unorganized foreign labor. The current and near future situation of Sunbelt agriculture   The Sunbelt now occupies a preeminent position in the national agricultural economy and international trade. The commodity mix of agriculture in the four-state study area is extremely diverse. With the exception of Florida citrus, there is no single, statewide monoculture or clear dominance by a single crop or commodity of entire regions. Leading commodities are cotton, sorghum, beef, wheat, citrus, row- crop vegetables, rice, sugar cane and beets, grapes, melons, avocados, strawberries, nuts, peanuts, and corn. Over nine million acres of cotton are now grown in these four states, amounting to over 70 percent of the U.S. total and about 30 percent of the world trade in cotton (U.S. Department of Agriculture, 1981a:30-31). After the war in Southeast Asia destroyed most of the rice fields of Vietnam and Laos, the U.S. moved from a negligible position to one providing about 25 percent of the world market in rice. Approximately one-third of the rice production in the U.S. is grown in the four-state study area (U.S. Department of Agriculture, 1984:44). One hundred percent of U.S. citrus production and 55 percent of all noncitrus fruits are grown in the Sunbelt (U.S. Department of Agriculture, 1982). California alone grows over 25% of the table fruits and vegetables consumed in the U.S. (Scheuring, 1982:2). Thirty percent of the U.S. wool production is in the study area.

Some of the new technologies currently under development will very likely accelerate the movement of food and fiber production to the Sunbelt and increase the economic pressure on agriculture in other regions of the country. The Office of Technology Assessment (OTA 1985:53) estimates that, while there are 303,710 farms in the U.S. reportedly raising milk cows, fewer than 5,000 "well-managed" dairies using current technologies are necessary to maintain current production levels. The favorable weather conditions in the Sunbelt and the historical norm of much large-sized dairy herds (mean of 532 cows for Florida vs. 125 in the Great Lakes dairy region), together with powerful new technologies (e.g., the bovine growth hormone) suggests the possibility in principle that the entire dairy production of the U.S. could shift to the four-state study area in a relatively short period. During the 1970s, milk production in the U.S. grew 11 percent, while the growth rate for the study area was 41 percent.

Already, half of the highest producing 100 agricultural counties nationwide are found in the four-state study area. Agricultural products are the principal industry and export of California, Arizona and Texas. In Florida, agriculture ranks behind tourism and manufacturing, but it still employs 77,000 workers and has an annual sales of $1.3 billion. (Carter, 1974:27) In Texas, the value added in agriculture is 1.3 times that of all manufacturing. (Texas Agricultural Experiment Station, n.d.: 5) The economic position of Sunbelt agriculture is all the more remarkable when the high level of industrial development of these same states is taken into consideration.

Industrial Agriculture Versus the Family Farm

Toward the end of the last book of *Capital*, Marx predicted the alignment of industrial style agriculture with manufacturing and the opposition of all forms of industry (agriculture and manufacturing) to the final remnants of a peasant mode of production. Marx's words anticipate in a curious way the arguments of current agricultural economists who claim that small farms are inefficient, should not therefore be subsidized, and should be allowed to pass out of existence (See, e.g., Barkley, 1978). Marx (1894/1967:807) wrote:

The free ownership of the self-managing peasant is evidently the most normal form of landed property for small-scale operation, i.e., for a mode of production, in which possession of the land is a prerequisite for the labourer's ownership of the product of his own labour, and in which the cultivator, be he free owner or vassal, always must produce his own means of subsistence independently, as an isolated laborer with his family. . . . It is a necessary transition stage for the development of agriculture itself. The causes which bring about its own downfall show its limitations. These are: Destruction of rural domestic industry, which forms its normal supplement, as a result of the development of large-scale industry; a gradual impoverishment and exhaustion of the soil subjected to this cultivation; usurpation by big landowners . . . ; competition, either of the plantation system or large-scale capitalist agriculture. Improvements in agriculture, which on the one hand cause a fall in agricultural prices, and on the other, require greater outlays and more extensive material conditions of production.

Of course, Marx saw the transition from small to large farms as salutary not merely because of the greater efficiency of the larger farms. In Marx's view, family farms emphasize individuality and independence, and discourage the development of social forms of labor and social forms of capital, and they are, therefore, ripe for takeover by larger operators. This takeover would be seen by everyone, including the small-scale farmers, as inevitable, a "natural" result of their own relative weakness, a position or standing which they themselves would know better than anyone. While the data on industrial agriculture in the U.S. Sunbelt appear to support Marx's general thesis on the evolution of farming systems, they leave unanswered the still intriguing question of why the oppositions between agribusiness and the community, and agribusiness and small-scale family farmers did not appear sooner after the industrial revolution in manufacturing, and why it is not more widespread.

The history of agriculture in America suggests that small-to moderate-scale family farming operations constitute an adaptation to an interlocked system of social, natural and economic conditions, and that this adaptation is specific and viable to the point that it takes substantial, external and artificial intervention to wipe them out. It will be argued that necessary and sufficient conditions for the destruction of the family farm system in America occurred for the first time in Sunbelt agriculture after World War II.

The Adaptive Significance Of The Family Farm

The Economic Question

How did the American family farm survive the growth of urban labor markets during the first phase of industrialization? It is obvious that Marx was wrong about the proletarianization of the rural sector as a result of urban-industrial development. His theoretical reasoning was precise enough: rural peasants are, in effect, "selling" their labor at below market prices if they persist in subsistence level farming. They could have earned more in the factories if they were willing to turn over their land and their independence. All this would suggest the rapid rise of industrial-scale farming at the beginning of the industrial revolution. But, in actuality, after about 1850, the rapid development of industries and cities world-wide, dramatically expanded markets for agricultural products. Peasant farmers and small landholders had more of a choice than Marx foresaw. They could let their land go and find factory work, or they could grow food for the ever expanding urban industrial market. So long as the system of industrial capitalism was expanding globally, those who stayed in agriculture, even small scale family farmers could be economically viable.

The Social Question

Can the family farm retain its independence and its centrality as the only universal human type? The new industrial worker was forced into often inhuman feats of specialization, had to work schedules which had nothing to do with social or natural rhythms, and were under constant supervision by others. Moreover, these workers were under threat of dismissal as a result of fickle and capricious forces which they could not see, understand or control. Those who stayed in farming operated in the framework of natural contingency—drought, flood, pestilence. But they understood the risks from almost ten millennia of collective experience, and could predict and guard against them in limited ways. Family farmers watched over themselves, their kin and their own lands, and could always hope for a bountiful harvest, a "good year," something of much greater potential significance than the Christmas bonus of the factory worker. They were neither exploited nor profiting from the work of others, so their communities were free from the kind of economic inequality which leads more or less automatically to revolutionary or criminal forms of class warfare. Finally, as the only universal human type, found in every epoch and every country, somehow surviving in the new industrial society which understands nothing of its own origins or prospects, the family farmer became a moral and ethical figure, not merely an economic but also a rhetorical entity, carrying much of the ideological baggage of modernity.

Today's politicians must ask themselves, Can American democratic institutions survive the death of the family farm, the last important economic activity not already concentrated in two or three international corporations whose board and management are neither representative of the general population nor accountable to it? Or is democracy itself like the family farm, an archaic concept, already an illusion that is artificially maintained by government programs? Either way, the "family farm" continues to have an essential sociohistorical role to play, a protected, perhaps even symbolic niche in contemporary society.

The Nature Question

What are the long-term environmental prospects of our current agricultural system? A case has been made that family farmers, because they have the long-term viability of their piece of land to be concerned about, for their own livelihood and that of their children who will inherit it, are more likely to conserve the land and soil than are large-scale operators . This argument is based on the assumption that industrial-scale farmers will place profits ahead of conservation in decision making, and are not much affected when the productivity of a piece of land is destroyed as they can find a nonagricultural use for it, and purchase or lease still viable agricultural properties elsewhere. This characterization of large-farm versus small-farm differences may be statistically true, but it is not a priori true. One can imagine counter cases wherein large corporations decide to place conservation ahead of short-term profits in order to maximize long-range profitability, and small-scale farmers who fail to practice costly soil conservation procedures when they are having difficulty making mortgage payments, etc. But there are some environmental problems specifically associated with large-scale agricultural operations; for example: soil compaction as a result of using machines weighing five tons or more; a drop in the water table to undesirable levels as a result of ground-water mining using thousand horsepower pumps to pull the water to the surface; the poisoning of entire rivers and lakes from pesticide and herbicide run-off; the leaching of selenium and other heavy metals from the soils as a result of multicropping and overirrigation; "chemical treadmills" (geometrically increasing amounts and types of pesticides are required with successive applications) which are both the cause and the effect of the emergence of pesticide resistant strains of harmful insects. These are environmental problems associated with large-scale agricultural operations. Small farm operators lack the resources necessary to engage in the excessive practices which lead to these forms of degradation. In so far as these practices are associated with industrial-scale agriculture, and they result in irreversible damage to the environment, they constitute additional reasons for the superior adaptability of the family farm, in this case to nature and the environment.

The Preconditions For Industrial Agriculture In The Sunbelt

A convergence of natural, social and economic conditions favoring the family farm explains its persistence as the dominant form of agriculture worldwide and in the U.S., against Marx's predictions, through the first hundred years of global industrialization. This pattern might have continued except for the appearance after World War II of a series of unique circumstances in the American Sunbelt favoring the establishment of industrial agriculture on a regional base. The current agricultural system of the study area was not fully established until after the war. In fact, some of its elements can be traced directly to wartime policies. A convergence of social, geographical, technical and political factors have permitted the development of a new form of industrial-scale agribusiness which is now powerful enough to operate mainly outside the constraints of nature, national policy, moral and ethical norms, and local markets. A brief account of these factors follows.

A Historical Pattern Of Large Sized Farms

The size of the largest landholdings in the 98 county study area results from the original nonirrigated uses of the land, and from its historical division into Spanish land grants, which still form the basis of ownership of many farms in the American West. Scheuring (1982:10) reports that between 1760 and 1822, 453 Spanish land grants ranging from 4,000 to 300,000 acres in the area now known as California were awarded. Most of these grants were between 5,000 and 25,000 acres. These large tracts were transferred to Anglo owners after the treaty of Hidalgo in 1848, and were therefore withheld from the public domain and were not subject to settlement in 160-acre parcels under the Homestead Act o f 1862. The average farm size for the entire study region in 1978 was 2,195. As has already been shown in Tables 1 A and B, this average figure is increasing.

State and federal water projects and subsidized irrigation The first crude irrigation systems were built at the beginning of this century by land developers and speculators. Irrigation systems are subject to problems such as silting and their maintenance is difficult and costly, requiring substantial communal effort as in Japan, or state intervention as eventually occurred in the study area. The early development of the irrigation in the American West was marked by abuses that intentionally prevented the establishment of a stable family farm type of agriculture in the areas that were irrigated first. For example, the Imperial Valley of California underwent a typical succession of events which began with a hastily constructed irrigation system and the division of a large property into small tracts. These tracts were sold to family farmers attracted by the good land, cheap and plentiful water and easy credit. But within a few years, the irrigation system silted up, the water cease d to flow, the crops failed, mortgage payments stopped and the land reverted to the original land and water company which had only to dredge the ditches in order to resell the land and repeat the cycle. In the beginning, the development and management of irrigation systems throughout the Sunbelt exhibited a conflation of "public" and "private" spheres of responsibility which seems essential to the unrestricted growth of new social forms (e.g., industrial agriculture). A current example of this conflation is the nonenforcement of the Federal Reclamation Law which restricts the delivery of subsidized irrigation water to small-sized farms. A recent example is the nonenforcement of federal immigration laws which, if enforced, might have reduced the availability of unorganizable labor to industrial-scale agriculture. An early example would be the California Wright Act of 1887 which enabled large landowners to take over private companies, issue bonds and levy taxes.

The abuses in California's Imperial Valley and elsewhere eventually brought federal intervention and public involvement in the construction and management of irrigation systems throughout the study-area states. Several of these water delivery systems and their associated dams and reservoirs are so complex and extensive as to qualify as the "eighth wonder of the world." Once dependable systems were built and managed at public expense, the original land companies and large property owners of the West became disinclined to subdivide and sell their lands. Many of them went into irrigated, row-crop agriculture on a scale unprecedented in human history. Acreages once associated only with range cattle operations, i.e., single farms of 2,000 to 5,000 acres, are now planted in vegetables, fruits, vines, and cotton. Current farm structure in the richest agricultural region of the study area, west Fresno county, California, fits this pattern and has only a fifteen year history. The San Luis Unit of the joint state and federal California Central Valley Project was completed in 1969, and full delivery of surface irrigation water to the farms in the region did not begin until five years later.

Today, industrial agriculture has a near monopoly on fresh water supplies in the Sunbelt. Most of the water in Florida (88 percent) is used for crop irrigation, the remaining 12 percent going for all other, i.e., industrial, rural and urban-domestic, uses (Carter, 1974:27). In California, 85 percent of the water supply is used in agriculture (Scheuring, 1982:13), and in Texas and Arizona 76 and 90 percent of the water are used, respectively (Texas Experiment Station Report, n.d.). This level of control of one of our most precious natural resources by a small segment of the population implies a distortion of general political processes. In California it is already commonly said that "politics is water politics." There are individual farms in the Sunbelt that use as much water each year as some cities with more than a million inhabitants. An annual 3 percent water savings on the part of Texas agriculture, a savings easily achieved without reduction in crop yield by the use of existing technologies and management practices, would be sufficient to provide for all the water needs of the city of Houston in perpetuity. Some California farmers are currently considering getting out of agriculture entirely, that is, earning their living by selling their annual water contract allotment to urban, industrial and other agricultural users.

Low Paid, Unorganized Foreign Labor

The war years' Immigration and Naturalization Act provided for temporary permits for otherwise inadmissible aliens to do seasonal agricultural work. The intent was to free the rural labor force to join the military without jeopardizing crop production, but the law was not repealed after the war. The the nascent industrial farm system had become dependent on foreign labor. In addition to documented workers who entered under the provisions of the Naturalization Act, substantial numbers of illegal (undocumented) aliens entered the U.S. to do agricultural labor. Workers from Jamaica, the Bahamas, British West Indies, Philippines, Laos, Cambodia, Thailand, and India are found in Sun belt agriculture. But the great majority of workers in the region are from Mexico and Central America.

The arrival of substantial numbers of foreign laborers, who would eventually dominate the rural labor force in the Sunbelt, corresponded precisely to the conversion of agriculture to the industrial form. After the war, they were no longer of strategic value, but they were an essential component to the emerging new agricultural structure. To the extent that the guest workers did not develop primary class, ethnic and community ties in this country, their treatment did not need to conform to U.S. norms for labor. They were hired on a seasonal, casual basis, paid minimal and subminimal wages, and worked without health, workman's compensation. and retirement benefits. In many, if not most, instances, these workers were arguably classifiable as "skilled," in that much of the practical knowledge requisite for the management of crops, irrigation, pruning, cultivation, etc., is found only among the members of this group. To the extent that the guest workers are illegal, they are unorganizable. Their presence in the Sunbelt depresses wages throughout agriculture and in other industries.

Foreign workers, both legal and illegal, found ways of settling out of the migrant labor stream and are now an absolute majority in many of the rural communities in the industrial agricultural areas of the Sunbelt. Current demographic projections indicate that each of the four states in the study region will have a nonwhite majority by the year 2000. While there are other migrations contributing to this ethno-demographic transformation, especially the arrival of post-Vietnam Southeast Asian refugees and people fleeing from conflicts in Central America, the change has been led by the immigration of agricultural labor. The dramatic demographic changes occurring as a result of the industrialization of Sunbelt agriculture have prompted the U.S. congress to express concern "that we have lost control of our southern border," and in 1986 to enact immigration reform legislation. The main provisions of the new law are to legalize certain categories of formerly undocumented aliens already living and working in this country, while specifying penalties to growers and other employers who hire illegals. The idea behind the law is to stop the flow of new illegal immigrants without disrupting current labor-management arrangements. Less than a year after its enactment, the new law was challenged by large growers who claim that they cannot operate under its provisions, and emergency administration and enforcement guidelines are now being considered which will permit the continued importation of new foreign workers.

Harvest mechanization and other uses of high technology The industrial farms of the Sunbelt are the most technologically sophisticated in the world. Among the advanced mechanical, electronic, genetic and chemical technologies in current use on the farms in the study area are: computers, lasers, embryo transplants, gene splicing, aerial and infrared monitoring. The Office of Technology Assessment (OTA 1986b:9-10) describes the application of biotechnology to agriculture in the following terms:

It focuses on two powerful molecular genetic techniques: recombinant deoxyribonucleic acid (rDNA) and cell fusion technologies. Using these techniques scientists can visualize the gene—to isolate, clone, and

study the structure of the gene and the gene's relationships to the processes of living things. . . One
major thrust of biotechnology in animals is the mass
production in microorganisms of protein-like pharmaceu-
ticals, including a number of hormones, enzymes, acti-
vating factors, amino acids, and feed supplements. . .
One of the applications of these new pharma-ceuticals
is the injection of growth hormones into animals. . . A
new technique arising from the convergence of gene and
embryo manipulations promises to permit genes for new
traits to be inserted into the reproductive cells of
livestock. . . Gene insertion will allow future animals
to be endowed permanently with traits of other animals.
. . On fusion of the pronuclei, the guest genes become
a part of the cells of the developing animal, and the
traits they determine are transmitted to succeeding
generations. Embryo transfer, which is closely related
to gene insertion, involves artificially inseminating a
super-ovulated donor animal [this is an animal which
has been injected with a hormone that stimulates more
than the normal number of eggs per ovulation, dm] and
removing the resulting embryos nonsurgically for
implantation in surrogate mothers which carry them to
term. Prior to implantation, the embryos can be treated
in a number of special ways. They can be sexed, split
(genetically to make twins), fused with embryos of
other animal species (to make chimeric animals or to
permit the heterologous species to carry the embryo to
term), or frozen in liquid nitrogen for storage.

Gene transfer in plants permits the use of DNA from one
plant in another without respect for normal species and
sexual constraints (OTA, 1986b:12). In addition to genetic
and embryo manipulation, OTA has listed and described over
100 new technologies ranging from the use of computers in
livestock production systems, in irrigation management, and
in disease management and chemical application, to radar
sensing in fertilizer application. Many of these technologies were developed for specific application in industrial
agriculture by the experiment stations in the state Universities. A federal district court has recently found that
the University of California violated its public trust by
failing to have internal policy to guard against its becom-

ing the "Research and Development" laboratory for private agribusiness interests.

As important as the technologies, and integral to them, are advanced systems of management, credit and marketing. Since the mechanization of the tomato harvest in the early 1970s, tomato growers of the California Central Valley have entered into delivery contracts and price agreements with the processing plants in the winter months before the crops are planted. The contracts now contain agreements on water and sugar content of and color of the tomatoes, on amounts to be delivered, and price penalties for deviation from the contracted standards. There are also price penalties, measured in hours, for early and late deliveries. These contracts, which also figure in the system of credit, are the results of the availability of new technologies, including the mechanical tomato harvester which can handle eight rows of plants simultaneously at speeds up to 35 miles per hour. A grower who signs these contracts must also have special tomato varieties that have been bred for, among other things, uniform maturation rates. He must also be prepared to run his machines and workers around the clock to meet his contract quotas and delivery times which were established by the processing industry to extend the harvest season for as long as possible and to maintain the smoothest possible flow of work during the season. In order to assure competitiveness at harvest time, California tomato growers must purchase an extra harvesting machine, which costs more than $200,000, to hold in reserve against the contingency of machine failure, as even a six hour repair could cause them to miss their delivery target and cost them enough in price penalties to make the operation unprofitable. A large grower with more than a thousand acres of tomatoes will plant several varieties with different maturation rates and develop a phased harvest plan and delivery contracts to make maximum use of his equipment, labor and time. Successful operation within this system requires masterful organization and full utilization of the most advanced technologies available. Similar complex integrations of technology, management practices, credit arrangements, and marketing is the norm for all other perishable crops in the region. (For more detail see the sociological studies of the tomato industry, particularly Friedland et al., 1978)

Farm Types In The Study Area

There are five types of operations in the industrial agricultural areas of the four state study region. I will discuss each briefly.

First are large-scale family-owned operations. These are otherwise indistinguishable from the most advanced, corporate industrial farms. These farms are closely held, i.e., non-public but corporate ownership. The owners of these farms do not work off the farms, except in other family owned businesses, and their farms are typically located in areas dominated by other similar, large operations of both family and nonfamily industrial farm types. This is the classic "pioneer family" type of farm that has been fully converted to a modern, rational industrial type.

Second are large corporate farms that are held in partnerships, shares or corporations which trade stock on the open market. These farms depend on full-time hired management and full-time and part-time labor, and have marginally better wage schedules and working conditions than the first type.

The *third* type are highly sophisticated "part-time" operations owned by noninstitutional investors (often urban-based professional) that have high gross sales. These farms grow specialty crops on small acreages. More of this type of farm are fully owned than is the case for the other types. Unlike the pattern found in other parts of the country, these are not marginal operations supported by the off-farm work of the owner(s). In fact, a higher proportion of these farms fall into the highest sales category ($100,000 plus) than the first two types.

Small-scale, unsophisticated part-time farming operations with low sales are the *fourth* type of operaton. These are sometimes called "hobby farms." Most of these farms in the four states are located outside of the most agricultural counties and they are marginal in other ways: i.e., they have outmoded equipment, they may have difficulty obtaining credit, etc. These farms are declining and disappearing at a rapid rate.

The *fifth* type are moderate sized family farms. There has never been a widespread tradition of moderate-scale family-operated farms in the Sunbelt, compared with the American Midwest pattern. Still, many such farms exist. The methodology used in the analytical sections of this report (below) assumes the presence of a range of farm types from marginal- and moderate-scale to super-scale operations. The assumption of variation is necessary to the form of the hypotheses which predict differences in social conditions associated with regional farm structure differences. Regional dominance by family farms cannot be assumed for any part of the study area, however. In California, marginally successful family farming, operating on a "break-even" basis, or slightly above, never existed statewide, as it has in so many other parts of the country. Researchers and policy makers must beware, however, that industrial-scale operators with annual payrolls exceeding several million dollars, often describe their operations as "marginal" using much the same rhetoric as a hard-pressed Midwestern family farmer.

Early wheat production in the Central Valley and western foothills of the Sierra, sometimes called the "second California gold rush," began as serious, large-scale operations organized around commercial markets serving the population boom of the 1850s. In Florida, a tradition of family-owned and -operated moderate-scale agriculture grew up alongside the larger holdings, but 1930s depression, the uncertain politics of swamp reclamation, and the emergence of a citrus monoculture have resulted in a trend toward increasing ownership concentration that started well before the current cost-price squeeze (Carter, 1974:26-27).

Even though once viable moderate-sized family operations have never been an important part of Sunbelt agriculture, their remnants constitute a visible and vocal group in the overall picture. Moreover, this is the only group which is permitted to speak publicly for the entire agricultural sector. It has already been noted that in the public pronouncements of industrial farmers, the rhetorical stance of the family farmer is adopted. The primary reason moderate-scale family farmers are permitted to dominate the system dramatically and rhetorically is easy enough to understand: the more effectively they complain about their impossible situation, the faster their marginalization. Programmatic relief in response to these complaints has so far tended to benefit the industrial farmers, accelerating the disadvantage of the smaller (but more vocal) operators. Family farmers are in a classic double-bind situation: the more effectively they communicate their problems to policy makers, the more they empower forces opposed to their interests.

The most distinctive feature of the current structure of farming operations in the study area is a pattern of part- and multiple-ownerships in which the "farmer" owns and/or operates more than one farm, or parts of several farms, and combines agriculture with other forms of investment and venture activity in real estate, hotels, light industry, food packaging and distribution, trucking, etc. The largest company in Yolo County, California, a tomato growing area of the Central Valley, makes it a point of pride that it owns no land. Instead, it prefers to lease land in much the same way that United Fruit does in its Central American operations. One California farmer purchased a well-known Las Vegas casino and hotel "to ease his cash flow problems." Even under conditions where the industrial farmer is a person rather than a board of directors, and even when he actually lives on or near one of his holdings, his unprecedented wealth and primarily urban orientation, combined with modern transportation and communication technologies, permit him to operate outside of the local community in all of his social, economic, political and cultural affairs, with the single exception of his need to obtain a steady supply of inexpensive labor. And even in this latter regard, international law and relationships are the ultimate determining factors in shaping local community and labor relations.

Measuring Agricultural Industrialization

This study uses nine indicators of agricultural industrialization as independent variables to predict social variation. First is the *percent of the farms in the county organized as corporations.* In the four-state study area, 5 percent of the farms are corporately owned. This includes the most productive farms of types 1, 3, and 5 (above). Many large-scale family-owned farms are incorporating without changing their overall approach to farming. The incorporation variable appears to reflect modern, rational management and economic values. For example, the wages and conditions on incorporated farms are marginally better than on unincorporated farms.

Second is *farm size in acres*. While this indicator seems self explanatory, it must be interpreted with caution. The meaning of acreage difference is sensitive to the crops that are produced. Three hundred acres of cotton is a "small farm," while three hundred acres of raisin grapes is large indeed.

Third is the *percent of the farms in the county with more than $40,000 in sales*. In the present 98 county context, this is probably a better measure of national rather than regional dominance. Regional patterns usually involve a few farms with large acreages and high sales dominating many small farms with a shrinking market share. The pattern in the 98 county study area is for all farms that stay in business to be increasing in size and sales.

Fourth is the *percent of farms with full-time hired labor*. Full time labor is defined as workers who work more than 150 days per year on the farm. This type of labor is associated with corporate ownership and is one of the only aspects of industrial agriculture that might lead to the development of an indigenous "middle class" in rural communities in the region. This middle class would be different from its historical rural counterpart in that it would be composed primarily of service employees and semi-professionals, not agricultural property owners. It is not yet sufficiently developed to observe its behavior or consciousness. Still, one would predict the full-time labor variable to be associated with positive social conditions, not negative, as would be hypothesized for most of the other industrial agriculture variables.

Fifth is the *cost of hired labor per farm*. This is a measure of dependence on off-farm labor. It is a strong indicator of the degree to which industrial agriculture has evolved away from family operated farms in the direction of large-scale commercial farming operations. In a theoretically ideal family farming system this figure would range from zero to no more than the market value of family member labor inputs.

Sixth is the *cost of contract labor per farm*. While some skilled labor is contracted in the four states, this is mainly an indicator of dependence on legal and illegal unskilled migratory labor.

Seventh is the *value of machinery per farm*. This is a measure of the degree of mechanization of production. It is sensitive to difference in machine costs by crop and therefore must be interpreted carefully like size in acres. It is useful for aggregate comparison between counties and also as an indicator of capital requirements, independent of crop differences.

Eight is the *cost of fertilizers per farm*. This measures the degree of capitalization of crop production and intensiveness and rationality of production practices.

Ninth is the *costs of other chemicals (including herbicides and pesticides) per farm*. This measures capitalization and intensiveness and rationalization of production practices as well as willingness to accept potential risks to health and the environment in exchange for higher immediate yields.

The relationship between the measures of agricultural industrialization. It is suggested above that all the necessary elements for the establishment of an industrial type agriculture came together in the study area during the last forty years, quickly bringing over a billion acres under this form of cultivation and management (see Table 1A).

Table 2 gives the correlations between the measures of agricultural industrialization in 1970. The overall pattern in the matrix clearly indicates that, with the possible exception of size in acres, the measures of industrialization were strongly and positively intercorrelated. The matrix suggests the presence of single, system-wide pattern of industrial agriculture. There is no evidence of a trade-off, for example, between machines and labor as would occur in regions where both traditional and industrial types of agriculture are practiced. In the 98 study counties, costs for machines, labor, chemicals, gross sales, incorporation, etc., increase together.

Table 3 gives autocorrelations between the nine variables and their own rates of change from 1970 to 1980. Most of these relationships are weak, but significant and negative. This indicates that it was the less industrialized of the 98 counties that underwent the most rapid change during the decade of the 1970s. What is now occurring in the Sunbelt is the most productive, industrialized counties are not increasing their advantage so much as the less productive counties are catching up. The result is a more uniform industrial agricultural system throughout the area, increasing its regional advantage over the other areas of

38

Table 2. Matrix of Intercorrelations Between Independent Variables, 1970

	1	2	3	4	5	6	7	8	9
1. Percent corporate		.18	.61	.46	.85	.83	.66	.83	.82
2. Average size			.42	−.13	.21	−.02	.06	−.06	−.02
3. $40K plus sales				.40	.72	.57	.74	.62	.64
4. Full-time labor					.65	.62	.39	.54	.60
5. Labor cost						.79	.80	.90	.91
6. Contract labor							.95	.95	.79
7. Machines cost								.85	.80
8. Fertilizer cost									.93
9. Chemical cost									

the U.S. and the world. The only deviation from this overall pattern is in the area of labor costs; those counties that had higher labor costs in 1970 were also those which underwent the sharpest increases in labor costs between 1970 and 1980. This is the first of several indications that increasing mechanization does not lead to decreasing labor costs—rather, the opposite appears to be true.

Another way of looking at the process of industrializing Sunbelt agriculture is according to farm size categories and ownership types which are given in Table 1B. The total number of farms decreased by 13 percent between 1970 and 1980. The number of large farms (with 1000 plus acres) increased by 4.6 percent, while the number of medium sized-farms (180 to 1000 acres) decreased 19.5 percent, and the average size of farms increased 5.6 percent. All small to moderate categories of size and sales declined during this period. The current structure is a dynamic but clear pattern of accelerating concentration and industrialization.

There has never been a more rapid or basic transformation of agricultural structure with the possible exception of Soviet collectivization programs. The most significant factor affecting the rapidity of the development was the absence of an earlier system of family or peasant farms that had to be displaced and/or absorbed by the new industrial type. Land holding sizes were already appropriate to the emerging system. The other requirements were also present, all feeding into one another synergistically: new giant water systems, an adequate mass of exploitable labor, and a strong institutional base for the ongoing development of new technologies.

Is This Postindustrial Agriculture?

The current pattern of agriculture in the area exhibits characteristics which suggest it may be qualified for classification as a "postindustrial" form or as a component of the emerging "world system." These characteristics are: (1) dependence on high technology and on advanced, hyperrational management systems; (2) a demonstrated capacity to subvert national policies to its own ends; and (3) to specialize and operate competitively in international markets by driving competitors out of business. The inclusion of U.S.industrial agriculture into this analytical framework

Table 3. Auto-Correlations: Concentration in 1970 X Change in
Concentration, 1970-1980

	Concentration Change
1. Percent corporate	−.29*
2. Average size	−.24*
3. $40K plus sales	−.43*
4. Full-time labor	.23*
5. Labor cost	−.15
6. Contract labor	.08
7. Machines cost	−.31*
8. Fertilizer cost	−.35*
9. Chemical cost	−.31*

* Significant at .05 level.

would, however, require some modification of existing conception. The most interesting problem in this regard has to do with the position of labor. What has occurred is the importation of a "Third world," "marginal," or "peripheral," labor population into a "developed" nation in such a way as to bring all of these concepts into question. The particulars of the development of U.S. industrial agriculture suggests that the internationalization of labor may be occurring alongside (perhaps hidden beneath) the already well-analyzed internationalization of capital (for a good discussion, see Marcussen and Torp, 1982 and Smith, 1987.)

Certainly any theory of "post-industrial" society which emphasizes the replacement of unskilled and semiskilled labor by technology does not apply (see, Gorz, 1982.) Marx always argued that land (and nature in general) is an imperfect form of capital which essentially stands outside of economic relations, or enters mainly as an obstacle.

Advanced technologies have transformed nature into a source of surplus value, putting it in the theoretical position of a new "industrial proletariat," setting in motion the same processes of degradation, irreversible except by revolutionary action, once the exclusive dominion of the working class. But far from replacing the worker, the interjection of technology into nature has simply broadened the scope of operation of late capitalism and produced a new "partnership" of subproletarian labor and high technology which is by no means restricted to agriculture. Whatever its theoretical base, the most salient feature of the rural communities in the industrial agricultural areas of the U.S. is they are composed of a growing majority of poor, nonwhite peoples, recently immigrated from Third World countries. One finds the same pattern conjoined with silicon microchip production, and advanced segments of the service sector.

The rapid rise of industrial agriculture in the U.S. occurred without significant public discussion, even though it has questionable moral contours that were fully visible well before the current "farm crisis." Our collective silence on this matter during the last decade may stem from a desire to deny that the industrialization of Sunbelt agriculture is an adaptation, on the part of the U.S. as a whole, to the outcome of the Vietnam War, the oil embargo and other signs of the increasing power and independence of

Third World nations. We can no longer exercise the kind of control over other countries, even poor countries, that makes them good environments for U.S. business. But apparently we can establish a simulacrum of a Third World economy, population, and class relationships within our own borders as the locus of high-tech industries, industrial agriculture, and modernized service delivery systems. This runs counter to the stereotype that features upper-income professionals as the most "characteristic" expression of current Sunbelt socioeconomic relations. But it fits first-hand observations of the actual groups and relationships found in Houston, Texas, Orange County, California, the silicon valleys, and the agricultural valleys of the region.

It is worthwhile to recall in this context that the farms of California, Arizona, Florida and Texas occupy a pre-eminent position in the production of food and fiber for foreign markets, and agricultural products, after World War II, are the U.S. principal export. It is probably not an exaggeration to suggest that what happened near the southern borders of the United States in the last three decades will prove to be as important in the formation of American character and institutions during the next 200 years as the pioneer experience was during the last 200.

There are changes occurring in the entire U.S. that are arguably traceable to the industrialization of Sunbelt agriculture. These include the departure of crops and commodity production from non-Sunbelt regions to the study area (e.g., cotton), market disadvantage to non-Sunbelt growers due to relatively greater subsidies to Sunbelt growers (e.g., the billion dollar state investment in water projects, 80 percent of the benefits of which go to Sunbelt farmers), and the appearance of industrial-type operations in non-Sunbelt regions in order to remain competitive, (e.g., the new "hog factories" of the Midwest). It is ultimately futile to attempt to establish a count of people affected by the changeover to industrial agriculture; the number would be as high as anyone would want it to be. However, it is possible to provide social and demographic profiles of the communities in the immediate proximity of the agricultural industrialization, and to estimate the numbers of peoples and communities already living within this historical process.

Small Communities Under Industrial Agriculture

There are almost 5.5 million people living in the 98 industrial agricultural counties in the sample. The number of communities in these areas is more difficult to determine. In California, excluding the cities of Fresno, Stockton, Sacramento, Madera, Bakersfield, and Merced, there are 83 towns with independent local governments located in the irrigated areas of the Central Valley. The populations of these towns range in size from about 700 to 45,000. There are approximately 150 additional small (under 1,500 population) unincorporated places in the same irrigated areas. About one out of seven California towns, located beyond the suburban fringes of the major cities, are found in the industrial agricultural areas. An estimate of 300 incorporated places and an additional 700 smaller unincorporated but named communities seems reasonable for the 98 sample counties in the four-state area—that is about 1,000 communities averaging about 5,000 population.

Tables 1 through 4 in CATF Appendix A present data on several of the most agricultural census tracts and counties. These counties and tracts were selected for closer observation if 20 percent of the labor force was classified as "farm laborers" in 1970, and/or 15 percent or more was classified as workers in "farming, fisheries and forestry" in 1980. This somewhat peculiar set of criteria was necessitated by a change in the categories of the U.S. Census between 1970 and 1980 which resulted in a much lower level of detail on questions in the 1980 Census. In the 1970 Census there was a specific count of individuals employed as farm laborers. In 1980, the farm-labor population was split between "employed as a laborer," and "employed in farming, fisheries, or forestry." The actual number of farm laborers is irretrievably lost in the 1980 Census, paradoxically at precisely the moment in time when their number became a necessary fact to know within the framework of policy debate over immigration laws, etc.

General Findings

On *every* social indicator, the people who live in communities embedded in the richest agricultural areas in the four-state study area are no better off, and in most instances are much worse off than their rural counterparts nationally.

Housing In Arizona, two of the rural tracts had slightly better quality housing than the state average using plumbing as an indicator. The other tracts were worse off with lack of plumbing running as high as four times the state average (2.6 percent lacking plumbing in the entire state). None of the Texas tracts have housing comparable to the state average, with lack of plumbing ranging from 25 to 41 percent of the housing stock in some areas. In Florida, where only county-level data are available, two of the industrial agribusiness counties slightly bettered the state average. The percent of homes lacking plumbing in the other counties ranged from 1.4 to 18.6 percent. In California, overall, only 0.2 percent of the housing stock lacks plumbing. While the rural California counties are relatively better off than their counterparts in the other states, none equal the California average. In Imperial County, lack of plumbing is 20 times greater than in the rest of the state; in west Fresno it is 100 times greater.

This same pattern appears in the data on crowding as measured by the proportion of the population living in houses with more than 1.5 persons per room. Only 0.4 percent of the population of the entire U.S. lives in crowded conditions according to this measure. The proportions of people living in crowded conditions in the industrial agricultural areas ranges from 2.0 to 10.2 percent in Arizona; 2.1 to 21 percent in Texas; 1 to 12 percent in Florida; and 1 to 16 percent in California. These same figures run about 30 percent higher for Spanish surname families in the rural agribusiness tracts. Up to 39 percent of the Spanish surname families live in houses with more than 1,5 persons per room in Arizona. The same figures are 21 percent in Texas and 23 percent in California. In Florida, 19 percent of black families in the industrial agriculture counties live in crowded conditions.

In summary, those communities that are surrounded by industrial farms have a bimodal income distribution with a few wealthy elites, a majority of poor laborers, and virtually no middle class. The absence of a middle class among these local societies has a serious negative effect on both the quality and quantity of social and commercial services (see analysis below), public education, local government, etc. Rothman et al. (1977) found that hired agricultural laborers are located on the bottom of community status hierarchies, are transient to some degree even if not technically migratory, and are not treated as full-fledged members of the rural community. On the other hand, the large-scale farm owner-operators tend to bypass local public and commercial services and establishments, preferring to shop in distant cities and to purchase education, police protection and recreations from the private sector for their own exclusive use. The public involvement of the largest industrial farmers is not based in the local community, but in lobbying and selling at the state, federal, and international levels.

Consequently, rural communities in the most productive agricultural areas of the U.S. do not share in economic or social benefits from increased production and sales. Instead, the rural community stagnates or declines in the context of increasing agricultural productivity. These structural conditions favor increasing dependence on foreign labor. Continued importation of labor, operating partly outside the economic value system of the United States, is the only possible support for an agricultural economy which has become disarticulated from the local community. The rural communities in the industrial agricultural areas are not "local" in the sense of participating in U.S. social and cultural traditions. They resemble more Honduran plantation communities or Laotian communities, than their rural counterparts in other areas of the U.S. These conditions cannot prevail for long without substantially altering the way the people of the U.S. view themselves and are viewed by others in the developed world. The day is rapidly approaching when the entire country will have to make a commitment to specific terms under which these newest Americans will be assimilated into American society. This problems is already a matter of concerned discussion in the affected groups. Maria Herrera-Sobek (1982:9) quotes Gregorio Cortez who remarks, not without irony, "The Anglos . . . saw us as abysmal savages—benighted by papistry (priest ridden, as that great Texas liberal, J. Frank Dobie, used to say) and debased by miscegenation (with ditchwater instead of blood in our veins, as another great Texas liberal and scholar, Walter Prescott Webb, once put it)."

Community Types In The Study Area

Field observations in California and analysis of the tract-level data for the other three states suggest that there are three main types of rural communities in the study area.

The first type is *wealth on-farm populations/impoverished rural communities*. This type is found in the California Central Valley and parts of Texas. Those owners who still maintain a residence in the area of their farming operations build a country estate which contains the amenities ordinarily found in the public and service sectors of society: swimming pools, guest houses, etc. They send their children to private boarding schools and shop in distant cities, maintain primary "civic" ties with the state and national capitals and otherwise abjure any local involvements not directly tied to the administration of their enterprise. The entire local community is left to the farm laborers and whatever minimal services and amenities they can support with their disposable incomes. In many instances, the only "services" found in these communities would be a bar, small grocery, and gasoline station.

The second type is *internally segregated communities*. This is the classic "two sides of the tracks" social phenomenon where rich and poor live in segregated neighborhoods within the same community. Examples of this pattern can be found in and near Lubbock and Brownsville, Texas.

The third type is *externally segregated communities*. This is a pattern in which entire rural communities come to be dominated by a single class or ethnicity. The result is a region within which some towns are lower working class, farm worker and transient communities, while other towns exhibit the classic pattern of rural a trade center with a range of available goods and services and a strong middle class.

This third type of community becomes the town of choice for ex-urban in-migrants and nonagricultural industrial relocation. The California Central Valley exhibits this brown-white checkerboard pattern and rural-to-rural "white flight" migration patterns. At the community level, there are important differences between subregions in the four-state area in terms of built-in expectations regarding equality in the arrangements between ethnic groups. California is economically richer than the other three states. California Chicanos aspire to leave agriculture and believe they have a right to a better future than agricultural work can provide. In Texas, there is more acceptance of the status-quo on both sides of the color line, i.e., more fatalistic belief in the inevitability of racial inequality. In Florida, the co-presence of blacks in the agricultural labor force, along with middle- and upper-class Cuban expatriates in urban areas, and rural enclaves of poor whites, confuses the picture, and places great strain on social institutions: the schools, police, etc.

Politically weak and impoverished rural communities provide industrial agriculture with a dependent pool of labor that is impervious to union organization. Moreover, such communities prevent greater integration and interaction between agriculture and other types of industry. Industrial agriculture is hyperspecialized, much like manufacturing in the nineteenth century. The lack of education, fear of authority, and the language barrier, which are such evident features of these communities, would make retraining, cross-training and the upgrade of tasks extremely difficult.

Similarly, any displacement of labor or reduction of the number of jobs resulting from new technologies could have potentially disruptive consequences. The data reported in the following section reveal a seeming paradox; namely, high levels of poverty in the same communities which have high levels of employment, approaching 100 percent employed in some tracts. The capacity of industrial agriculture to employ is almost as well-known as the capacity of nineteenth century industrialized manufacturing to employ. Urban-based welfare caseworkers routinely refer their clients to employment opportunities on nearby farms. There is a seasonal migration of over 15,000 welfare recipients from the city of Fresno to the west side of San Joaquin Valley, for example. However, this is subject to change, and there is some evidence that it is beginning to change; i.e., there is some evidence of unemployment even in the most industrialized agricultural areas (although it is chemical use, not mechanization which is associated with labor displacement—see below). Any change in agricultural structure which substantially reduces its capacity to employ will drive up welfare roles and increase crime rates in rural areas, thereby increasing costs to local government and potentially producing a social environment that is unfriendly to agriculture itself.

Agriculture And The Small Community:
A Causal Analysis

The evidence presented has shown a strong association between industrial agriculture and the degradation of rural communities. Certain justifiable methodological questions can be raise d against it, having to do with accidental association: it is possible that "things are rough all over" in rural areas of the U.S. and that the "relationship" between industrial agriculture and rural community conditions as so far described is mainly accidental. This concern is mitigated by the regression analysis in the following sections which show increasing and decreasing community pathology correlated with increasing and decreasing agricultural industrialization variables. In other words, things may be subjectively rough "all over," but objectively they are the roughest in areas of greatest agricultural industrialization. The relationship is not accidental. The discovery of this relationship requires us to rethink current theory and policy.

Policy makers in the U.S are adept at thinking in terms of an opposition of interest between large-scale industry and the urban community. But this same kind of understanding does not characterize thinking about the rural community and the agricultural economy. Much of the current stereotype of rural America is based on the historic, Midwestern, family farm experience. In one of his Saturday radio chats, President Reagan said, "Every American should have the opportunity to live in a small, rural community." He certainly could not have had in mind Rio Grande City, Texas, or Three Rocks, California. The conditions which favor unified agricultural and rural policies probably never existed in the most productive agricultural areas of the Sunbelt. Today, the presence of industrial agriculture near the small communities in rural areas of California, Arizona, Texas, and Florida make them the opposites of their of their ideal image. In the place of towns which could be described as providing their residents with a clean and healthy environment, social equality, local autonomy and democratic institutions, we have pesticide container dumps, wiring by extension cords strung from house to house, multihouse water supply from a single faucet, workers on minimum wage giving kickbacks to employers in order to keep jobs, teenaged children who have never been to school, and a range of related social pathologies. Few Sunbelt industrial agricultural communities support a local middle class or the businesses and services demanded by that class.

The industrialization of agriculture and concentration of land and capital in the study area have produced a new and clear division within the rural sector; namely, policies that benefit agricultural businesses do not automatically improve the life of agricultural laborers and rural nonfarm peoples. Current policies and technologies designed to promote agriculture, insofar as they lead to the expansion of existing operations and greater concentration, in actual practice, also promote the deterioration of rural community life. This can be demonstrated by an analysis of the relationship of agribusiness to poverty in the 98 sample counties.

Agribusiness And Rural Poverty

The federal poverty standard (or "poverty line") has been criticized both for being ungenerous (i.e., for underestimating actual poverty), and for producing inflated figures (i.e., for failing to take into account income from food stamps, welfare payments, etc). In California, less than 15 percent of those persons below the poverty line are served by the social programs for which they qualify (food stamps, etc.), so it is likely that overall we are underestimating actual poverty. For purposes of this analysis, poverty is used only as a social indicator, not a measure of individual need. Even if the federal poverty standard provides an underestimate of actual poverty, it is a good social indicator because it is intercorrelated with numerous other measures of social well-being; i.e., infant mortality, ethnic inequality, low wages, absence of quality social institutions, etc. Poverty levels in urban areas of the Sunbelt average around 8 percent of the population. In rural tracts dominated by moderate- and family-sized farms, the average is about 10-12 percent. Poverty figures in rural agribusiness tracts of the Sunbelt indicate much larger proportions of all segments of the population (families, unrelated individuals, Spanish surname families), live below poverty in these areas. In Arizona rural agribusiness tracts, family poverty affects about 20 percent of the overall population and up to 40 percent of the families in one tract. Spanish surname family poverty runs 5 to 20 percentage points higher in all the tracts. The poverty figures for unrelated individuals are as high as 60 to 70 percent. In Texas agribusiness tracts, family poverty ranges from 5 to 40 percentage points higher than national averages; up to 47 percent of the population in poverty. The figures for Spanish surname families are consistently higher, varying from a few points up to 15 points higher than the total population figures. Four of the 10 Texas tracts have Spanish surname poverty exceeding 45 percent.

Tables 4 and 5 give scatter plot diagrams of the relationship of poverty to agribusiness at the county level. The "California pattern" noted in previous studies by the macrosocial accounting project appears in Table 4. California exhibits a low-dispersion linear relationship in which increases in income from agriculture are associated with increasing levels of poverty. (The Pearson's correlation between the two variables is .47 for all the counties in California and it doubles when only rural counties are analyzed.) This relationship, when considered outside of the theoretical framework being developed here, is remarkable for two reasons: (1) it is counter intuitive because increasing wealth (from agriculture) is associated with increasing poverty, and (2) it reveals poverty to be a rural and agricultural, not an urban, phenomenon as it is widely thought to be. Within the framework of the industrialization-degradation thesis, the positive correlation between agricultural wealth and poverty is precisely what would be predicted. It was only the persistence of the family farm pattern throughout America during the last one hundred years that masked the relationship which is now beginning to appear in these data. [Table 5 about here]

Table 5 shows that the positive relationship between agribusiness and poverty has two forms. The first form is the California pattern in which substantial increases in income from agriculture are associated with small increases

Table 4. Agribusiness and Poverty in California

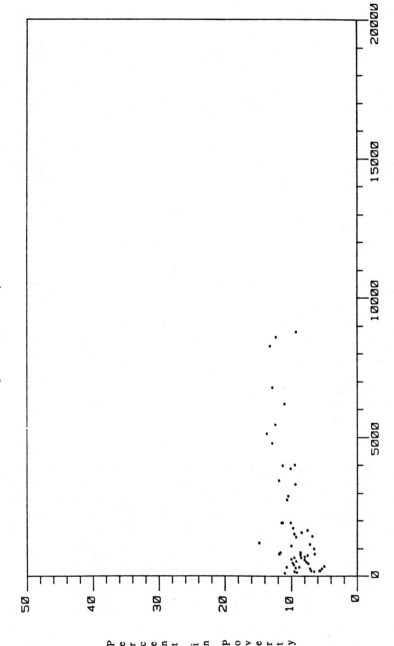

Per capita income from agriculture - CA - 1974

Table 5. Agribusiness and Poverty in the Sunbelt

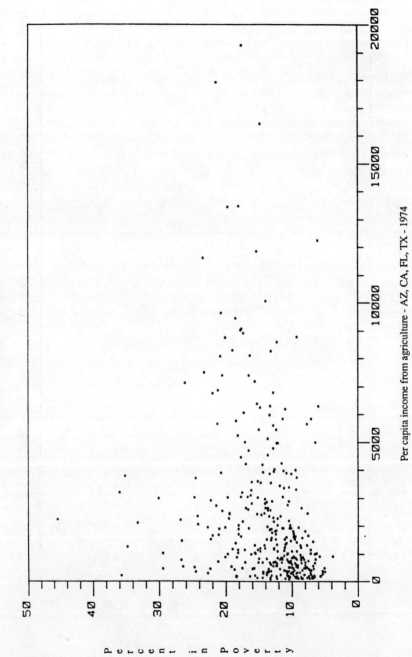

Per capita income from agriculture - AZ, CA, FL, TX - 1974

in poverty. The second pattern, associated with the other states in the analysis, exhibits a steeper slope in which slight increases in agricultural income, up to a restricted limit, area associated with sharp increases in poverty.

A second way to look at the same relationship is via regression analysis. Tables 6, 7, and 8, give the relationships of farm size to poverty in 1970 and 1980 and to the change in poverty from 1970 to 1980. Table 5 shows a weak, negative relations hip between farm size and poverty in 1970. In other words, there was still some evidence for a direct linkage between agricultural structure and community conditions in the study area in 1970: as farm size increased, poverty decreased. By 1980, this relationship had reversed. Table 7 shows a weak but statistically significant positive relationship between farm size and poverty. By 1980, the farm system and rural community conditions had become disarticulated and the first evidence appears suggesting that increasing development of agriculture leads to deteriorating social conditions. Table 8 shows a strong and highly significant relationship between farm size and the rate of increase in poverty from 1970 to

Table 6. Farm Size and Poverty in 1970

Analysis of Variance

Source	DF	Sum of Squares	Mean Square	F Value	Prob > F
Model	1	720.4597	720.4597	7.144	0.0106
Error	43	4336.246	100.8429		
C Total	44	5056.706			

Root MSE		10.04206	R-Square	0.1425	
Dep Mean		48.08222	ADJ R-Sq	0.1225	
C.V.		20.88518			

Table 7. Farm Size and Poverty in 1980
Analysis of Variance

Source	DF	Sum of Squares	Mean Square	F Value	F Prob >F
Model	1	120.5261	120.5261	4.103	0.0491
Error	43	1263.237	29.3776		
C Total	44	1383.763			

Root MSE		5.420111	R-Square	0.0871	
Dep Mean		15.53556	ADJ R-Sq	0.0659	
C.V.		34.88843			

Table 8. Farm Size and Increasing Poverty: 1970–1980
Analysis of Variance

Source	DF	Sum of Squares	Mean Square	F Value	F Prob >F
Model	1	4392.325	4392.325	32.613	0.0001
Error	43	5791.217	134.6795		
C Total	44	10183.54			

Root MSE		11.60515	R-Square	0.4313	
Dep Mean		−66.2719	ADJ R-Sq	0.4181	
C.V.		−17.5114			

1980. In the 98 study counties, over 40 percent of the increase in poverty is directly attributable to farm size differences with the greatest increases associated with the largest farm sizes. The results of this analysis provide support both for the general relationship of industrialization to community degradation, and to the historical point that this form of agricultural is a relatively recent, regional specific phenomenon.

Industrialization And Social Conditions

The following sections discuss the results of analysis of the affects of farm structure and changing agricultural technology on rural community conditions. The analysis is based on regression models in which farm structure and agricultural technology indicators are entered as independent or causal variables, and measures of social conditions (median income, services per capita, etc.) are entered as dependent variables. It can be noted that the discovery of any relationship between farm structure and community conditions at the county level is highly unusual. There are many kinds of social and economic activities, other than agriculture, which occur within these counties, which potentially buffer and obscure whatever connections may exist between farming systems and community life. Nevertheless, the following tests of the industrialization— community degradation hypothesis assume that there are no other variables intervening between agricultural structure and social conditions in the 98 sample counties. We know this is a false assumption. The presence of many and medium-sized cities with relatively low rates of poverty, higher family incomes, and job opportunities in nonagricultural work, certainly obscures the depressing effects of industrial agriculture in any Sunbelt county-level analysis. (Note that this would not necessarily be true for other areas of the nation where urban-industrial sectors are as depressed as agriculture.) The following regressions demand, in effect, that variation in agricultural structure predict all the variation in social conditions in the study sample, not just those conditions experienced by the people and communities embedded in the matrix of industrial agriculture. Thus, when it is shown, for example, that 18 percent of the variation in median family income at the county

level is a function of farm size, with the larger sized
farms predicting smaller family incomes, we are looking at
the incomes of every family in the county; i.e., the doctor
in town as well as the farm owners, and not just the families of farm laborers. This approach has been dictated by a
lack of readily available data at a more precisely delim-
ited community level of analysis. But the results, even
diluted form serve to indicate the power of industrial
agriculture to pull down social conditions for the entire
county and region, not merely for the nearby, small farm
worker communities.

Specifying The Goldschmidt Model

In an early study, which set the terms for the debate
on the relationship of agriculture to social conditions in
the U.S., Goldschmidt (1944) found a series of negative
social effects associated with large scale agriculture in
the Central Valley of California. Goldschmidt's research
was based on a matched pair comparison of a large farm community (Arvin) and a small farm community (Dinuba). He
found higher family incomes, lower poverty, more retail
trade, better schools, more recreational opportunity,
stronger institutions including churches, and more newspa-
per readership in the small farm community than in the
larger one. Goldschmidt's study has been heavily criticized, especially by apologists for agribusiness, for methodological inadequacy and because it violates conventional
socioeconomic reason. Conventional logic suggests that as
the dominant economic activity of a region (in this case
agriculture) increases in size and volume, and modernizes
and becomes more efficient and profitable, the entire
region and all the communities—eventually every class and
ethnic group within the region—will benefit in the form of
improved living standards. Following this logic, Goldschmidt's critics have argued that the differences he found
between Arvin and Dinuba were only temporary, that the
large farm community would eventually catch up with and
surpass Dinuba on all indicators of the quality of community life. Other critics have suggested that something
other than the structure of agriculture was responsible for
the better living conditions in Dinuba, or for the
depressed condition of Arvin. All of these critics have

missed a primary point of the study, that industrial work-places in agriculture are harmful to farm workers. This conclusion is unassailed by the critiques.

In actuality, Arvin has not surpassed Dinuba in the forty years since Goldschmidt's study. In fact, original differences between the two communities have become accen-tuated. But in fairness to Goldschmidt's critics, it has been difficult to replicate his findings until recently (see Green, 1985). The present study suggests some reasons for the inconclusive nature of the "large farm—small farm debate." What is needed is a more powerful theory and empirical methods. Specifically, what is suggested here is the idea of the industrial farm as qualitatively different from previous forms of small- to moderate-scale family farming. Earlier studies and discussions have been based on the assumption of a linear relationship between farm size and community conditions. Small farm "advocates" have claimed that increasing farm size leads to community dete-rioration, a position which appears to be similar to the hypothesis guiding this study. Until recently, large farm "advocates" have been able to suggest, without much fear of contradiction, that there was precious little evidence, beyond anecdote and Goldschmidt's original finding, for the small farm position. What is the actual situation?

The theory behind the present research suggests that the relationship of farm structure to community conditions is curvilinear. Specifically, one would hypothesize that in areas dominated by small- to moderate-sized family farms, farm size differences are either randomly associated with community conditions, or, if there is a relationship, it would be positive; namely, increasing farm size would be associated with community improvement. However, in an industrial farm context, where the agricultural economy is integrated into the world system and becomes detached from the local rural community, increasing the size, technologi-cal sophistication, and power of agriculture leads to declining social conditions at the local community level.

In sum, the overall relationship between agricultural economy and community conditions is hypothesized to fit an inverted "J" curve, with general conditions remaining unchanged, or improving with increases in farm size up to approximately 300 acres under conventional forms of family management, then dramatic declines in the general welfare with further increases in size under an industrial administrative model. Goldschmidt tapped into this relationship perhaps by accident when he included Arvin (one of the first Sunbelt communities to practice irrigated agriculture on large acreages using an industrial management model) in his study. But within the framework of the theory presented here, one would not expect to be able to replicate his findings in a comparison of small versus large family farms. In fact, the results of such a study might appear to contradict Goldschmidt. The present study was able to replicate Goldschmidt's findings because it was looking at the relationship between agriculture and the community in a region dominated by industrial agriculture, that is, at relationships on the "downside" of the inverted "J" curve.

THE REGRESSION MODELS

The relationship between agricultural industrialization and community conditions was tested in two ways: (1) the static relationship between agricultural structure in 1980 and social conditions in 1980, and (2) the dynamic relationship of agricultural structure in 1970 and the rate of change in social conditions from 1970 to 1980. The tests appear as a series of regression models in CATF Appendix B. All nine agricultural industrialization variables were originally entered in to each model as causal variables. Only those agricultural measures which significantly and independently predict variation in the social variables are retained in the final analysis. In other words, the absence of an agricultural variable from the model does not necessarily mean the absence of correlation with social conditions, only lack of predictive power in the overall context of the agricultural industrialization model.

Population The measures of percent urban, rural farm and rural nonfarm tend to be associated with agricultural industrialization as would be expected. Average farm size is negatively correlated with percent urban but positively with percent rural , for example. But there are some agricultural industrialization—population relationships that require closer scrutiny. Specifically, full-time workers on farms is positively correlated with urbanization. This finding suggests that farms organized in such a way as to use stable, long-term labor are found most frequently in regions with closer rural-urban ties. Similarly, corporate ownership of farms is negatively correlated with farm population as a percent of the total population but positively correlated with nonfarm population as a percent of rural. These findings suggests that the stability of the farm work situation and incorporation are occurring in those areas that are less rural farm in character; i.e., with closer urban ties and a higher proportion of nonfarm people living in the countryside. This finding is consistent with the hypothesis that incorporation and stable labor practices reflects participation in a generalized value structure which supports wage and work condition standardization between rural and urban sectors, and higher expectations for community quality. The correlation of farm incorporation with favorable community conditions does not wash out the negative independent effects of farm size, mechanization, etc.

In the dynamic relationship of industrialization to community conditions, high levels of corporate ownership and gross sales in 1970 predicts total population increases from 1970 to 1980, while farm size and mechanization predicts population stagnation or decrease. The use of machines and chemicals in agriculture also drives down both rural farm and general rural populations. This finding is consistent with earlier studies (see, e.g., Goldschmidt, 1944; MacCannell and White, 1984) which show that increasing farm size and industrialization is antithetical to organized rural community life.

Family Income

Farm size is the strongest—although negative—predictor of median family income in the static relationship: as farm size increases median family income decreases. Full-time workers in agriculture is the only other variable to enter into a n independent significant relationship with income. Full-time work is positively associated with median income, supporting the idea that this group might constitute the base for an emergent middle class in some high-agricultural-influence counties.

The only 1970 agricultural variable which predicts the rate of change in median family income from 1970 to 1980 is proportion of the farms in a county with annual sales of

more than $40,000. This variable accounts for 18 percent of
the variation in change in median income and the association is negative; i.e., high sales in 1970 predicts low
growth of income from 1970 to 1980. In sum, the measures of
agricultural industrialization which enter into a relationship with income are inversely associated with median family income at the county level. This finding is counter-
intuitive from the standpoint of common sense and standard
economic reasoning, but it supports the industrialization—
degradation hypothesis. Employment In an earlier study,
MacCannell and White (1984) found that the pattern of
employment in high-agricultural-influence counties to be
one of high employment and substandard wages. The present
study brings greater specificity to our understanding of
this relationship. Unemployment is negatively associated
with both farm size and mechanization as previously determined; i.e., large industrialized farms are major employers
of unskilled workers earning low wages. This is a problem-
atical finding from a policy and planning standpoint
because it suggests that job training is not an answer to
the wage and employment problems of industrial agricultural
areas. Rather, wages, working conditions, and the mix of
jobs now available must be targeted for change if there is
to be any reasonable expectation of an improvement in the
situation of farm worker families. At the present time,
pubilic policy is not prepared to deal with this issue.

The proportion of farms with gross sales in the highest
sales category (more than $100,000 per year) is correlated
with unemployment. This is the first evidence we have found
in these kinds of farming systems for a relationship
between an aspect o f industrialization and unemployment.
Overall, 31 percent of the variation in unemployment in
these high-agricultural-influence areas is accounted for by
the industrialization model.

Poverty

Ten percent of the variation in families living below
the federal poverty standard and 14 percent of the variation in individuals below the poverty standard is predicted
by the industrialization model in the 1980 static analysis.
Average farm size is the strongest predictor for both families and individuals and the relationship is positive. That

is, again in support of the industrialization-degradation hypothesis, as average farm size increases so does poverty. Industrialization may be a better predictor of individual (as opposed to family) poverty because of a relatively high proportion of "unrelated individuals" in the migrant labor population. Corporate ownership has a weak but significant negative relationship to poverty suggesting that marginally better wage structures are found in those areas (already determined to be more urban) where there are relatively more corporate farms. This might be traced to alternative employment opportunities in nearby urban and suburb an areas driving up expectations and wages.

The same patterns are stronger in the analysis of the change of poverty from 1970 to 1980. Twenty-four percent of the variation in change in individual poverty between 1970 and 1980 is accounted for by the operation of a single industrialization variable: average farm size in 1970. Again, the relationship supports the industrialization-degradation hypothesis; poverty persists and increases in the large farm counties. Change in family poverty is correlated with expenditures for machines, also in an industrialization-degradation direction: the most mechanized counties have the most persistent family poverty. This is also entirely consistent with Marx's prediction of the effects of the mechanization of production processes on wages.

Local Government

Evidence for the disarticulation of agriculture from the rural community appears in the absence of any relationship of farm size and sales to local taxes and per capita expenditures by local government. However, both taxation and levels of expenditure are related to the proportion of farms with full-time hired labor. This is further evidence for existence of institutions supportive of a local middle class and generalized (rural and urban) social values associated with stable patterns of management-labor relations. In the dynamic analysis, high levels of corporate ownership in 1970 predicts increasing local government revenues from 1970 to 1980. However, high levels of mechanization in 1970 had a depressing effect on the revenues of local governments.

Manufacture, Wholesale, And Retail Trade

Average farm size and high sales have a consistently depressing effect on measures of nonfarm and off-farm economic activity. In the static analysis, farms with sales of $100,000 or more is negatively correlated with retail sales and retail establishments per capita. Farm size in acres is negatively correlated with employment in the service and manufacturing sectors. All these relationships are significant and supportive of the industrialization-degradation hypothesis. The overall picture that emerges is that as farm size and sales increase, other occupational opportunities and community amenities constrict. Corporate ownership and full-time labor continue to act as buffers between the negative social impact of farm size, gross sales, and mechanization.

With but one exception, the agricultural structure variables did not predict change in wholesale and retail trade and other employment opportunities between 1970 and 1980. The industrialization model did predict 48 percent of the variation in the change in the numbers of retail trade establishments. Mechanization and the use of chemicals on farms is correlated with declining numbers of retail establishments, while corporate ownership and full-time labor is associated with increasing retail trade establishments.

Conclusion

With some qualification, the relationship of agricultural structure to rural community conditions throughout the study area supports the industrialization—-degradation hypothesis: as the degree of agricultural industrialization increases social conditions in the rural communities become worse. This test of the hypothesis can be considered rigorous because (1) it measures social impacts of agricultural structure at the county level where any such impacts are weakened by other economic and sociodemographic factors, (2) it tests for the relationship across four states, 98 counties and over five million people, and (3) it is restricted to rather small variations between counties preselected to represent only the highest levels of industrialization and intensiveness of agriculture found in the U.S. today. All these factors would tend to obscure the strength of the relationship between agricultural industrialization and community conditions. Nevertheless, many such relationships have been found at statistically acceptable levels of significance. Repeated tests have consistently shown that increasing farm size, mechanization, and gross sales significantly predict declining community conditions not merely at the local agricultural community level, but in the entire county.

The industrialization variables that do not predict in the hypothesized direction are corporate ownership and full-time workers. The behavior of the full-time workers variable relative to community quality measures is understandable and requires no modification of the industrialization-degradation hypothesis. Where industry curtails its exploitation and abuses (in this case of labor) social conditions improve. The corporate ownership question is more complex. Critics of large farms have of ten seized upon the term "corporate farm" as the best label for the pathologies that they want to oppose. It is now evident that there are several different forms of corporate farming ranging from farms that become subsidiaries of major food conglomerates to incorporating for tax purposes, even perhaps as an intermediary step to delay eventual economic failure. Incorporation in an of itself appears to represent a neutral form of modernization of the farm enterprise that may bring with it better and more stable relationships with banks, unions, nonunion labor, consumers and environmental groups. Rural community problems are associated with farm size and measures of industrialization, not incorporation per se.

AGRICULTURAL TECHNOLOGY AND COMMUNITY CONDITIONS

The adoption and diffusion of new technology is especially important in the framework of agricultural industrialization. The specific impacts of agricultural technology on community conditions was tested in the following way. We selected two technology variables, machine costs per farm and chemical costs per farm, and created a typology of farming systems based on their characteristics in 1970 and patterns of change from 1970 to 1980. The system types, are defined as follows:

MachHiHi = Counties in which both machine costs in 1970 and growth in machine costs from 1970 to 1980 were above the mean for all counties

MachHiLo = Counties in which machine costs in 1970 were above the mean for all counties and the growth of machine costs from 1970 to 1980 were below the mean

MachLoHi = Counties in which machine costs in 1970 were below the mean for all counties and the growth in machine costs from 1970 to 1980 was above the mean.

A parallel set of types were constructed for chemical use: *ChemHiHi, ChemHiLo*, and *ChemLoHi*. In addition, for purposes of verification, a similar set of types was constructed for the farm size variable. That is, we looked at the position of the counties relative to one another in terms of average farm size in 1970, and the growth in farm size between 1970 and 1980: Size HiHi, SizeHiLo, and Size LoHi. These large and/or increasing technology and size types were contrasted with the "LoLo" counties in the following regression models. These procedures permitted us to examine the social impacts of high and persistent, or recently growing, use of two forms of agricultural technology. The large and persistent, or growing, size in acres models permit a parallel test of the affects of a variable known to be associated with adoption of new technologies, and also the affects of increasing concentration of land ownership in agriculture.

The resulting nine types of technology use and concentration were entered as causal variables in a series of regression equations using the measures of social conditions as dependent variables. Unlike the analysis discussed in the previous sections, all nine technology and size types were retained in the final regression equations, not just those which entered into statistically significant relationships with community conditions. The results of this test are presented in CATF Appendix B and discussed in the following sections.

Population

In general, agricultural technology types are not strong predictors of changes in county population configurations (e.g., rural/urban ratios). This is understandable in light of the fact that virtually every variable used in constructing these models has, including the technology variables, has a population size control built in. As a result, there is not much variation left to explain. Increasing mechanization from a low base (MachLoHi) is found in counties with low rural population. High and increasing farm size (SizeHiHi) is found in counties with low rural population. High and increasing farm size (SizeHiHi) is also associated with declining farm and rural nonfarm populations. These relationships make sense conceptually but they appear as isolated "hits" in the regression models.

There is one strong model: 26 percent of the variance in the change of farm population is accounted for by the size model (see CATF Appendix C; Table 1). Increasing farm size from 1970 to 1980 is associated with decreasing farm population, mainly independent of conditions in 1970. On the other hand, high chemical use in 1970 in conjunction with continued high growth in chemical use between 1970 and 1980 predicts increasing farm population. We are not fully confident that the direction of causality is from agricultural structure to community conditions in these models. It is possible that only those farms located at a distance from population centers can increase in size, and/or that those farms near population centers practice a different kind of agriculture or grow a different crop mix involving the use of more chemicals.

Income And Employment

The technology and size types do not predict income differences between counties in the static analyses, but they prove to be occasionally good predictors of changes in median family income from 1970 to 1980. Thirty percent of the variance in changing family incomes is accounted for by five technology and size types, all supporting the industrialization—degradation hypothesis. High mechanization and chemical use in 1970 are the best predictors of declining median family income. (See CATF Appendix C; Table 2.)

CATF Appendix C, Table 3 shows the relationship between agricultural technology and unemployment. The only significant relationships here are with chemical use. High chemical use in 1970 and high growth (from a low base—ChemLoHi) in chemical use between 1970 and 1980 is associated with increasing unemployment.

Technology, Farm Size, And Family Poverty

Throughout this study, family poverty, as opposed to individual poverty, has proven to be difficult to predict using agricultural structure variables. There are good sociological reasons for this. The working family serves as a buffer against poverty in industrial agricultural areas. Cultural factors may contribute to this. In Hispanic families, there is a longer period of child-parent interdependence, and a greater willingness on the part of children to turn over earnings to their parents, than would be the case for Anglo families of the same social class.

The technology and size types predict 15 percent of the variation in the change in family poverty from 1970 to 1980. Three out of four of the significant relationships are with the "HiHi" patterns, all supportive of the industrialization-degradation hypothesis. In other words, relatively high technology use and large farm size in 1970, coupled with continued high increases in technology use and increasing farm size between 1970 and 1980, drive families into poverty. This is an important finding from the standpoint of public policy affecting farm structure and technological development. It suggests that stable family relationships cannot ultimately withstand the pressures of continued increases in farm size and use of technology in industrial agriculture. Increasing numbers of families are succumbing to poverty under intense technological development and increasing concentration of land ownership in industrial agriculture.

Individual poverty is predicted by large and increasing farm size (SizeHiHi), and by high chemical use in 1970.(See CATF Appendix C; Table 5.)

Retail Trade

The retail trade models are given in CATF Appendix C, Tables 6 and 7. Increasing farm size and increasing chemical use between 1970 and 1980 predict declining numbers of retail establishments and declining per capita sales. Those counties with large farms in 1970 that did not continue to increase the size of their farms between 1970 and 1980 at a rate greater than the average, actually increased their retail sales on a per capita basis.

Discussion

The results of the foregoing special analysis of farm size and farm size increase, and technology use and acquisition, overwhelmingly support the industrialization—degradation hypothesis. Every significant relationship in the predicted direction. The general conclusion to be drawn from these tests is that there is already advanced community deterioration in those Sunbelt counties which have achieved the highest levels of industrial agricultural development. This deterioration can be traced directly to the structure of agriculture as it is practiced in the region; i.e., high and increasing concentration of land ownership and high and increasing use of technology. the current trend toward increasing farm size and concentration (see Table 1A and B) and use of new technologies (see U.S. OTA, 1986) will accelerate the social degradation of these communities unless there is substantial programming which addresses the problem.

The implications of these findings are chilling in the context of current projections of agricultural and technological change. Production scientists have argued persuasively "that American agriculture is poised in the threshold of another technological revolution." Currently, there is concern that this technological revolution may have unforeseen and undesired negative impacts on soil, air, and water quality, and on wildlife and human health. On the basis of the evidence now before us, it is reasonable to add the rural community and rural family to this list.

Labor Displacement

A greater risk to the already over-stressed and fragile rural communities of the Sunbelt is posed by labor displacement from new technologies. Traditionally and at the present time, work in industrial agriculture has been readily available. The government of Mexico estimates that its greatest source of dollars is the money sent home by Mexican nationals working in agriculture in the study area. While farm labor jobs are plentiful they are also the last resort for many workers; i.e., industrial agricultural jobs are the lowest status and lowest paying in American society. Young Greencard workers in California repeatedly express their desire to leave the valley and find a "good job" washing cars or dishes in a city. When these agricultural jobs disappear there are no others for us to fall back upon, either individually or as a society concerned about the disorganizing effects of mass unemployment in an important sector of the economy; e.g., unpredictable migrations, organized crime, and the appearance of articulate anti-American sentiments within our own society.

Our research suggests that under current conditions, the risks of labor displacement are greater for chemical-based technologies than for machine-based technologies. This finding should be reexamined in light of the basic features of the 28 new technologies described in a recent (1986) Office of Technology Assessment report—15 are chemical-based technologies. Eleven of the technologies are machine-based, but most of these 11 are actually computer-based. We have not been able to measure the effects of computers on farm structure and community conditions. It is possible that computers may resemble chemicals more than traditional machinery when it comes to their social impacts. In any event, most of the new technologies will be labor displacing, perhaps all of them will be. There are substantial risks of labor displacement that will stress rural communities to the breaking point, i.e., generate problems which demand substantial public intervention.

Scale Neutrality and New Technologies

Our size and technology models provide clear evidence that as farm size increases community conditions deteriorate. In reviewing the adoption curves of new technologies and packages of technology provided by OTA, none are projected to be scale neutral. While we realize that their adoption projection figure may not be perfectly accurate, we think there is little reason to doubt the general conclusions about these new technologies reached by the production scientist teams: large farms will be the first to adopt new technologies and adoption will be the norm in the largest -sized farm category; small-to-moderate sized farms will adopt slowly or not at all. There is only one possible social impact of this pattern. The larger farms will increase their market advantage and grow in size and numbers, while the social conditions of agricultural labor and the small communities will continue to deteriorate.

Public Policy Alternatives

The so called "large farm" future condition described in discussions of public-policy alternatives has already been achieved in the Sunbelt study counties. This gives us an opportunity to study effects of "large farm scenarios" on present day communities as we have done in this report. But it also restricts the range of public policy options aimed at improving the situation and increasing numbers of moderate-sized farms in the Sunbelt region. In other areas of the U.S. it is possible to increase the numbers of moderate-sized farms by developing policy which favors such farms. However, in California, Arizona, Texas, and Florida, the only way to increase the numbers of moderate-sized farms is by scaling down existing large farms. Also, to the extent that there is a national agricultural system, any restrictions on Midwestern agriculture may stimulate further growth of industrial-scale farming in the Sunbelt.

One of the clear lessons learned in the course of the research leading to this report is that the entire farm size debate has been badly framed, at least from the standpoint of the scale of agriculture that is found in the four state study area. In OTA analyses of technology packages, "large farm" most often falls in the 600-800 acre range. The 2,000-acre average farm size for the 98-study counties casts these estimates in a new light. The distinction we should be making for policy purposes is not between moderate- and large-scale farming but between super-sized industrial farms as found in the Sunbelt and the small- to large-sized farms found in other areas of the U.S. Much of the reason for the current crisis in other areas of the U.S. agriculture stems from domestic and international market domination by industrial superfarms. These farms, starting out on large nonirrigated acreages have, since World War II been able to exploit a series of advantages including longer growing seasons and milder winters, new sources of subsidized irrigation water, cheap foreign labor, and access to commodity support programs intended for normal farms. The strongest policy recommendation to be derived from these findings is the need for a policy focus on "farms" which are much larger than those currently labeled as large farms—the superfarms.

Controlling The Negative Impacts Of Agricultural Concentration And Technological Change

Following are eight recommendations for future action which would have the affect of slowing, arresting, and possibly reversing the degradation of rural communities associated with the development of industrial agriculture.

First, the federal government should define and move to separate superscale farming operations (farms which own their own banks, trucking companies, processing plants, etc.) from other types of freestanding farming operations that are operated as small business.

Second, the social responsibility (i.e., workplace standards and contributions to community infrastructural improvements) of superscale farms should be spelled out.

Third, special taxes on superscale agriculture based on sales volume and/or profits should be considered as a way of financing the community development work required to repair the social damage which has already been done.

Fourth, the Reclamation Law governing access to federally subsidized irrigation water should be strictly interpreted and enforced and fines collected for violation should be reinvested in community improvement and social programs.

Fifth, current laws against hiring illegal aliens should be enforced at the farm level and employer fines for violation of these laws should be increased until the practice stops.

Sixth, minimum-wage laws for all workers (alien and U.S. citizens) should be strictly enforced with particular attention given to "job costs," i.e., growers' practices of charging for transportation to and from the fields.

Seventh, the extension services and experiment stations of the land-grant universities should be charged with the responsibility of adapting all new technologies to small- to moderate-scale farms and rewarded for success in delivering technological expertise to small- to moderate-scale farmers.

Eighth, commodity programs should continue to be sales volume sensitive as they are now (i.e., increasing supports with increasing sales) up to the threshold of super-scale farming, then all support should come off, i.e., no super-farms should benefit from any such programs.

REFERENCES

Agriculture and Human Values
    1984   Special issue on "Land Reform and Land Use Ethics,"
           Vol. 1 No. 3 (Summer).

Barkley, P. W.
    1978   "Some Nonfarm Effects of Change in Agricultural
           Technology." *American Journal of Agricultural
           Economics*, Vol. 58: pp. 812-19.

Bergland, Bob
    1981   A Time to Choose. Final report of the Secretary of
           Agriculture, Washington, D.C.: U.S. Government
           Printing Office.

Bertrand, Alvin, and Floyd Corty
    1962   *Rural Land Tenure in the United States.* Baton Rouge:
           Louisiana State University Press.

Borgers, Peggy
    1980   "The Hidden Link: Agricultural Structure and the
           quality of Rural Life," Perspectives on the Structure
           of American Agriculture. Vol. II. Rural
           America/Community Services Administration
           Newsletter: Pp. 49-53.

Buttel, Frederick H.
    1983   Agricultural Communities: The Interrelationship of
           Agriculture, Business, Industry, and Government in the
           Rural Economy. Committee Print. Prepared by the
           Congressional Research Service, Library of Congress for
           the Committee on Agriculture, U.S. House of
           Representatives, 98th Congress. Washington, D.C.:U.S.
           Government Printing Office. Pp. 150-173.

Carter, Luther J.
    1974   *The Florida Experience: Land and Water Policy in a
           Growth State.* Baltimore: Johns-Hopkins University
           Press.

Cernea, Mihail
    1975   "The Large-Scale Formal Organization and the Family
           Primary Group," *Journal of Marriage and the Family*,
           November: 927-936.

Coughenour, C. Milton and Gregory S. Kowalski
  1977   "Status and Role of Fathers and Sons on Partnership
         Farms," *Rural Sociology*, V 42, (2): 180-205.
Doeksen, Gerald A.
  1987   "The Agricultural Crisis as it Affects Rural
         Communites," *Journal of the Community Development
         Society*, V 18 (1): 78-88.
Friedland, William H. et al.
  1978   *Manufacturing Green Gold: The Conditions and Social
         Consequences of Lettuce Harvest Mechanization.*
         Publication Number 2. California Agricultural Policy
         Seminar, Department of Applied Behavioral Science,
         University of California at Davis. (July)
Geisler, Charles C. and Frank J. Popper, eds.
  1984   *Land Reform American Style.* New Jersey: Rowman
         and Allenheld.
Goldschmidt, Walter F.
  1978   *As You Sow.*   Montclair, New Jersey: Allanheld,
         Osmun and Co.
Gorz, Andre
  1982   *Farewell to the Working Class.*   Boston: South End
         Press.
Green, Gary P.
  1985   "Large-Scale Farming and the Quality of life in Rural
         Communities: Further Specification of the Goldschmidt
         Hypothesis" *Rural Sociology* 50(2): 263-272.
Heffernan, William D.
  1979   "The Structure of Agriculture and the Rural
         Community," *AgWorld* September/October: 18-20.
Herrera-Sobek, Maria
  1979   *The Bracero Experience: Elitlore Versus Folklore.*
         University of California at Los Angeles Latin American
         Center.
  1982   "The Acculturation Process of the Chicana in the
         Corrido" *De Colores*   6(1-2): 7-16.
Hollander, Rachelle D.
  1986   "Values and Making Decisions About Agricultural
         Research" *Agriculture and Human Values* 3(3): 33-40.
Kessler, Ronald C.
  1981   *Linear Panel Analysis: Models of Quantitative Change.*
         New York: Academic Press.
Koning, Neik
  1983   "Family Farms and Industrial Capitalism" *The*

Netherlands' Journal of Sociology 19(1): 29-46.

Leary, Mary Ellen
  1974 "Paul Taylor: The Power of a Tenacious Man" *The Nation* October 12: 353-358.

MacCannell, Dean
  1978 "The Elementary Structures of Community: Macrosocial Accounting as a Methodology for Theory Building and Policy Formation" pp. 32-48 in E. Blakely (ed.), *Community Development Research.* New York: Behavioral Sciences Press.

MacCannell, Dean, and Edward Dolber-Smith
  1985 "Comunidades rurales, estructura de la agricultura y tecnologias agricolas en zonas de agricultura industrializada," *Agricultura y Sociedad* 36-37 (Julio-Diciembre): 93-121.
  1986 "Report on the Structure of Agriculture and Impacts of New Technologies on Rural Communities in Arizona, California, Florida and Texas" Background Paper 2 in Technology, Public Policy, and the Changing Structure of American Agriculture, V ol II. Background Papers. U.S. Congress, Office of Technology Assessment.

MacCannell, Dean and Jerry White
  1984 "The Social Costs of Large-Scale Agriculture" pp. 35-54 in C. Geisler and F. Popper (eds.), *Land Reform American Style. New Jersey: Rowman and Allanheld.*

Mann, Susan A.
  1987 "The Rise of Wage Labor in the Cotton South: A Global Analysis." *Journal of Peasant Studies* 14(2) (January): 226-241.

Marcussen, Henricher, and Jens Erik Torp
  1982 *The Internationalization of Capital Prospects for the Third World.* London: Zed Books, Ltd.

Martin, Philip L.
  1977 "The Rural Labor Force: Disadvantaged But Growing," Economic and Social Issues newsletter. Cooperative Extension, University of California at Davis. (December).
  1978 "Agricultural Mechanization and Public Policy." Paper presented at the Southwest Labor Studies Conference, Berkeley, California, March 17.

Martin, Philip L., and Alan L. Olmstead
  1985 "The Agricultural Mechanization Controversy' *Science* 227 (8 February): 601-606.

Marx, Karl
  1967 *Capital* vol. 3. New York: International Publishers.
Rodriguez, Nestor P., and Joe R. Feagin
  1986 "Urban Specialization in the World System: An
        Investigation of Historical Cases." *Urban Affairs
        Quarterly* 22 (2) (December): 187-220.
Rohwer, Robert A.
  1951 "Family Farming as a Value," *Rural Sociology* 16(1-4):
        331-38.
Rothman, Robert A., et al.
  1977 "The Undulating Community: A Typology of Recurrent
        Migrations," *Rural Sociology* 42(1): 93-100.
Sassen-Koob, Saskia
  1983 "Recomposition and Peripheralization at the Core" pp.
        88-100 in Marlene Dixon and Susanne Jonas (eds.),
        From Immigrant Labor to Transnational Working Class.
        San Francisco: Synthesis Publications.
Scheuring, Ann F.
  1982 *California Agricultural History.* Berkeley: University of
        California Press.
Smith, Michael Peter
  1987 "Global Capital Restructuring and Local Political Crises
        in US Cities" pp. 234-250 in Jeffrey Henderson and
        Michael Castells (eds.), *Global Restructuring and
        Territorial Development.* New York: Sage Publications.
Texas Agricultural Experiment Station
  N.D. Texas Agriculture in the 80s. Unpublished report.
U.S. Congress, Office of Technology Assessment (OTA)
  1985 A Special Report for the 1985 Farm Bill. OTA-F-282
        (March) Washington, D.C.: U.S. Government Printing
        Office.
  1986a Technology Public Policy and the Changing Structure of
        American Agriculture. OTA-F-285 (March).
        Washington D.C.: U.S. Government Printing Office.
  1986b Technology, Public Policy, and the Changing Structure
        of American Agriculture: Summary. OTA-F-286
        (March). Washington, D.C.: U.S. Government Printing
        Office.
U.S. Department of Agriculture
  1981a Cotton and Wool Outlook and Situation. Washington,
        D.C.: Economic Research Service (March).
  1981b Livestock and Meat Outlook and Situation.
        Washington, D.C.: Economic Research Service (March).

1981c Vegetable Outlook and Situation. Washington, D.C.:
Economics and Statistics Service (March).
1982 Fruit Outlook and Situation. Washington, D.C.:
Economic Research Service (April).
1984 Rice Outlook and Situation Report. Washington, D.C.:
National Economics Division, Economic Research
Service (October).
Villarejo, Don
1981 New Lands for Agriculture: The California State Water
Project. Davis, California: California Institute for
Rural Studies.
Wallerstein, Immanual
1974 *The Modern World System: Capitalist Agriculture and
the Origins of the European World Economy in the
Sixteenth Century.* New York: Academic Press.
1979 *The Capitalist World Economy.* Cambridge: Cambridge
University Press.
Young, Frank W.
1972 "Macrosocial Accounting for Developing Countries"
Sociologia Ruralis XIII/3-4: 288-301.
Young, Ruth C. and Dean MacCannell
1979 "Predicting the Quality of Life in the USA," *Social
Indicators* 6: 23-40.

3
Public Policy, Farm Size, and Community Well-Being in Farming-Dependent Counties of the Plains

Cornelia Butler Flora and Jan L. Flora

This study examines how changes in the structure of agriculture affect the welfare of agricultural communities in the Great Plains and West of the United States. This area of the country has the largest concentration of farming-dependent counties and the most clearly identifiable farming systems. It also has been until recently the last bastion of the Jeffersonian ideal of the family farm, a production unit combining labor, management, and land ownership. Except for the cattle areas in Texas, there were no concentrated land holdings. The farms employed little non-family labor. The occasional hired hand could aspire to rent, then own, a farm. As a result of that relative equality, communities in this part of the country have maintained a relatively high level of community services. Schools, hospitals, libraries, parks, and other locally controlled institutions thrived as a result of local initiative and a willingness to provide local resources for their maintenance and improvement.

These counties have shown steady population decline since the settlement period, although a few counties experiencing a population turn-around in the 1970s, which again reversed to continued out-migration by the mid-1980s. Out-migration was viewed as the result of young people exercising their multiple employment options, which pulled them to cities to work. The good education available in local communities facilitated out-migration, although lack of opportunity in agriculture, deriving from growth in farm size due to the substitution of capital for labor, was a push factor. The farms were relatively large and family-owned. Farm work was performed by family members, who also made the major management decisions. The relative prosperity of the farms contributed to the well-being of the local community. This, in turn, provided the base for family farmers to develop and thrive.

Agricultural structure can vary according to different ways of combining the major factors of production: labor, management, land, and capital. In industrial production, all of these factors are separated, provided by different sectors of society. The result of that separation, in the view of some scholars, is increasing concentration of wealth, as represented by capital, at the expense of those who provide the labor.

In industrial societies, land becomes ever less important, and is generally considered simply as a subcategory of capital, albeit a relatively immobile and nonliquid form of capital. By contrast, in agricultural production (as with urban real estate), land becomes a key symbol and source of wealth. That notion of land as the basic indicator of wealth has caused populists to focus on land ownership as the main indicator of agricultural structure. But such a view neglects the more dynamic aspects of wealth and the structure of production that are more dependent on capital and management than on land or labor. However, it is important to recognize the symbolic nature of land ownership, despite increasing evidence that surplus value can be extracted from agriculture by these who do not own land.

The structure of agriculture can be influenced by large number of factors: natural, policy related, or technology driven. Often, impacts of nature, policy, and technology interact in changing agricultural structure. Such combinations provide differential sources of labor, management, capital and land in farming, implying different repositories of accumulated wealth. For example, high real interest rates (in part of result of monetary and fiscal policy) provide an impetus for depending upon outside providers of capital (stockholders) for a farm operation.

Technology can be viewed as a form of capital that has direct implications for the other factors of production. Technology is not an independent variable, operating outside the policy sphere or market. Instead, technology responds to the policy climate, both in its development and its adoption (see Ruttan and Hayami, 1972, on induced innovation as well as Koppel and Oasa's critique (1987) of that theory. We will examine the major technologies employed in each of the farming systems we analyze and relate them to public policy and changes in the structure of agriculture. Technology does not necessarily cause increasing concentration of wealth nor the increasing imposition of the industrial model of organization of the factors of production in agriculture. But neither can we assume that technology is "size neutral" and thus has no impact on the way the factors of production are combined in various farming systems in the areas under consideration.

Technology in agriculture is often enterprise specific. Certain enterprises and enterprise mixes tend to become systematized into farming systems, implying different mixes of land, capital and labor, as well as differential technology and responses to technological innovation. These farming systems evolve in part in response to the ecology of an area (rainfall, soil quality, climate and topography) and in part to the history of an area, which determines differential access to land and capital and differential availability of labor (Pfeffer, 1983). Thus the analysis linking structure of agriculture to community welfare is specified by type of farming system, allowing greater precision in assessing the impacts of technology and policy.

In order to more precisely isolate the interaction between agricultural structure and community, we have chosen to separately analyze specific farming systems which predominate in farming dependent counties west of the Mississippi River. We chose not to analyze counties which changed farming systems, such as those counties that went out of cotton or into sunflowers during the time period under examination. Those shifts in farming system were influenced by technology and have had an impact on the structure of agriculture (and presumably community well being), but they require separate analysis.

Despite the emphasis on change in agricultural structures in this analysis, it should be recognized that many other factors have affected agricultural counties in the region, including Federal transfer payments (particularly to retired individuals), declining service sector wages, the rural retail revolution, and changing mineral costs. Thus the models of changes in community viability are only partially specified.

The generalizability of findings, then, is limited by the specific nature of our sample. But it is also limited by the time period for which the data analysis was carried out. Because it was the most recent "clean" data available, we examined changes in agricultural structure and community between 1969 and 1980. The decade of the 1970s presented some enormous changes in the macro-economic structures in which farms and rural communities existed, conditions that have been dramatically reversed in the 1980s. Current analysis suggest that the 1970s were probably an aberration in that the positive conditions influencing agriculture are not likely to be repeated, particularly for the farming systems represented in this region.

The Macro Economic Setting

The 1970s were marked by a distinct shift in the world terms of trade. In 1971 the U.S. stopped exchanging gold for dollars in response to the first U.S. trade deficit since the Second World War. In 1973, President Nixon's administration allowed the value of the dollar to float in the world financial market. These events allowed for the value of the dollar to decline relative to other currencies, which increased the competitiveness of American exports in the world market.

But the main trigger for changes in the world terms of trade, which shifted purchasing power to oil-exporting countries, was the formation of OPEC and the sharp increase of oil prices beginning in 1973. While this increased energy costs for farmers, it also drove up all commodity prices. More land went into crop production around the world, including the U.S., reversing commodity limitation programs in place in the U.S. in one form or another since the 1930s. The increase in commodity prices was part of world wide inflation, fueled by the need to recycle petro-dollars. As a result, real interest rates declined.

In the early part of the decade, low interest rates and a weak dollar were an impetus for growth world-wide. Farmers in the Great Plains and West utilized cheap capital to expand, and, as a consequence, to become more capital intensive through increased use of the technology. Some of that capital invested was turned over in local communities. Land prices increased dramatically, further driving up rural debt. The end of government price support programs led to great variations in farm incomes during the last half of the 1970s. It was possible to make a living through farming, although price variation tended to lead to market capture of profits (Grant et al,1984). The average age of farmers declined, while the average education level of farmers went up.

However, although systematic census data are not yet available, it is clear that the "good times" of the 1970s have been reversed in 1980s, particularly in the Great Plains (although states with corn-belt farming systems—Iowa, Minnesota, and Wisconsin—are the hardest hit). Fiscal and monetary policy of the early 1980s combined to increase real interest rates, which in turn drove up the value of the U.S. dollar vis-a-vis other currencies. In 1979, new leadership at the Federal Reserve Bank, spurred by the political pressures of stagflation, undertook control of inflation as its major function. In 1981, federal spending sharply increased at the same time government revenue declined as a result of tax cuts. These new conditions—high real interest rates and loans that had to be repaid in now-high priced dollars—meant that the debts incurred during the 1970s by the developing countries, including oil exporting ones, became the debt crisis of 1980s. The international terms of trade again shifted, and commodity prices dropped as demand for all commodities fell and international competition increased. The shifting factor cost of capital led to a sharp decline in land prices, undercutting the assets that secured the loans that spurred the farm growth of the 1970s. Farming-dependent communities in the farming systems under analysis were hit by the twin crises of farm driven debt that endangered community financial institutions and low farm incomes resulting from low commodity prices. These conditions hit local businesses in farming dependent counties particularly hard. While these shifts have implications for the structure of agriculture, the exact interaction of the variables—and the resulting structures—are not yet well documented.

Definition Of Rural Farming Communities

We examined communities located in primarily farming dependent and federal lands counties which have a strong agricultural component. The two types of counties are identified by Bender, et al., (1984). We limited our analysis to those counties whose agriculture is currently dominated by wheat or livestock or both. However, summary descriptive statistics regarding the importance of wheat and livestock to the region will be based on all agriculture in the region. Counties which are candidates for inclusion in the study are those located in any of the Western or Great Plains states, excluding the industrial agriculture counties of California and Arizona, and south Texas. While agriculture may have an impact on communities in counties in which agriculture is not a principal economic base, we have chosen to include only those counties for which agriculture contributed an average of at least 20 percent of total labor and proprietor income for the period 1975-79 (the definition used by Bender, et al., 1984). Counties which had at least 25 percent of their economically active population in agriculture in 1980, but did not appear in Bender's list, were added to our sample. The sample was limited to predominantly farming counties, because secondary analysis of structural relations is not likely to show significant results unless only "extreme" cases are examined. Generally there are too many possible causal variables contributing to changes in diversified counties. The rural communities involved are relatively small, with relatively large and diffusely populated hinterlands; approximately 1,200 rural communities are to be found in the sample counties.

Major Forces Potentially Affecting Rural Communities

Land and resource policies, deregulation, fiscal policy, monetary policy, tax policies, and commodity programs have affected the development of rural communities, both in terms of farm structure and ideology behind the structure that has emerged. Water policy, particularly the separation of water rights from land use rights, will prove a major factor in an increasing portion of the region, as both ecological factors (depletion of non-renewable aquifers) and political factors (urban demands for control of the water) will make water an even more scarce resource than it has been in the past. Wheat has been a heavily supported commodity over time, with state and more recently, national wheat associations lobbying hard for Federal support programs. However, the decline of the farm coalition in the U.S. Congress implies a future decrease in wheat-based transfer payments.

Because of the rapid post-World War II consolidation of farm holdings and attendant outmigration of young persons, many communities of these regions derive a large portion of their income from transfer payments to the elderly, which in turn generates off-farm income for farm families. As a result, any federal policy changes that in any way lead to a decline in social security and other social transfer payments may mean the decline of the small cash margin that has kept family farms viable during times of low commodity prices.

Except for times of war, wheat has until recently been marketed domestically in the United States. Different parts of

the region specialize in different types of wheat for different
end-use products. By the early 1970s, the destination of the
majority of U.S. wheat shifted from domestic to foreign markets. Much of this growth was spurred by less developed countries, particularly those whose oil wealth provided foreign
exchange, either directly or through bank credit. Such purchases
helped those countries maintain a cheap food policy. For
developing countries, the error of a cheap food policy has been
made evident through declining domestic food production and
increased foreign debt. The debt crisis of many of the new U.S.
cash customers, such as Nigeria and Indonesia, is unlikely to be
reversed in the foreseeable future. Further, the strong American
dollar between 1981 and 1986 overpriced our wheat on the
world market. The fact that our major competitors peg their
currency to the dollar makes it unlikely that high U.S. international wheat sales will increase, despite a fall in value of the
dollar vis-a-vis the Japanese yen or German mark. The lack of
government controls on the quality of our wheat exports has led
to charges of selling dirty wheat abroad, which has further
disturbed our markets. Finally, the trend for most wheat on the
world market is for sales to occur through government-to-
government purchase contracts. The U.S. until 1986 had only
one—with the Soviet Union. Unless there is more activity on
the part of government in marketing, not just in promoting,
U.S. wheat, the U.S. share of the international market will
continue to fall.

Beef has been a highly protected U.S. industry in terms of
foreign import competition, both directly through tariffs and
indirectly through high health standards, particularly those
health problems arising from low capital input, such as foot and
mouth disease and tapeworm. Until recently, the U.S. has
largely been immune to the imposition of standards related to
potential health hazards of high technology beef production,
such as the use of growth hormones and antibiotics in feed.
Any change in these standards, domestically or internationally,
could change the conditions for beef production and for the
communities that depend on it. In addition, a secular decline in
the demand for beef, plus a shift in the type of beef preferred
by consumers, could lead to a shift away from feedlots to
grass-fed beef. Such a change in production practices could cut
production costs, but decrease the employment generated and
the capital circulated in feedlot activities in many rural
communities.

**Wheat- and Livestock-Based Farming Systems,
Community Welfare and Public Policy**

Methodology of County Selection

We analyzed farming dependent counties in the Great Plains and the West. The end of the Great Plains and the beginning of the West is defined chiefly by amount of rainfall. Annual precipitation in the Great Plains ranges from more than 40 inches in eastern Texas to less than 20 inches along the western border of the region. In areas of the West considered agricultural, annual precipitation ranges from 25 inches or less in most river valleys to 6 inches or less in intermountain basins and southern desert areas. Much of the land outside the river valleys is owned by Federal or state governments, which regulate access by agriculturalists. Grazing is the principal agricultural land use.

The tier of states from Texas to North Dakota are included in the Great Plains, as well as northeast New Mexico, the eastern half of Colorado, the eastern portion of Montana, and the westernmost part of Minnesota. The western half of South Dakota and northwestern Nebraska, areas in which grazing on federally owned public land is common, are considered part of the West. The frost-free period in the areas under consideration varies from less than 100 days in North Dakota to over ten months in southern Texas.

Wheat production (spring wheat in the north and winter wheat in the south) dominates the Great Plains. Corn, an increasing proportion of which is irrigated from east to west, is an important crop in southeastern South Dakota and eastern Nebraska and Kansas, which, when rotated with soybeans and integrated with hog-cattle operations, makes the dominant farming systems in those areas most like those in the corn belt. Grain sorghum is an important crop further west in Nebraska, Kansas, Oklahoma and Texas and is often a secondary crop in a wheat-dominated cropping system, whereas cotton dominates in parts of Oklahoma and Texas. However, much of the land, especially in the western half of the region, is in native range, whose productivity is limited by low precipitation.

The 17 states of North Dakota, South Dakota, Nebraska, Kansas, Oklahoma, Texas, New Mexico, Colorado, Montana, Wyoming, Idaho, Utah, Arizona, Nevada, California, Oregon, and Washington potentially had farming dependent counties in which farming systems of grains, livestock (excluding dairy), or

combined grains and livestock predominated. In these 17 states,
351 counties were classified as farming dependent by Bender, et
al. (1984). Using crop and livestock data from the 1974 and
1982 agricultural censuses, the farming system predominating in
each county was determined, as well as whether or not irrigation was an important factor in that farming system. Initial
analysis indicated that irrigation was indeed important in a
number of the counties, but that the presence of irrigation was
reflected in the emergent farming system.

Small grain/livestock counties with irrigation tended to
diversify into mixed grain/livestock (corn, sorghum, wheat, and
cattle), whereas livestock counties with irrigation simply
increased hay production for cold weather feeding. Thus, four
major farming systems were identified for analysis: wheat,
livestock, small grains/livestock, and mixed crops/livestock. The
livestock in small grain/livestock counties were cow-calf, and in
some instances ewe-lamb, operations, while the livestock in
mixed crop/livestock counties were chiefly feedlot cattle.
Counties were eliminated from the analysis that obtained 25
percent or more of their production value from dairy, poultry,
cotton, potatoes, sugar beets, rice, vegetables and fruits, and oil
seeds, particularly sunflower seeds and soybeans. These two
crops have had a substantial impact on a number of counties in
the region and require separate analysis. Counties on the eastern
edge of the area that had predominantly corn belt agricultural
systems, in which soybeans and hogs mix predominated (with
over 50% of income coming from the two combined) also were
eliminated from this analysis.

These commodities have different technologies and organizational constraints on production, as well as different ecological
factors influencing their presence or absence. One hundred
thirty-four counties were eliminated because their dominant
farming systems were too ideosyncratic for inclusion in the
analysis. To the remaining 217 counties were added 16 counties,
which Bender, et al. did not classify as agricultural counties,
but which in 1980 had at least 25 percent of their economically
active population engaged in agriculture, and two counties in
the northeast corner of Minnesota which were part of a wheat-
dominated farming system. One livestock county in Texas was
eliminated because of its very small population and the fact that
it was consistently an outlier on most important variables. These
234 counties then were classified as 1) wheat, 2) livestock, 3)
small grains/livestock or 4) mixed crops/livestock. No county in

Arizona or California was classified under one of these four farming systems.

A county was classified as a wheat county if wheat was its primary grain and small grains provided at least 75% of the value of agricultural product sold in 1974 and 1982. Thirty-three counties were predominantly small grain counties. Counties were classified as livestock if at least 75% of the value of agricultural products came from livestock, excluding hogs, poultry, and dairy. These counties had cattle and sheep as their major livestock. Eighty-four counties were classified as livestock counties. Counties that had less than 75% of their products sold as either small grains or livestock were classified as mixed. One hundred seventeen counties were classified as mixed.

Mixed crop and livestock counties with over 25,000 acres in irrigation in 1982 were tentatively defined as irrigated counties. The cropping mix was then examined. If the irrigation did not change the farming system to emphasize corn production over wheat and sorghum production, it continued to be classified as either wheat or small grain/livestock. However, if the mix of grains in the mixed counties shifted toward corn, it was assumed that feedlots predominated in the livestock sector. Then it was deemed appropriate to distinguish a different mixed farming system. Forty-five of the mixed counties were classified as mixed crops/livestock. The remaining 72 were classified as small grains/livestock counties. In the livestock counties, irrigation means irrigated pasture and/or hay. Although 19 of the livestock counties had over 25,000 irrigated acres, the farming system was not substantially changed.

Technology and the Four Major Farming Systems Of The Region

The four major farming systems — livestock (Figure 1), wheat (Figure 2), small grains/livestock (Figure 3), and mixed crops/livestock (Figure 4)—differ according to use of capital, labor, land, and management. As a result, they differentially utilize available technology and have differing potentials for technology adoption in the next 15 years.

Wheat Production and Wheat Counties

There are three major areas of wheat production in the region, growing different types of wheat under three different kinds of land use. The hard red winter wheat region, including

Figure 1: Livestock Counties.

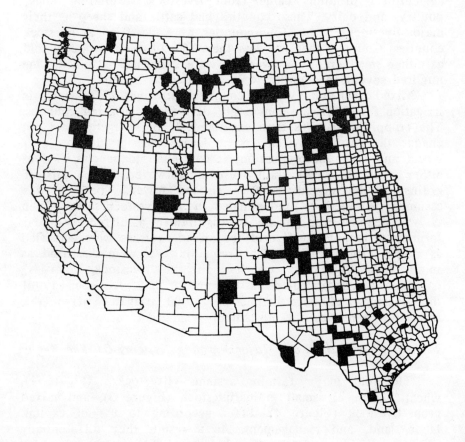

Figure 2: Wheat Counties.

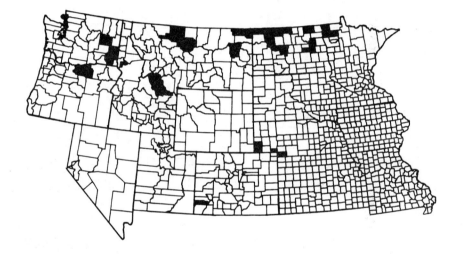

Figure 3: Wheat and Livestock Counties.

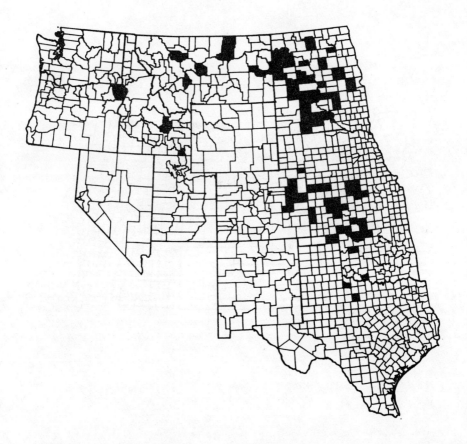

Figure 4: Mixed Crop and Livestock Counties.

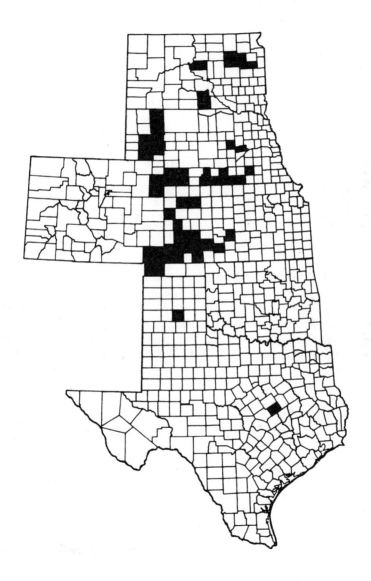

Kansas, Nebraska, Oklahoma, and Texas, accounts for 50 percent of total U.S. production. Hard red spring and durum (also
a spring wheat) are produced in Minnesota, Montana, North
Dakota, and South Dakota. The Pacific Northwest produces most
of the U.S.'s soft white wheat. (A fourth region - Illinois,
Indiana, Ohio, and Missouri -produces soft red winter wheat.)
Wheat in the region is grown under three main land use situations: 60 percent is continuous cropped dryland wheat grown in
the eastern part of the Great Plains; 33 percent is produced on
summer followed land in the Western Great Plains and Pacific
Northwest and 7 percent is grown on irrigated land, mostly in
Kansas, Oklahoma, and Texas (the Ogalala Aquifer) (Heid,
1980:17 and 19). Figure 1 shows the wheat counties, Figure 3
the small grains/livestock counties (wheat is the crop around
which farming system is organized), and Figure 4 shows the
location of the mixed crop/livestock counties, where most of the
irrigated wheat is grown.

Technological Development and Change

The technology generated since World War II, with the
exception of mechanization, has come primarily from the public
sector and has been area specific. Shifts in cultural practices in
wheat production over the past 50 years have been based on: 1)
fertilizer application (which was massively adopted for wheat
between 1955 and 1965), 2) reduced tillage practices (which for
wheat can be considered to have begun on a significant scale in
the late 1970s), and 3) breeding innovations to control disease,
pests, and ameliorate the effects of environmental hazards, such
as hail, heat, and drought (initiated in the 1920s, but greatly
accelerated after World War II; see J. Flora, 1986).
New varieties have been consistently introduced in all the
areas under consideration, with each succeeding variety usually
increasing yields. The risk-reducing aspects of the breeding
program were as responsible for the increased yields as the
direct yield-enhancing breeding efforts. Breeding for stronger
straw and shatter resistance began with the use of combines for
harvesting, which gained momentum in the 1920s. The combination of mechanization with varieties amenable to mechanical
harvesting greatly reduced labor use. Capital substituted for
labor, either directly by purchasing equipment or indirectly by
hiring combine harvest crews. However, the combine required
that the grain remain longer in field in order to dry adequately

for storage. Mechanical harvesting increased pressure to expand land holdings to make machinery investment economical. With the increased use of nitrogen fertilizer on wheat in the 1960s, wheat breeders responded with even shorter, thick-strawed varieties in order to resist lodging.

Cultural practices in the wheat areas are aimed at moisture storage, nutrient release and availability, erosion control, and proper timing of operations. Management is also a critical component of erosion control, which is a particularly serious problem in the western and high plains wheat areas. Mechanisms to reduce erosion, including increasing ground cover and minimum tillage practices, require management commitment. Such dependence on management limits the potential effectiveness of very large wheat operations, as less attention can be paid to the crucial variable of timing of cultural practices. However, it is possible that sophisticated sensing devices combined with appropriate computer software could reduce dependence on a farm operator's own knowledge of particular fields.

Biological fixation of nitrogen by the wheat plant, a technology which is not on the near horizon, could also reduce input costs in wheat production if developed within public sector. Otherwise, maintenance research will probably continue to lower input costs and increase output. Direct marketing by individual farmers or cooperatives might increase the proportion of wheat-generated income accruing to farmers and remaining in local communities.

A major technology shift that is occurring in wheat areas is the increased use of herbicides and minimum tillage implements to diversify cropping patterns and to get a greater number of crops off the land in a given time span, using the moisture thus conserved. This technology requires a higher management input than conventional farming, and thus favors full-time over part-time farmers. Computer technology that can stimulate agronomic and economic conditions can help fine-tune introduction of new systems for small farming operations and standardize good management strategies. The wheat-fallow rotation, with one crop in two years, is being replaced by including sunflower, sorghum, and even corn in a dryland farming sequence, giving up to four crops in five years.

Commodity programs, such as the 1985 Food Security Act, which limit acreage which can be planted to wheat and feed grains encourage maximum production per acre through high input agriculture. Field work in small grain/livestock counties of western Kansas indicates that farmers will plant a non-allotment crop in rotation with one which is covered by the farm program to increase total production. Thus sunflower production expanded significantly in the Central and Northern Plains in the mid 1980s. Those that planted sunflowers the first year did quite well. In subsequent years, the price fell dramatically, as supply exceeded demand. Political pressure was then exerted to make sunflowers a supported crop to be included in the farm program.

Livestock Counties

Cow-calf operations predominate in the counties classified as livestock counties (See Figure 2). These are extremely low management operations, where little technological innovation has occurred in the past 20 years. Much of the technology that exists for these operations, such as hormonal synchronization of estrus, artificial insemination, improved or fertilized pastures and even controlled breeding programs, has not been adopted, in part because of the management factor. The major capital investment on many of these operations is a pickup truck with a gun rack. Federal tax policies through 1987 tended to favor investments in equipment and physical plant, rather than investment in other types of technology.

A minor technological innovation affecting cow-calf operations was the change in forage harvesting technology. Mower-conditions were introduced in the western part of the region under analysis, whereas in the Great Plains, where rain is more of a threat, there was a move to package hay in large round bales, which are less susceptible to damage from precipitation when stored outdoors than are conventional rectangular hay bales.

Two potential technologies may have implications for the livestock counties. The first one is a bovine growth hormone, which increases the efficiency of weight gain in cattle. Its adoption will depend on the ease of application and complexity of management. Its use could decrease the time between calving and fattening, resulting in selling larger calves at a younger age. Assuming that larger operations would adopt growth hormones first, the smaller, later adopting operations would be disadvantaged due to price declines resulting from greater, more efficient, production (i.e., over production). Since major costs, such as breeding stock and land, are fixed, the impact of such an innovation on farm size should be less for cow-calf operations than for feedlot or dairy cattle.

A second new technology is computer-based telemarketing. Many cattle fattened in western feedlots are imported from the South from the U.S. or from Mexico. More efficient marketing procedures could reduce the costs of transportation by better distributing locally produced cattle to local feedlots. This would result in a greater return to the producer. It could also serve as a brake on further increases in farm size among livestock counties, since smaller operators could pool their feeder cattle to form regular marketing lots.

Small Grain/Livestock Counties

Small Grain/Livestock counties are dominated by farming systems that combine the cultivation of wheat with cow-calf operations and limited production of feed grains or forages. (See Figure 3 for the geographic distribution of these countries). This combination of crop-animal enterprises allows for a rationalization of labor, land, and machinery use. As with the single-enterprise systems, little technological innovation during the past 20 years in livestock production (i.e. artificial insemination, control of estrus, etc) has been adopted on a substantial scale. Innovations in wheat production technology during the same period have been readily adopted. Because of the generally higher management inputs already present in this farming system, compared to the straight livestock system, these farmers might be more likely to adopt the bovine growth hormone, particularly since, with continuing low grain prices, the number of calves raised on a given piece of land could increase considerably. This could off-set the current trend in increase in farm size. As with the livestock counties, adoption would depend on the management demands of the technology, as well as its dependence on the local development of subsidiary provider enterprises, such as those required for artificial insemination.

Telemarketing, aided by computer communication, could increase profitability for medium-sized small grains/livestock farms by helping owners not only to market their calves and grain, but better decide when to feed wheat or milo to their livestock, when to market grains commercially, and how to "farm" the farm program.

Mixed Crops/Livestock Counties

The mixed crop and livestock system is the most complex and integrated of all the farming systems in the counties analyzed (see Figure 4 for their geographic distribution). These counties generally have irrigation from ground water, which has been shown in cross-sectional studies by Albrecht and Murdock (1985), and J. Flora, et al. (1977) to be associated with smaller farm scale and larger populations than is true for surrounding dryland counties. Their argument is that technology substitutes for land. While it is important to acknowledge the importance of adoption of irrigation technology in these counties as a technological strategy that requires higher initial capital investment and more intensive management and labor inputs, it is also important to understand the change in land use that takes place. Farm operator flexibility is increased and the risk for the family is reduced.

A major market change that has accompanied the increase in irrigation in these counties during the 1970s is an increase in the number of feedlots that have the potential of utilizing the variety of crops and animals produced in the counties. During this time period, there was a change in location of the feeding-out of cattle from farm to feedlot. Further, feedlots, along with the meat packing industry, moved west. These market shifts were due less to technological innovations than to capital incentives and the lower cost of labor in non-union states.

The move to feedlots transferred labor from the farm operator and unpaid family members, who managed cattle in conjunction with other production activity, to hired labor. Labor per head of cattle is 75% less in large feedlots than in small farmer-fed cattle operations (Van Arsdall and Nelson, 1983:31). This labor efficiency is due to 1) more mechanization, 2) more efficient year-round use of labor, and 3) shorter feeding periods per animal.

Successful feedlots innovations over the past 20 years have facilitated an increase in the weight gain per animal per day while decreasing animal loss. Such technologies as antibiotic feed additives and other pest control mechanisms, while initially applied universally as preventatives, are increasingly used selectively in integrated pest management programs. In terms of profitability of a feedlot, which generally receives a fee for each head fed per day with a premium for fast weight gain, management of the disease and pest control technologies have been as important as availability of the technologies themselves. In addition, technologies that increase feed efficiency, both hormonal injections or implants and feed additives, such as rumensin that allows for use of more diverse feeds by decreasing acidosis and the resulting bloat, have been important for feedlots in the last decade. These have had positive impacts that lead to greater integration of the farming system. For example, rumensin allows for the feeding of wheat to feeder cattle when wheat prices are low.

New technologies of importance will increase feed efficiency and consistency. Bovine growth hormone could greatly increase the capacity and efficiency of feedlot operations. Biotechnology in sorghum (milo) breeding could increase the feed value of that grain while decrease its nutritional variability. This would allow milo to be substituted for corn as the feed grain of choice of feedlots, a substitution that may be inevitable as the ground water supply decreases in the Ogalala Aquifer, thus leading to a decline in the availability of local corn.

Computer software technology that can rationalize feeding procedures is making it increasingly possible for western farm feeder operations to compete with commercial feedlots. Thus, use of computer software technology for larger family-size operations can help invest community-produced resources locally and maintain medium-sized diversified operations. However, meat packers, by giving premium price for large homogeneous lots of slaughter animals, discriminate against farmer feed lots. Although farmer feed lots could utilize local products, most large feedlots currently import a great deal of feed and cattle. The advent of computer-based marketing linking farmer and feedlot could allow for more effective use of local supplies and thereby decrease transportation costs for the feedlot operator.

Comparison Of Results Among Counties
For Different Farming System Types

The four types of counties, defined by the dominant farming system in each county, are arranged in the tables according to diversity of that farming system. Livestock counties are the least diverse, while the mixed crop livestock counties (cattle-wheat-sorghum-corn counties) are the most diverse (see Table 1 for means on cropland, pastureland, and sales by commodity which validate the typology). This ordering also corresponds to the intensiveness of land use, with the exception that the two

TABLE 1.   DEFINING CHARACTERISTICS OF AGRICULTURAL COUNTIES
CLASSIFIED BY PREDOMINANT FARMING SYSTEMS,
GREAT PLAINS AND WESTERN U.S., 1978

Agricultural Characteristics	Live-stock	Wheat	Small Grain/ Livestock	Mixed Crop/ Livestock
		(m e a n s c o r e s*)		
Pasture and range-land as percent of total farm sales	72	29	48	35
Percent of total agricultural sales from livestock	76	21	54	54
Cropland as percent of total farm acres	25	66	50	62
Percent of total sales from grain	8	69	31	35
Percent of land in farms which is irrigated	5 (79)	3 (29)	3 (69)	15
Number of cases	(84)	(33)	(72)	(45)

* Means of county means.

middle groups of counties would be reversed. Land in wheat counties is more intensively used than that in wheat/livestock counties, as is suggested by value of land and buildings per acre and value of machinery and equipment per acre in Table 2.

Table 2 also shows statistical means for farm size and production variables for the four county types. (It should be recognized that we are using county averages, which ignore the substantial variation within counties.) Physical farm size is inversely related to diversity, although farm sales positively relates to diversity. Farm sales (total and per acre) are greatest for the mixed crop livestock farms, because of the high capital-to-land ratio of this type of agriculture, and the resulting high production per acre. Capital intensity, as measured by irrigation, is highest in the mixed counties, even though only 15 percent of the land is irrigated. Irrigation permits higher levels of production per acre and justifies a larger per-acre investment. Mixed crop-livestock production in irrigation areas or areas of abundant rainfall allows for more flexible cropping and live-stock combinations. It also provides the opportunity to expand production without purchasing more land. Irrigation allows for incremental expansion, while the purchase of land does not.

Livestock counties, like mixed crop/livestock counties, had a majority of farm sales from holdings that produced over $100,000 in farm sales in 1978 (in contrast to wheat and small grain/livestock counties). Livestock monoculture historically and currently has attracted large producers partly because of its relatively low management input. However, modest management requirements also make it a viable option for small, part-time operators. This has contributed to the bimodal distribution of farm numbers by farm size for livestock counties (See Flora and Flora, 1986:Table 8). Stock cattle production also has been an attractive investment for persons with large nonfarm incomes, because of the significant capital-gains tax provision regarding stock cattle raising.

Community and Farming Systems

Retail and wholesale services are positively related to farming system diversity, as is indicated in Table 3. However, the difference by county type in per capita retail services narrowed over the decade from 1967 to 1977. The decline in service availability was least in the livestock counties and largest

TABLE 2. FARM CHARACTERISTICS OF AGRICULTURAL COUNTIES
CLASSIFIED BY PREDOMINANT FARMING SYSTEMS,
GREAT PLAINS AND WESTERN U.S., 1978

Farm-Related Variables	Live- Stock	Wheat	Small Grain/ Livestock	Mixed Crop & Livestock
	(m e a n	s c o r e s*)		
Average size of farm (acres)	3410	1740	1619	1203
Value of land and buildings per farm $1000	554	525	397	495
Value of land and buildings/acre ($)	243	351	316	458
Value of machinery and equipment/ acre, $	26	54	44	67
Value of agri- cultural products sold per farm, $1000	103	63	60	137
Value of agri- cultural products sold per acre, $	60	41	50	125
Agricultural sales from farms with $100,000+ sales, %	62	47	48	68
Number of cases	(84)	(33)	(72)	(45)

* Means of county means.

TABLE 3. POPULATION AND COMMUNITY-RELATED CHARACTERISTICS
OF AGRICULTURAL COUNTIES CLASSIFIED BY
PREDOMINANT FARMING SYSTEMS, GREAT PLAINS AND
WESTERN U.S., 1967-88

Community Variables	Live-stock	Wheat	Small Grain/ Livestock	Mixed Crop & Livestock
	(m e a n		s c o r e s*)	
Total county population, '80	4202	6261	4616	6044
Retail sales per capita, $, '77	1995	2422	2286	2929
Wholesale sales per capita, $, '77	2821	6071	3717	5844
Percent change in:				
total population, '70-'80	+5.1	-3.1	-2.1	-0.7
rural non-farm pop., '70-'80	+31	+10	+19	+13
rural farm pop., '70-'80	-20	-25	-27	-25
# of retail estab. '67-77**	- 8	-13	-15	-17
retail sales volume, '67-'77**	+3	-14	- 7	-15

* Means of county means. ** The consumer price index in 1977 was 181.5 when 1967 was set at 100.

in mixed crop/livestock counties, though the latter continued to have the greatest sales per capita. It would appear, as suggested by the rapid growth of rural non-farm population, that the livestock counties are experiencing some population growth which is unrelated to ranching. These may simply be a spillover effect from the more generalized population growth taking place in the West. Farm population, as a proportion of all types of farming-dependent counties, declined from one-fourth to one-fifth over the decade of the 1970s.

Measures of income and unemployment in farming dependent counties are rather unreliable, since income measures are so dependent on level of farm prices and farm production, which vary considerably from one year to another. Unemployment is generally low in western farm areas. Of all income measures, the percent of families below poverty seems the most stable. Livestock counties show the most poverty, but also the greatest improvement in the reduction of the proportion of the population in poverty during the decade of the 1970s (see Table 4). This improvement may be related to economic activities independent of agriculture. The high initial rate of poverty is related to the fact that hired labor per farm is greatest in livestock counties, even though hired labor shows the greatest increase in mixed crop/livestock counties (see Table 5). The low unemployment rate in 1980 in mixed crop/livestock counties indicates a labor shortage in those counties.

Indications of an increased separation of labor, management, and/or capital among farming units suggests that farming is becoming part of the modern capitalist economy. Table 5 shows changes in these indicator variables. There was an increase of off-farm work by farm operators, an increase in hired labor, and a growth in part ownership at the expense of full ownership. On the other hand, the proportion of farms that are family or individually operated (in contrast to those that are partnerships, corporations, trusts, or other legal-corporate forms) has increased notably. The enormous increase in land values during the inflationary 1970s encouraged new legal land title arrangements to decrease tax liability, especially inheritance tax.

While use of hired labor is expanding (from an average of one in three farms having a season-long hired worker to about one in two farms), capital investment in machinery and equipment grew much more rapidly, as indicated by changes in the ratio of expenditures for hired and contract labor to value of machinery and equipment (Table 5). This is a great degree a

TABLE 4. SOCIOECONOMIC CHARACTERISTICS OF THE
POPULATION IN AGRICULTURAL COUNTIES CLASSIFIED BY
PREDOMINANT FARMING SYSTEMS, GREAT PLAINS AND
WESTERN U.S., 1969-1980

Socioeconomic Variables	Live- stock	Wheat	Small Grain Livestock	Mixed Crop & Livestock
(m e a n s c o r e s*)				
Families below poverty, %, '69	19	11	16	14
Families below poverty, %, '79	16	11	15	12
Change in percent of families in poverty, 1969-79	-2.8	+0.1	-1.1	-1.1
Percent pre-1940 year-round housing				
1970	47	51	53	53
1980	42	47	49	48
Percent unemploy- ment, '80	4.0	4.6	3.5	2.0
Number of cases	(84)	(33)	(72)	(45)

* Means of county means.

reflection of the "cheap money" (i.e., low or negative real interest rates) in late 1970s, as well as tax laws favorable to the substitution of capital for labor. It also suggests that substitution of capital for labor has limits. Increased use of hired help implies an internal differentiation of both field labor (hired) and management (owner/operation).

Farm operators in 1978 among livestock counties are much less likely to consider their principal occupation to be farming than are operators in the three other types of counties. Likewise, livestock-county operators are more likely to work off the farm 100 or more days per year, and their rate of increase in off-farm employment is greater than for the other types. Livestock counties are also somewhat less likely to have family or individually owned farms, although they are more likely to be operated by full owners.

Analysis of Change of Medium and Large Farms Within Farming System Types

Goldschmidt, within the limited research design of case study, attempted to measure the impact of farm size on community and family well-being while controlling for most other relevant factors, including total agricultural product and size of the community, centrality, and ethnicity (Goldschmidt 1978:289-90,304,321). However, as Hayes and Olmstead (1984) point out, there were numerous dissimilarities in the communities that could lead to both differences in farm size and differences in community quality. Moreover, Goldschmidt was unable to control for farming system differences, a definite intervening factor. This is important since particular farming systems lend themselves to specialized labor patterns and, hence, to difference in farm size. This has already been noted in the earlier examination of the four farming systems.

This study seeks to overcome this limitation imposed by Goldschmidt's case study by analyzing census data for a large enough number of counties so as to examine the impact of change in farm size within types of farming systems. Nationwide, the period of the 1970s and 1980s has been characterized by a new phenomenon—a bifurcation in the size of agricultural holdings. Medium-sized farms decreased in number and acreage, while very large commercial and very small subcommercial farms increased. However in the western region the absolute increase in acreage and farm sales represented by small farms is

TABLE 5. INTEGRATION OF FARMING INTO THE MODERN ECONOMY,
FOR AGRICULTURAL COUNTIES CLASSIFIED BY PREDOMINANT
FARMING-SYSTEMS, GREAT PLAINS AND WESTERN U.S., 1969-78

Modern Economy Variables	Live-stock	Wheat	Small Grain Livestock	Mixed Crop & Livestock
	(m e a n	s c o r e	s*)	
Operators whose principal occupation is farming, %, '78	65	82	77	80
Operators who worked 100+ days off farm, %, '78	31	22	24	22
Change in percent of operators working 100+ days off farm, '69-78	+3.5	+1.7	+1.7	+0.7
Number of workers working 150+ days on farm per farm				
1969	.40	.26	.17	.21
1978	.58	.48	.31	.42
Percent change in number of workers working 150+ days/year, '69-'78	69	80	89	95
Expenditures for hired labor/farm, $, '78	3,995	3,939	1,960	3,542
Percent change in expend. for hired labor, '69-'78 ** ('78 dollars)	128	130	111	168
Expenditures for contract labor/ farm, $, '78	430	410	180	240

104

(Table 5, cont'd)

Modern Economy Variables	Live-stock	Wheat	Small Grain/ Livestock	Mixed Crop & Livestock
Expend. for hired & contract labor/ value of machinery and equipment:				
1969	.21	.10	.11	.14
1978	.11	.05	.04	.05
Farms which are family or individually owned, %:				
1969	67	75	74	75
1978	71	76	80	80
Change in percent of farms family or individually owned, '69-'78	+4.6	+1.4	+5.6	+4.6
Full owner-operated farms, %, 1969	45	35	37	30
1978	38	31	32	28
Change in percent by full owners, '69-'78	-7.7	-4.1	-4.1	-2.2
Number of cases	(84)	(33)	(72)	(45)

* Means of county means.
** The Consumer Price Index was .562 in 1969 when 1978 was placed at 100.

inconsequential relative to the medium and large farms (see Flora and Flora, 1986, Table 7). Thus, although the percentage growth in small farms (those of less than 180 acres) is quite substantial, the 1969 base from which that percentage is calculated is quite small (Flora and Flora, 1986:Table 8). While the number of very large farms is also not great, particularly in the case of mixed crops/livestock counties, it still represents a substantial proportion of total acreage. In this region, a growing number of small farms makes little contribution to either total farm acreage or total production, and only moderately greater contribution to total farm numbers. Their association with community structure and well-being was not analyzed.

Relation Of Medium and Large Farms To Community Well-Being

In order to understand the accumulated history of the relationship between farm size and various population, community, socioeconomic, and farm variables, this study examined the zero-order correlations between percent of farmland in medium and in large farms in 1969 and indicators of the initial level of community well-being. The relationship of these two farm size variables with subsequent change in the other variables was also examined. Percent of land in farms of 500-999 acres was chosen to represent medium-sized farms and percent of land in farms of 2000+ acres was chosen to measure large farms. The two farm size variables correlated highly negatively with one another. The correlations for the four types of counties range from -.93 to -.98. This clear multicolinearity led us to use only one size category at a time in further analysis.

As expected, counties in which medium-sized farms predominated over large farms had larger populations (see Table 6). The greater population base of counties with a predominance of land in medium farms over large farms is due in part to more intensive agriculture among the medium-farm counties. The medium-farm counties also had a larger proportion of their population living on farms than did the large-farm counties.

For counties with more diversified farming systems (small grains/livestock and mixed crop/livestock), the medium farm counties in the 1970s experiences significantly greater loss in total population than did the large-farm counties. For the medium-farm wheat counties, the loss in total population was due largely to a loss in their rural farm population.

TABLE 6. ZERO–ORDER CORRELATIONS OF PERCENT OF FARMLAND
IN MEDIUM FARMS IN 1969 BY POPULATION CHARACTERISTICS
OF AGRICULTURAL COUNTIES CLASSIFIED ACCORDING TO
PREDOMINANT FARMING SYSTEMS, GREAT PLAINS AND
WESTERN U.S., 1969–80

Population Variables	Live-stock	Wheat	Small Grain Livestock	Mixed Crop & Livestock
	% of land in medium farms in 1969 (Pearsonian R)			
Total county population, '70	.35*	.25	.62*	.15
Percent change in total population, '70–'80	−.13	−.17	−.25*	−.30*
Rural farm population as % of total population, '70–'80	.28*	.41*	−.10	.31*
Percent change in rural farm population, '70–'80	−.17	−.40*	−.22	−.21
Number of cases	(84)	(33)	(72)	(45)

* Significant at the .05 level.

Note: The correlations between percentage of land in large
farms (2000 or more acres) and the variables in the table
above are of approximately the same magnitude and of opposite
sign from the correlations presented between percentage of
land in medium sized farms (500–999 acres) and the same
variables, since the two land size variables are correlated
nearly perfectly negatively with one another. The
correlations between the two land variables are as follows:

    Livestock counties   −.93
    Wheat counties   −.97
    Wheat-livestock counties   −.98
    Mixed crop-livestock counties   −.94

Table 7 shows changes according to different farm size categories in the succeeding decade for the medium-farm dominated counties and large-farm dominated counties of 1969. Counties with a high percentage of land in medium-farms were most likely to experience a decline in numbers of farms in all size categories below 1000 acres. An exception were crops/livestock counties below 500 acres. Areas of predominance of medium-farm agriculture in 1969 were associated with growth in numbers of farms of 1000+ acres by 1978. For the large-farm counties the relationship was reversed. The percentage of land in large farms in 1969 was positively associated with change in numbers of farms in size categories below 1000 acres, and negatively associated with change in number of farms over 1000 acres. Once again, the mixed crops/livestock counties are an exception, with threshold of about 500 acres. These patterns suggest a homogenization of predominant farm size, regardless of farming system. This observation is important for interpreting results that immediately follow.

Table 8 shows the relationship between percent of land in medium and large farms and various measures of the integration of agriculture within the modern capitalist economy. As expected, there is a strong positive relationship between use of season-long hired labor and large-farm agriculture. However, those counties dominated by medium-sized farms in 1969 experienced a greater increase in hired labor than did the large-farm counties (except in the case of the wheat counties). This is at least partially associated with the decline in the number of middle-sized farms over the 1970s decade. Hence, many of the counties that in 1969 were medium-farm dominated became large-farm dominated.

A high ratio of hired and contract labor to machinery and equipment was strongly associated with large-farm counties in 1969. This difference in capital use between large and medium farm counties declined over the succeeding decade, suggesting that growth in machinery purchased in the medium-farm counties during the 1970s was greater than in the large-farm counties. Therefore, not only did the medium-farm counties experienced a more rapid increase in hired labor than the large-farm counties, their increased investment in farm machinery was even faster. Mechanization, then, was the key factor facilitating the decline in the numbers of medium-sized farms and their replacement by large farms. It would appear that medium-farm counties, up to at least 1969, lagged behind

TABLE 7. ZERO–ORDER CORRELATIONS OF PERCENT OF FARMLAND
IN MEDIUM FARMS IN 1969 BY FARM SIZE CHANGES IN
AGRICULTURAL COUNTIES CLASSIFIED BY PREDOMINANT FARMING
SYSTEMS, GREAT PLAINS AND WESTERN U.S., 1969–78

Farm Size Variables (1969–78)	Live-stock	Wheat	Small Grain Livestock	Mixed Crop & Livestock
Percent change in number of —	% of land in medium farms in 1969 (Pearsonian R)			
farms of 50–179 acres	$-.15$	$.13$	$-.37*$	$-.34*$
farms of 180–499 acres	$-.39^*$	$-.56^*$	$-.52^*$	$-.44^*$
farms of 500–999 acres	$-.31^*$ (N=82)	$-.38^*$	$-.51^*$	$.07$
farms of 1000–1999 acres	$.51^*$ (N=79)	$.63^*$	$.44^*$	$.67^*$
farms of 2000+ acres	$.49^*$ (N–81)	$.76^*$	$.79^*$	$.66^*$
Number of cases	(84)	(33)	(72)	(45)

Note: The numbers in parentheses indicate the number of
counties without a zero in the denominator; that is,
missing data is due to there being no farms in that size
category in 1969 (or so few that the data were suppressed).
See also the note at the bottom of Table 6.

* Significant at the .05 level.

TABLE 8. ZERO-ORDER CORRELATIONS OF PERCENT OF FARMLAND IN
MEDIUM FARMS IN 1969 BY INTEGRATION OF FARMING INTO THE
MODERN ECONOMY, AGRICULTURAL COUNTIES CLASSIFIED BY
PREDOMINANT FARMING SYSTEMS, GREAT PLAINS AND
WESTERN U.S., 1969-78

Modern Economy Variables	Live- stock	Wheat	Small Grain/ Livestock	Mixed Crop & Livestock
	--% of land in medium farms in 1969 -- (Pearsonian R)			
Number of workers working 150+ days on farm/number of farms, '69	-.49*	-.60*	-.60*	-.73*
Percent change in number of workers working 150+ days/ year, '69-'78	.46*	-.16	.24*	.35*
Expend. hired & contract labor/ value of machinery and equipment, '69	-.50*	-.44*	-.35*	-.75*
Change in expend. for hired & contract labor/value machinery & equipment, '69-'78	-.37*	-.11	-.29*	-.73*
Number of cases	(84)	(33)	(72)	(45)

* Significant at the .05 level.

Note: See note to Table 6.

large-farm counties in the adjustment of farm size to the scale
of machinery then available. In the 1970s, that adjustment was
made. It was facilitated by the high-inflation, cheap-money
financial policies of the federal government during 1970s.
Medium-sized farm operators, who had previously been cautious
about over-extending themselves, succumbed to the proposition
that the good farmer was highly leveraged and used the tax
laws to buy machinery which in turn encouraged them to rent
more land. In Salamon's terms, many commercial yeoman farmers became risk-taking entrepreneurs (Salamon, 1985).

Table 9 suggests that within each county type there is a
positive association between proportion of land in medium-sized
farms and number of retail and wholesale establishments. The
more intensive use of the land, and the resulting larger
population supported by agriculture in the medium-farm
counties than in the large-farm counties, supported more trading
establishments but not necessarily greater trade volume. This
would indicate more local ownership of retail, and perhaps
wholesale, trade in the medium-farm counties than in the
large-farm counties at the beginning of the 1970s.

There was no association between predominant farm size
and per capita retail or wholesale sales, except that the
proportion of land in large farms was positively associated with
per capita wholesale sales in livestock counties. Counties with a
high proportion of land in medium-sized farms in 1969 experienced a greater decline in wholesale and retail establishments
and sales (and, as we saw above, in population) in the succeeding decade than did counties with a high proportion of land in
large farms. This is probably because medium-farm counties
experienced more rapid growth in farm size than did the large-
farm counties over the decade of the 1970s. Paradoxically, the
purchase of more machinery and expansion of farm size in
what were initially medium-farm counties had a negative effect
on local commerce. It is easy to speculate that farmers in these
counties tended to bypass the local dealers in making large
machinery and other input purchases.

The data analysis further suggests association between farm
size and a county's socioeconomic well-being. Median family
income was positively associated with land in large farms and
negatively associated with land in medium farms in 1969 (Table
10). The relationship was moderately significant for wheat and
mixed crop/livestock counties and strongest in wheat counties.
In the wheat counties, the relationship of medium-farm agricul-

TABLE 9. ZERO-ORDER CORRELATIONS OF PERCENT OF FARMLAND
IN MEDIUM FARMS IN 1969 BY COMMUNITY-RELATED
CHARACTERISTICS OF AGRICULTURAL COUNTIES CLASSIFIED
BY PREDOMINANT FARMING SYSTEMS, GREAT PLAINS AND
WESTERN U.S., 1967-77

Community Variables	Live-stock	Wheat	Small Grain/ Livestock	Mixed Crop & Livestock
	-- % of land in medium farms in 1969 -- (Pearsonian R)			
Retail establish-ments, #, '67	.35*	.33	.64*	.15
Percent change in number of retail establishments, 1967-77	-.28*	-.23	-.31*	-.01
Percent change in retail sales volume, 1967-77	-.23*	-.08	-.23	-.20
Wholesale estab-lishments, #, '67	.47*	.32	.61*	.14
Wholesale sales per capita, '67	-.26*	-.04	-.03	-.07
Number of cases	(84)	(33)	(72)	(45)

* Significant at the .05 level.

Note: See note to Table 6.

TABLE 10.   ZERO-ORDER CORRELATIONS OF PERCENT OF FARMLAND
IN MEDIUM FARMS IN 1969 BY SOCIOECONOMIC CHARACTERISTICS
OF THE POPULATION IN AGRICULTURAL COUNTIES CLASSIFIED BY
PREDOMINANT FARMING SYSTEMS, GREAT PLAINS AND
WESTERN U.S., 1969 AND 1970

Socioeconomic Variables	Live-stock	Wheat	Small Grain/ Livestock	Mixed Crop & Livestock
	-- % of land in medium farms in 1969 -- (Pearsonian R)			
Median family income, '69	-.19	-.61*	-.15	-.30*
Percent families below poverty, '69	.04	.40*	-.23	.07
Percent year-round housing built before 1940, '70	.34*	.30	.38*	.64*
Number of cases	(84)	(33)	(72)	(45)

*   Signifcant at the .05 level.

Note: see note at bottom of Table 6.

ture with change in median income (1969-79) was nearly as strong but reversed. That is, the gap in median family incomes between median and large-farm counties tended to close from the beginning to the end of the decade. This may be related to the fact that in wheat counties rural farm population, as a proportion of the total population, was most strongly associated with medium-farm agriculture in 1970, and that the rural farm population tended to experienced a greater decline in wheat counties than in other counties in the succeeding decade (Table 6). Again, this may be due in part to the process of many medium-farm counties subsequently becoming large-farm counties.

In wheat counties, there is a positive correlation between poverty and percent of land in medium farms, while poverty is negatively correlated to percent of land in large farms. The situation for mixed grain/livestock counties was different. Percent of land in large farms was significantly and positively correlated with poverty (r=.27). For the other two types of counties, dominant size of farm was unrelated to poverty.

With respect to housing stock built before 1940, percent of land in medium farms was more highly correlated with percent older housing than percent of land in large farms. This was true for all county types. The older housing in the medium-farm counties in 1969 is consistent with commercial yeoman farmer dominance. Yeoman farmers would tend not to engage in "conspicuous" consumption, but would save for a "rainy day" (risk reduction) or to help the next generation get started in farming (Salamon, 1985).

Change In Numbers Of Moderate And Large Farms
And Change Among Communities' Characteristics

This study analyzes the relationship between change in numbers of large and medium farms, on the one hand, and change in variables that indicate community vitality, individual or family well-being, and other farm characteristics, on the other. The time period over which the two sets of variables were measured was approximately the same for both independent and dependent variables. No lagged variables were included. It was assumed that response was relatively immediate. Change in numbers of medium or large farms were the independent variables, and, in general, were assumed to be causal. Where it appears that the direction of causality could be reversed, this will be noted. The initial value (i.e., around 1970) of the dependent change variable was included an independent control variable.

It was hypothesized that the growth in numbers of medium-sized farms (or more accurately the lesser decline in numbers of medium-sized farms) had a higher association with positive changes in community vitality and family well-being than did growth in the number of large farms. A linear regression model was chosen. The difference in the slopes of the two regression lines for percent change in numbers of medium and large farms were each regressed against a dependent variable. The relationships among counties of each type were examined to determine if there were differences according to county type. In general, there were not. Therefore, all four county types were combined in the regressions reported in Table 11. Only the livestock counties were significantly different from counties with other dominant farming systems with respect to population change. (The reasons are discussed later in this section.) The correlation between percentage change in number of medium farms and percentage change in number of large farms ranged between -.08 and -.32 for the four farming systems types. Thus, there was no problem with multicolinearity between these two variable in the regression equation.

The regressions for which there was a significant difference between the slopes of the regression lines relating the dependent variable to changes in each of the two farm size variables are presented in Table 11.

An assumption of this study is that medium-sized farming contributes to greater economic vitality of the local community than does large-scale farming. This was tested by relating percent change in numbers of medium-scale and numbers of large-scale farms to percent change in number of retail establishments and in retail sales volume, on the assumption that diverse retail activities were the best barometer of such economic viability. The results suggest that growth in numbers of medium-sized farms and/or a lack of growth in numbers of large farms is positively associated with local purchasing (equations 1 & 2 of Table 11). Retail trade appears to be much more sensitive to farm size change than is wholesale trade. Both the measures for retail activities, most notably change in volume of sales, are positively associated with growth, or a lesser decline, in number of medium-sized farms and negatively associated with growth in number of large farms.

TABLE 11. REGRESSIONS OF LINEAR RELATIONSHIP BETWEEN
"PERCENT CHANGE IN NUMBER OF LARGE OF MEDIUM FARM" BY
POPULATION, LABOR FORCE, COMMUNITY, AND LAND
OWNERSHIP CHANGE VARIABLES, AGRICULTURAL COUNTIES
IN GREAT PLAINS AND WESTERN UNITED STATES

Change Variables	Slope Estimate & Standard Error	Significance Levels	F Value-- $H_o:B_3=B_6$
1. % change in # of retail establishments, '67-77:			
Medium farms (X3)	+.116 $\pm$ .051	.025	7.45
Large farms (X6)	-.029 $\pm$ .033	.39	(p =
# retail estab.,			.007)
1967	-.039 $\pm$ .023	.10	
R^2	.056		
F value	4.38	.005	
2. % change in retail sales vol., '67-'77:			
Medium farms	+.507 $\pm$ .183	.006	16.22
Large farms	-.238 $\pm$ .111	.033	(p =
Retail sales vol.,			.0001)
vol. '67	+.0003 $\pm$ .0006	.61	
R^2	.077		
F value	5.71	.001	
3. Change in ratio of expend. for hired & contract labor to mach. & equip. value, '69-'78			
Medium farms	+.0003 $\pm$ .0001	.008	6.99
Large farms	-.00002 $\pm$ .00006	.81	(p =
Labor expend./			.009)
machinery &			
equip. value,'69	-.41 $\pm$ .03	.0001	
R^2	.47		
F value	61.8	.0001	

Table 11. (cont'd.)

Change Variables	Slope Estimate & Standard Error	Significance Levels	F Value-- $H_o:B_3=B_6$
4. % change in rural non-farm population, '70-'80:			
Medium farms	+.145 + .090	.11	6.56
Large farms	-.087 + .056	.12	(p =
Rural non-farm			.011)
pop., '70	-.0015 + .0007	.05	
R^2	.046		
F value	3.55	.015	
5. % change in total pop. '70-'80:			
Medium farms	+.190 + .044	.0001	33.56
Large farms	-.072 + .028	.011	(p =
Total pop, '70	+.0006 + .0003	.026	.0001)
R^2	.137		
F value	11.60	.0001	
6. Change in % of housing built before 1940, '70-'80:			
Medium farms	-.049 + .014	.001	24.08
Large farms	+.022 + .009	.014	(p =
% pre-1940			.0001)
housing, '70	-.053 + .024	.030	
R^2	.104		
F value	8.49	.0001	
7. Change in % of farms w/full owners, '69-'78:			
Medium farms	+.038 + .016	.019	9.11
Large farms	-.010 + .009	.25	(p =
% full-owner farms,			.003)
'69	-.43 + .03	.0001	
R^2	.51		
F value	71.5	.0001	

This is due to a number of factors. First, medium-sized farms have a higher labor-to-capital ratio and use more labor per unit of agricultural product than do larger farms, if family labor is accounted for. Table 11 provides very modest, though statistically significant, support for the assumption that growth in medium-sized farms is associated with a more rapid increase in expenditures for hired labor than in investment in machinery and equipment. (See the third equation in Table 11.) That is, medium-sized farms retard the substitution of labor by capital, contributing modestly to community population retention.

Second, medium-sized farmers tend to buy locally, while large farmers are more likely to buy in bulk, bypassing the local in-put suppliers. A similar pattern may also occur with respect to the sale of livestock.

Third, counties with growth in large farms are more likely to have absentee farm operators or ones who do much of their consumer purchasing and recreating outside the county.

Farm size change was also related to population change. One would expect that the greatest impact of farm size change would be on rural farm population. If medium-sized farms use more labor (on a per acre or per unit of product basis) than do large scale farms, one would expect that the rural farm population would increase with a growth in medium-sized farms and decrease with a growth in large farms. Surprisingly, no significant relationship was detected between the farm-size change variables and change in rural farm population. Rural farm population continued to decline regardless of the type of change in farm structure. However, there was an important impact on the rural nonfarm population, the largest population category in most of the counties. Since in many counties the largest town is rural (i.e., less than 2,500 population), the results presented in Table 11 provide support for the hypothesis that growth in medium-sized farms contributes to the development of associated economic activities centered in rural towns, while growth in large-sized farms occurred to the detriment of rural town economic activity.

The impact of farm structural change on total population of the county follows the same pattern, and the relationships were equally strong (see regressions 4 and 5 of Table 11). The relationship between change in number of medium farms and change in the two population variables was even stronger when the livestock counties were excluded, since for the livestock counties there are no significant relationship between the population variables and change in medium-sized farms. This may be because there was little change in the technology of pastured livestock production in the 1970s, particularly with respect to introduction of labor-saving technology.

No significant relationship was found between change in numbers of medium or large farms and change in median family income and change in percent of families in poverty. Median family income in agricultural counties was considered to be so dependent on cyclical changes in the agricultural economy so as to be an unreliable variable. Because none of the counties in the sample had high levels of poverty, the variance was not great and no association was found. None were classified as poverty counties under the USDA classification system we are utilizing.

Three other reasons may exist for the lack of relationship between income measures and change in farm size. First, in the post World War II period and at least until the beginning of the 1970s, farm size growth tended to promote increased family income as increased scale generally brought greater net per-farm incomes. This was particularly true in wheat counties and mixed crop/livestock counties (see Table 10). In the former, poverty was exported and unemployment remained low. Of the four types of counties, the mixed crop/livestock counties experienced the greatest economic growth during the period. Since they have not been in the main migrant labor streams, they tended to experience a labor shortage which has kept wages up.

Second, and more generally, economic activity generated by the maintenance of medium-farm agriculture does not necessarily enhance family income throughout the economy of the community, since both on-farm and off-farm jobs in rural communities continue to be non-unionized and generally low paying. The greater multiplier effect of more moderate sized farms as opposed to a smaller number of large farms means more economic activity, but did not necessarily higher incomes or reduced poverty. Population is retained, but income does not rise.

Third, the expansion of the service sector, much of which is independent of the farm economy, even in farming dependent counties, has reduced the impact of farm-generated income on the community or county as a whole.

The variable percent of housing built before 1940 was a more stable indicator of standard of living than was median family income. A relationship was found between percent of pre-1940 housing and change in numbers of medium and large farms (see regression number 6 in Table 11). At first blush, this would appear to suggest that general economic vitality based on moderate-sized farming contributes in a limited way to improved standard of living. An equally plausible explanation is that medium-sized farmers who previously had carefully reinvested net income in the farm, under conditions of easy money, were willing to spend some of that liquidity on major consumption items such as a new home. The more entrepreneurial farmers, representing the increase in larger farms, already possessed newer homes, e.g. ones built since 1940.

Maintenance of medium-farm agriculture contributed to a modest increase in full ownership of farms, although overall there was a decline in full ownership of farms (see Table 5). Full ownership in medium-farm counties was achieved at the expense of partial ownership, not complete tenancy. There was no relationship between change in tenancy and change in numbers of medium or large farms. Land purchase was a major use of expanded liquidity based on high commodity prices, inflation, and low interest rates. The results are consistent with the interpretation that operators of medium-sized farms in the 1970s used that liquidity to purchase land they were already farming. The mechanism to become a large farmer appears to have been a mix of purchasing and renting additional land. Some medium sized farmers, by seeking to pass land on to their children (appropriate yeoman farmer behavior), went into debt in the 1970s, thereby exposing themselves to serious financial difficulties when land prices (their collateral) fell precipitously in the 1980s.

The thrust of the results are consistent with those obtained by Goldschmidt 40 years ago. This study has resolved his principal methodological problems and extended his conclusions beyond the industrial agricultural zone of the Central Valley of California to commercial family farm agriculture of the Great Plains and West. Where, because of his case study approach, Goldschmidt was unable to control for the type of farming system and for the related problem of differences in age of the two communities (Hayes and Olmstead, 1984), this study was able to do so through the use of macrostructural secondary analysis. The patterns of relationship were quite similar for all four farming systems types, with the partial exception of livestock counties. The farming systems analyzed, although covering a major part of the United States, are more similar to each other than to the orchard system in Dinuba and the row crop in Arvin. Public Policy, Agricultural Structure and the Rural Community

During the 1970s, macro economic policies, as discussed above had more impact on agriculturally dependent counties in the Great Plains and the West than did agricultural policies per se. A cheap dollar paved the way for increased exports, including farm commodities as well as rural-based light manufacturing, to newly wealthy developing countries.

Increased availability of capital and high inflation caused by the expansion of the capital supply resulted in shifting factor costs, particularly cheaper capital. In response, land increased in value, as capital sought investments which hedged against inflation. Investment in agriculture in the 1970s, compared to the 1950s and 1960s, was guided by speculative and tax rationales, not by the direct productive potential of the land. However, in the farming systems under consideration, major land investors tended to be rural residents, not outside corporations. Tax policy favored land investment and indebtedness over saving. Furthermore, the high rates of inflation meant that loans could be repaid with ever-cheapening dollars.

Land values, pushed up by the increasing demand, helped fuel the trend toward increased farm size. Farmers now had increased equity, providing collateral to borrow more money to buy more land. Low real interest rates and inventive bankers helped farmers in the Great Plains and West leverage themselves into ever-larger farms. It was far more profitable to buy than to rent. Moreover, during the 1970s farmers found that it had become unfashionable to pay income tax. Tax laws favoring farm investment encouraged increased indebtedness to reduce tax liability. While farmers increased long-term indebtedness to buy land, they also increased their medium-term indebtedness to buy machinery. These debts, too, brought with them special tax advantages, including rapid depreciation and the writing off of all interest payments.

There is also evidence from the analysis that the inflationary period of the 1970s encouraged farmers in counties where medium sized farms predominated to expand particularly rapidly and enticed medium sized farmers to become full owners, perhaps in what in retrospect was often a vain effort to preserve the family farm for the next generation. Farmers in medium farm counties shifted from a relatively labor-intensive strategy to a more capital intensive strategy. Fiscal and monetary policy encouraged an intensified substitution of capital for labor (Eginton, 1980). Between 1969 and 1978 the farm size gap between medium farm counties and large farm counties began to close. As farm size grew, hired labor replaced family labor, but labor expenditures grew more slowly than did investment in machinery, as the factor cost of capital was lower than that of labor, compared to previous post-war decades.

The demise of the farm programs in response to the unprecedented world demand and high commodity prices in the mid-1970s had an important impact on grain farmers. There were economic and legal incentives to plant fence row to fence row, and thus tear our the terraces, windrows, and other conservation structures that made the use of large machinery difficult. The use of fertilizers and pesticides increased as more intensive cropping encouraged weeds and pests and robbed the soil of natural fertility as the restorative fallow period was dropped by many farmers now encouraged to getting three crops every four years, rather than one crop every two years.

The termination of production control oriented farm programs, coupled with the high world demand, also set up the grain farmers of the area for a major price collapse in the 1980s. All around the world—in the region, in the United States, and in developing countries—new, often marginal land was brought into grain production. A tax code that gave capital gains advantages to those who brought virgin land into cultivation encouraged the planting of a great deal of marginal and highly erodible land, particularly in wheat. Once the initial investment in machinery was made, costs of production were often lower in the new areas. This was because land could be farmed more intensively in such "new" wheat areas as California and the South of the United States. Furthermore, land was even cheaper in developing countries, leading to environmental degradation on a world scale.

U.S. farm programs would not have ended if the specter of over-production had not been removed by the shift in the world terms of trade, as indicated by the low value of the dollar, and the entry into the world market of new buyers of grain in the form of developing countries and centrally planned economies. These new buyers produced oil and sought to increase the well-being of their poorest citizens through cheap food. But even oil exports were not enough to pay for the imported grain. Much of the foreign exchange came from international loans, particularly private sector loans. Just like the farmers whose grain they were buying, developing countries counted on continuing inflation and the ability to pay back with ever-depreciating dollars.

When dramatic shifts in the U.S. monetary and fiscal policy in the 1980s brought U.S. inflation to a halt, causing a spectacular rise in real interest rates, and dramatically strengthened the U.S. dollar, the borrowing ability, and therefore the purchasing power, of the new customers of the grain grown in the Great Plains and the West was abruptly terminated. In order to continue to borrow money, often from multilateral banks, such as the International Monetary Fund, to pay back the private ones, country after country had to agree to domestic austerity measures. The end of subsidized food, and thus the end of grain imports, was part of the austerity package. The debt crisis in the Third World and the farm crisis in the United States were intimately linked together.

Technology, Farm Size and Policy

A principal assumption of this study is that policy, rather than technology, caused the rapid shift in agricultural structure that took place in the region during the decade of the 1970s. One of the major production technologies, irrigation, slowed the growth in physical farm size in the mixed crop and livestock areas, although it increased gross sales per farm substantially. Some of the technologies in beef production, particularly those related to cow-calf production, favored moderate and large-sized farms equally, since a very small proportion of either size beef producer applied such technology as artificial insemination and induced estrus (Gilliam, 1984:17-18). However, shifts in the structure of the beef packing industry, fueled by policies favoring consolidation in non-unionized areas, meant that farm feeders, profitable in the Great Plains and the West in the 1970s, could no longer market competitively in the 1980s, although their rates of gain were comparable or better than those of large feedlots. Technologies associated with marketing, rather than production, gave advantages to corporate beef fattening by the 1980s.

Even in grain production, the study did not indicate technology to be the root incentive of farm size expansion. Although the introduction of large-scale machinery certainly hastened the consolidation of farms, the increased use of that machinery must be evaluated in the light of the policy-generated negative interest rates and the tax policies that made machinery purchase profitable beyond any production efficiencies it might provide. There was a machinery-land treadmill fueled by cheap credit, as larger machinery required more land, and more land larger machinery, in search of a never-reached equilibrium. Eventually this increased scale required relatively expensive non-family hired labor, thus introducing capitalist (industrial) relations of production.

Tax policies allowing large write-offs against nonfarm income and a short holding period on farm property for capital gains exemption tended to favor operators of large and small farms. For farmers who had neither investment earnings nor income from off-farm jobs, common characteristic of medium sized farms, such tax advantages are almost worthless.

Community Viability and Policy

The analysis has shown that moderate sized farms contribute to rural community vitality. This occurs because the capital-labor ratio for medium-sized farms is slightly lower than for large farms, given the same or similar farming systems. More importantly, medium size farms contribute to community vitality because families with medium-sized farms tend to generate a higher local multiplier from their income than do either the hired workers or the owners or managers of larger farms. This means more retail firms and sales in the local community. This may also be associated with more local ownership of retail firms than is true in large-farm communities. In turn, this results in greater population retention. Given these patterns, what farm policies are most likely to contribute to vital rural communities?

It must first be recognized that current farm programs favor large-farm agriculture, although they have in an immediate sense helped keep many moderate-sized farmers in business. For large farms, hired labor is a larger portion of total inputs than is true for medium or small farms. As Schultze points out, "Much of the small farmer's input is his [or her or their] own labor, the return to which is treated not as an expense but as part of income" (1971:17). Large farms operate on smaller margins than do moderate and small farms with a large family labor component. Family operations often reduce their own wages, making variable capital truly variable. Since price supports or target prices raise prices and receipts the same proportion above free market levels for both size groups, such programs will increase large farms' net income by a greater percentage than the income of medium and small farms. Two types of alternative policies would tend to redress that balance and increase the competitiveness of the moderate-sized farmer. Either eliminate the subsidies and price supports, the free market approach, or impose a dollar ceiling on payments or provide for graduated payments according to farm sales, family income, and/or quantity of the commodity on question produced.

A radical version of the latter approach would be to completely decouple payments from production or limitations on production by having a generalized income maintenance approach. As long as assets which are part of one's business were not used to deny farmers and other small businesspersons the appropriate benefits, such persons would be free to choose either farming or living in rural areas, where wages are historically lower than in urban or metropolitan communities. This type of policy would guarantee a basic income. Stated another way, such a policy would be oriented toward rural people, since the standard of living in rural areas is lower than in metropolitan areas.

Both of the policy options noted above would have a major advantage over the New Deal farm programs as practiced up to the present, since they would not unduly encourage high-input agriculture. The coupling of acreage limitations with subsidy payments or price supports has not only favored larger farms, but also has encouraged high input agriculture and unnecessary yield maximization. This has had substantial adverse ecological consequences (similar to the impact of high commodity prices in the 1970s), including pesticide pollution and poisoning, contamination of ground and surface water by nitrates, and a disincentive for crop diversification. It has also been a very blunt instrument for reducing surpluses, since the capacity to expand yields seems to have usually outstripped the impact of acreage limitation on total production.

It is highly unlikely that finding the "ideal" farm program would ipso facto result in viable rural communities. It is equally important to reverse the prevailing assumptions concerning causality. The development of an appropriate rural nonfarm policy and the strengthening of rural communities could contribute to the strengthening of moderate sized agriculture. This is an important question to consider, even though this analysis has examined only the impact of farming on community well-being.

As in the case of non-agricultural policies having an impact on agriculture, policies not specifically aimed at rural communities have a greater impact on those communities than do those developed with such communities in mind. For instance, a national income policy could result in viable rural communities, as well as a healthy moderate-sized agriculture. More generally, there is a need to provide a "level-playing field" so rural communities can compete effectively with urban areas. There are four policy issues that merit examination.

The first are issues arising from the 1980s trend toward deregulation. Deregulation has disadvantaged rural areas in the access to markets. This is evident in transportation, where the long haul can be cheaper than the short haul in the railroad, trucking, and airline industries. Deregulation has disproportionately increased rural telephone rates. The assault during the Reagan administration on regulations protecting unions, although perhaps initially providing comparative advantages to rural areas, has negatively affected wage rates nationally, encouraging rural communities to make even greater concessions than before to attract branch industry. Relaxation of an anti-trust law has resulted in mass and massive mergers and the closing of branch plants in rural areas for reasons unrelated to their profitability. While the farming-dependent counties examined in this study had little industry in the 1970s, they are frequently near counties which did have such plants, which provided employment for some persons in farming-dependent counties.

Second, there exists an urban bias in the regulations for qualifying for federal program. This bias is evident in the inclusion of a population density requirement, as is the case with much formula funding such as for (1) state aid to schools, (2) basing programs on unemployment rate (rural areas have under-employment), (3) denying benefits to individuals or families using a means test which precludes ownership of property (though that property may be necessary for earning one's living), and (4) the decrease in medicare payments. The latter has hit rural communities hardest, since they have a disproportionate percentage of elderly.

Third, the ideology of low taxes, which spread from the national to state governments during the Reagan years, has reduced federal and state aid to localities as well as reduced local revenue. It is again the smaller, and hence more rural, localities which have been least able to fend for themselves. This has been exacerbated by the fact that decline of rural infrastructure like roads and bridges, much of it built after World War II, coincides with the decreasing fiscal capacity of small local governments to make the needed investments.

As Schoening points out (1986:87-88), the shift of federal spending from income maintenance and other people-related programs to defense programs, and passage of the 1981 tax act, have disadvantaged rural areas. Few defense contracts go to rural areas. The tax changes favored capital-intensive over labor-intensive activities, disadvantaging both labor intensive rural industrial activities as well as the more labor-intensive medium-sized farms vis-a-vis capital-intensive large farms. Furthermore, increases in social security and unemployment insurance tax rates expanded the tax burden on labor-intensive industries which continue to be major rural employers. While the 1986 tax act has corrected some of the inequalities in taxation of labor versus capital, a policy which positively rewarded firms for substituting labor for capital would help rural areas. Moreover, this might also have the effect of reducing unacceptable levels of unemployment and under-employment throughout the rural economy.

Fourth, the long-term population shift to metropolitan areas have disadvantaged rural areas politically. It is surprising the amount of political pressure those areas are able at the national level. The 1985 Food Security Act is easily the most expensive farm program in our history. However, it is a program that benefits well-to-do farmers the most, consequently making it an inefficient approach to revitalizing rural areas. The political price of such an effort is the failure to develop an effective rural non-farm policy, which with appropriate alliance-building could be sold to urban workers, consumers, legislators, etc., and which could strengthen medium-sized farming in the process.

There is an equally deep reservoir of good will toward rural communities as there is toward family farms in this nation. A substantial proportion of urbanites have rural backgrounds and many express a desire to live in smaller communities than their current urban residence. The population turnaround of the 1970s indicated that there was a willingness to act on such preferences when comparable economic opportunities are present. A rural policy that favors job creation, infrastructural development, and service delivery in rural areas could bring about a more desirable population distribution in this country, and would be more democratic, allowing more choice in the kind of community a family or individual would like to live in. Such a policy would have to be accompanied with a willingness of rural people through their communities to organize themselves. Such new community institutions could develop and expand locally-controlled economic enterprises, creatively design services to both improve quality of life and increase employment by selectively seeking branch firms of service and industrial companies. Such a combination of local effort, technical and organizational assistance from state agencies and universities, and a national rural non-farm policy would help dynamic rural communities to flourish, while others would continue to wither on the vine. Most importantly, people would have greater opportunity to choose the environment in which they live and raise their children.

REFERENCES

Albrecht, Don E., and Steve H. Murdock
  1985 "The consequences of irrigation development in the Great Plains," College Station: Texas Agricultural Experiment Station. Department of Rural Sociology, Technical Report 85-1.
Bender, Lloyd, D., Bernal L. Green, Thomas F. Hady, John A. Kuehn, Marlys K. Nelson, Leon B. Perkinson, and Peggy J. Ross
  1985 "The diverse social and economic structure of nonmetropolitan America," Rural Development Research Report No. 49. Washington, D.C.: Agriculture and Rural Economics Division, Economic Research Service, U.S. Department of Agriculture.
Center for Rural Affairs
  n.d. "Modified flat tax proposals: their treatment of agriculture and impact on family farm survival and profitability," mimeographed publication, Walthill Nebraska.
Eginton, Charles W.
  1980 "Impacts of federal tax policies on potential growth in size of typical farms," *American Journal of Agricultural Economics* (December): 929-939.

Flora, Jan L.
   1986   "History of wheat research at the Kansas Agricultural
          Experiment Station," in Lawrence Busch and William B.
          Lacy (eds). *The Agricultural Scientific Enterprise: A
          System in Transition.* Boulder, Co: Westview Press,
          1986: 186-205.
Flora, Jan L., Ivan Brown and Judith Lee Conboy
   1977   "Impact of type of agriculture on class structure, social
          well-being, and inequality." Presented at the Rural
          Sociological Society meeting, Madison, WI (August).
Flora, Jan L., and Cornelia Butler Flora
   1986   "Emerging agricultural technologies, farm size, public
          policy, and rural communities: the Great Plains and
          the West," Office of Technology Assessment.
          Technology, Public Policy and the Changing Structure
          of Agriculture. Volume II -Background Papers, Part
          D: Rural Communities. Washington, D.C.: U.S.
          Congress (May).
Gilliam, Henry C., Jr.
   1984   "The U.S. beef cow-calf industry," Agricultural
          Economics Report No. 515. Washington, D.C.: National
          Economics Division, Economic Research Service, U.S.
          Department of Agriculture (September).
Goldschmidt, Walter
   1978   *As You Sow.* Montclair, N.J.: Allanheld, Osmun and
          Co.
Grant, W.R., J.W. Richardson, B.W. Brorsen, and M.E. Rister
   1984   "Economic impacts of increased price vulnerability: a
          case study with rice," *Agricultural Economics Research*
          36,4 (Fall): 17-27.
Green, Gary P.
   1985   "Technocratic strategies of control: the case of the
          multibank holding company in rural areas," *The Rural
          Sociologist* 5,1 (January): 10-14.
Hayes, Michael N., and Alan L. Olmstead
   1984   "Farm size and community quality: Arvin and Dinuba
          revisited," *American Journal of Agricultural Economics*
          66 (November): 430-436.
Heid, Walter G., Jr.
   1980   "U.S. wheat industry," Agricultural Economics Report
          No. 432. Washington, D.C.: Economics, Statistics, and
          Cooperatives Service, U.S. Department of Agriculture
          (April).

Koppel, Bruce and Edmund Oasa
  1987 "Induced innovation theory and Asia's green revolution: a case study of an ideology of neutrality," *Development and Change* 18(1): 29-67.

Melichar, Emanuel
  1979 "Capital gains versus current income in the farming sector." *American Journal of Agricultural Economics* 1085-1092.

Ruttan, Vernon W., and Yujiro Hayami
  1972 "Strategies for agricultural development," Food Research Institute Studies in Agricultural Economics, Trade and Development 9,2: 129-148.

Pfeffer, Max J.
  1983 "Structural origins of three systems of farm production in the United States" *Rural Sociology* 48 (4): 540-562.

Salamon, Sonya
  1985 "Ethnic communities and the structure of agriculture," *Rural Sociology* 50 (3): 323-40.

Schoening, Niles C.
  1986 "Federal policies and rural growth patterns," *Forum for Applied Research and Public Policy* (Fall): 84-100.

Schultze, Charles L.
  1971 "The distribution of farm subsidies: who gets the benefits?" a staff paper. Washington, D.C.: The Brookings Institution.

Tweeten, Luther
  1984 "Causes and consequences of structural change in the farming industry," in *Research in Domestic and* International Agribusiness Management *5 (Greenwich,* Conn: JAI Press): 27-106.

Van Arsdall, Roy N., and Kenneth E. Nelson
  1983 "Characteristics of farmer cattle feeding," Agricultural Economics Report No. 503. National Economics Division. Economic Research Service. Washington, D.C.: U.S. Department of Agriculture (August).

Watts, Myles J., Lloyd D. Bender, and James B. Johnson
  1983 "Economic incentives for converting rangeland to cropland," Cooperative Extension Service Bulletin 1302. Bozeman: Montana State University (November).

4
Agricultural Technologies, Farm Structure and Rural Communities in the Corn Belt: Policies and Implications for 2000

John C. van Es, David L. Chicoine, and Mark A. Flotow

Agriculture is often referred to as the main economic activity of rural America and in certain respects the hegemony of agriculture in rural areas cannot be challenged. Historically, ically, except in those few locations where extractive industry or trade dominated, agriculture has been the foremost economic activity in rural areas. This historical dominance has had a strong impact on the culture and institutions of rural areas.

Even now, farming is the dominant use of space in most rural areas, and though the number of farmers may be few, their activities are very visible. Finally, the economy of agriculture is characterized by cyclical ups and downs because of strongly fluctuating market prices and inconsistent weather patterns. The sometimes violent swings of the farm economy may or may not coincide with the general business cycle. This has given agriculture great notoriety as a local economic factor. The farm financial crisis of the 1980s is an example of the volatility of the farm economy and the significance of a healthy agricultural sector for the general well-being of rural economies.

The objective of this chapter is to investigate the impact of changes in agricultural structure on rural communities, utilizing data for 1970 and 1980. In the 1940s Goldschmidt (1978) studied two communities in California and determined that a large scale, more concentrated agricultural structure, which was dependent upon hired farm labor, was associated with negative effects on the well-being of rural communities. Subsequent research (Sonka and Heady, 1974; Tweeten, 1984) tends to confirm that the nature of the structure of agriculture has an impact on local communities, as well as on numerous other items, such as the value of agricultural exports, the price of food and the income obtained per farm. As Tweeten (1984:50) points out:

> In short, consumers pay more for food, but rural communities are favored with a superior social and economic base under a system of small farms. Such a system would require considerable off-farm employment to supplement limited income per unit from farm sources

A declining number of farmers has repercussions for the community through the loss of employment in the public service sector: such persons as teachers, ministers, and retail store employees are likely to lose employment the number of farms declines. However, as noted above, smaller scale farms are usually associated with lower income per family and thus by themselves do not provide for enhanced community well being.

Changes other than those taking place in agriculture, such as shifts in the labor force from the industrial to the service sector, affect contemporary rural communities. Because of different degrees of economic diversification in rural communities, the importance of agriculture can vary dramatically by location. Farmers and their families are almost always outnumbered by other residents. Presently, while in many communities farming still contributes substantially to local income, few rural economies in the Midwest are dependent on agriculture. During the decade of the 1970s, non-agricultural employment in rural areas grew substantially, as did the nonmetropolitan population.

> Rural communities have shown remarkable vitality in the face of declining farm employment. Industries have located or expanded in rural areas to utilize underemployed labor freed from farming. In the 1970s, employment and population grew more rapidly in rural communities than in metropolitan communities. The well documented demographic transition is characterized by employment and population growth not only in counties adjacent to metropolitan counties but also in hinterland counties.(Tweeten, 1984:51).

United States Department of Agriculture economist Bluestone has noted that during the recent decades rural economies have become dominated by manufacturing, construction, and service-producing industries. Although Bluestone expects employment growth in the rural and small town communities to lag behind metropolitan areas, Bluestone argues that:

> . . . rural employment growth during the 1980s will probably be more rapid than in the three decades following 1940, when nonmetro areas were adjusting to the large job losses in agriculture and other natural resource industries (Farmline, 1985).

Certainly, future changes will not take place uniformly throughout the country. Consequently, rural communities will be affected in varying degrees.

The chapter is organized into three sections. First, we present a brief review of the history of change in the region's agriculture. This is accomplished by focusing on the structure of farming and the changes that have taken place nationally and in the North Central Region. Second, we turn our analysis toward the rural counties of the Corn Belt, specifically those dominated by grain, dairy or mixed agricultural enterprises. In this way we are able to make judgments on the likely impact of changes in the structure of agriculture on rural communities. Third, we discuss the implications for rural communities of future technological changes in production agriculture.

Structural Change and Technology

For the purpose of this chapter it is important to sharply distinguish between changes in the structure of farming and general changes in the agricultural economy and other sectors important in rural areas. The purpose of this chapter is not to study the overall importance of agriculture to the economic viability of rural communities, the impact of the farm financial crisis of the mid-1980s, or the consequences of federal commodity program changes on rural communities. Rather, the objective is to analyze the likely consequences of changes in the structure of agriculture, driven by technology, on the well-being of rural communities in the Corn Belt. The ability of the analysis to effectively measure farm structure and to identify those community characteristics associated with structural change is limited by available data and conceptual frameworks.

For example, sudden changes in federal commodity programs may severely impact rural communities, but such changes are not the direct result of technologically induced modifications in the structure of agriculture. The impacts of the farm financial crisis and federal commodity program changes on rural communities are important issues, but are also outside the intent of this chapter and beyond the scope of the project to which the chapter contributes.

Finally, one basic assumption of this analysis is that similar regional and agricultural economic conditions will exist under various alternative structures. One implication of the interaction of weak economic conditions and advancing technologies is that any social and economic adjustments are likely to be accelerated; while a strong farm economy faced with advancing technologies may allow for a slower rate of adjustment. The focus of this chapter, however, is on isolating the association between farm structure and community well-being, assuming similar underlying economic conditions.

Definition of Agricultural Structure

Agricultural structure is not a well-defined concept (Penn, 1979), but most authors refer to agricultural structure in terms of the organization of, and control over, agricultural resources and production. Certain authors have referred to the structure of agricultural in terms of the existence of certain types of farms such as family farms or corporate farms. However, the most common concerns with the structure of agriculture deal with the distribution of farms within agriculture in terms of their access to resources, their ability to support the farm operator economically, and the consequences of such distribution for agricultural production and agricultural communities. While not entirely acceptable, the structure of farming will be measured by the distribution of farm size in agriculture. It is recognized that size may not always be a good proxy for structure, but given the data and resource limitations of the present study, it is the one selected.

The two most commonly used operationalizations define farm size either in terms of the amount of farm sales or in terms of acres operated. Farm sales, when the information can be related to expenditures, provides a better measure of the ability of farms to support the operator economically. However, no national statistics are available which provide good sales and expenditure measures.

Number of acres on a farm provides as a general measure of size, but it is very dependent on such agronomic considerations as soil productivity and type of enterprise. However, within regions where agricultural conditions tend to be similar, acreage is a measure which provides useful information on the number and size distribution of farms. For purposes of the historical discussion, the trends in numbers of farms will be used to represent the changes in agricultural structure in the United States.

Historical Developments

Number of Farms

The number of farms by regions in the United States reflects the historical pattern of the major forces operating in agriculture. Until the first decades of the twentieth century the number of farms in the United States expanded, reflecting the westward expansion and the increased settlement of the United States, especially in the Central states. However, only the Pacific region (Washington, Oregon, and California) grew in the number of farms after 1930 and only for an additional decade (see Table 1).

It should be noted that the decline in farm numbers is not a recent phenomenon. Farm numbers have been declining for a half a century or more in all but one region, including periods of decline of more than a century in New England and the Middle Atlantic region (see Table 1). These regions also have undergone considerable change in the types of commodities that are produced.

The decline in the New England and Middle Atlantic states is not only of longer duration, it has also proceeded further than has been the case for the other states (see Table 1). The degree of the decline in farm numbers is most pronounced in the East and gradually diminishes as one moves toward the West. New England's contemporary farm numbers account for less than 15 percent of the number it attained in 1880. The reductions in numbers have been least pronounced in the West North Central, Mountain, and Pacific regions. These are the regions in which the homesteading of farms got underway much later. In general, the average farm size in these Western regions has tended to be somewhat larger.

The growth in farms until early in the twentieth century was accompanied by a similar increase in acres farmed (see Table 2). By 1930 the decline in farm numbers had commenced,

Table 1. Decline in Number of Farms Since Highest Count Year
for Regions of the United States

Region	Year of Highest Number	Highest Number	1978 Number	1978 as Percent of Highest Number
New England	1880	207,232	30,036	14.5
Middle Atlantic	1880	488,907	119,110	24.4
East North Central	1900	1,135,823	452,470	39.8
South Atlantic	1920	1,158,976	352,273	30.4
Mountain	1920	244,109	127,698	52.3
West South Central	1930	1,103,134	371,330	33.6
East South Central	1930	1,062,214	318,701	30.0
West North Central	1930	1,112,755	575,253	51.7
Pacific	1940	276,173	158,771	57.5

Table 2. Number of Farms, Number of Acres in Farms, and
Percent Change During Preceding Decade for the United States

Year	Number of Farms	Percent Change During Preceding Decades	Number of Acres in Farms (in millions)	Percent Change During Preceding Decade
1850	1,459,073		293,561	
1860	2,044,077	40.1	407,213	38.7
1870	2,659,985	30.1	407,735	0.1
1880	4,008,907	50.7	536,082	31.5
1890	4,564,641	31.9	623,219	16.2
1900	5,737,372	25.7	841,201	35.0
1910	6,361,502	10.9	878,798	4.5
1920	6,448,343	1.4	958,677	9.1
1930	6,228,648	-2.5	990,112[1]	3.3
1940	6,096,799	-2.1	1,065,114	7.6
1950	5,382,162	-11.7	1,161,420	9.0
1959	3,710,503	-31.1	1,123,378[1]	-3.3
1969	2,730,250	-26.4	1,062,892[1]	-5.4
1978	2,478,642	-9.2	1,029,694[1]	-3.1

[1] Includes Alaska and Hawaii

while total acreage in farms still continued to grow for several decades. During the last three decades acreage in farms has decreased by more than one million acres, but the rate of decline in numbers of farms has always been larger than the rate of decline in land in farms. One of the results has been, of course, the well-known growth in average farm size.

Distribution of Farms by Size

The decline in number of farms has not affected different size classes equally (see Table 3). Nationally the numbers of farms in the size classes of less than 500 acres have declined since 1940. Only 30 percent of the number of farms of less than 100 acres that existed in 1940 was present in 1978. On the other hand, by 1978 farms of more than 1,000 acres numbered 161 percent of farms that size in 1940.

In 1978, the total number of farms equalled approximately 40 percent of the number of farms existing in 1940. The shift in the number of farms from small scale toward the larger scale becomes more impressive when it is taken into account that the number of large-scale farms is a very conservative estimate of their presence. Table 4 indicates that, for the nation in 1978, although farms of less than 500 acres constitute 85 percent of all farms, they account for 27 percent of the land in farms. On the other hand, farms of more than 1,000 acres account for 6.5 percent of all farms, but for 58.5 percent of all farmland. The growth in number of larger farms thus in effect is a very significant phenomenon on the American rural scene.

Reasons for the Changes

Changing structure of agriculture can be attributed to a large number of factors, none of which can be considered a single cause in explaining the changes but all of which have contributed to the transformation that has occurred in agriculture. In the following section, the main factors contributing to the changing structure of agriculture will be discussed.

Technology

Changing technology has been a necessary condition for the restructuring of farming in the United States. Without the technological change, the transformation in agriculture could not

Table 3. Number of Farms by Size of Farm in Acreage for the East North Central and West North Central Regions and for the United States, 1940-1978

Region and Year	< 99 Acres N	%	100-499 Acres N	%	500-999 Acres N	%	1,000+ Acres N	%	Total Number of Farms
East North Central									
1940	537,809	53.4	460,514	45.7	6,895	0.7	877	0.1	1,006,095
1950	427,053	48.2	446,657	50.4	10,240	1.2	1,221	0.1	885,171
1959	270,147	40.5	379,386	57	15,016	2.3	1,638	0.2	666,187
1969	196,084	38.2	288,487	56.2	25,352	4.9	3,372	0.7	513,295
1978	190,492	42.1	220,857	48.8	33,480	7.9	7,641	1.7	452,470
West North Central									
1940	319,129	29.3	675,814	62	67,887	6.2	27,744	2.5	1,090,574
1950	257,683	26.2	614,598	62.6	75,698	7.7	34,432	3.5	982,411
1959	167,264	21	503,286	63.3	82,141	10.3	41,827	5.3	794,518
1969	129,562	20.3	369,594	57.9	87,575	13.7	51,858	8.1	638,598
1978	144,453	25.1	286,818	49.9	85,387	14.8	58,595	10.2	575,253
Total U.S.									
1940	3,583,649	58.7	2,254,861	37	163,675	2.7	100,531	1.6	6,096,716
1950	3,003,090	55.8	2,071,184	38.5	183,913	3.4	183,913	2.3	5,379,250
1959	1,709,618	46.1	1,658,006	44.7	197,383	5.3	197,383	3.7	3,703,922
1969	1,091,906	40.1	1,267,685	46.5	215,613	7.9	215,613	5.5	2,726,022
1978	1,072,141	43.3	1,023,603	41.3	215,058	8.7	215,058	6.5	2,472,801

Table 4. Land in Farms and Number of Farms by
Farm Size for the United States, 1978

Farm Size	Land in Farms		Number of Farms	
(acres)	Acres	%	Acres	%
Less than 499	41,890,127	4.0	1,077,351	43.4
500-999	237,400,433	23.0	1,024,023	41.3
More than 1,000	650,403,975	72.9	377,268	15.2
Total	1,029,694,535	100	2,478,642	100

have taken place (Lu, 1979). The primary types of technology were labor- and land-saving.

The replacement of human and animal labor (or the increased production per unit of labor) by mechanical power was the first great technological force shaping changes in U.S. agriculture. It allowed existing acreage to be worked by many fewer hands. Inexpensive energy, mass production of mechanical equipment, declining profit margins per unit produced and the competition for labor with a rapidly industrializing urban sector facilitated the migration of labor out of agriculture, and allowed the remaining labor force to handle larger acreage than had before been possible. Without the competition from the urban labor market, especially during the period 1940-1970 (Binswanger, 1978), there might have been little incentive to reduce the agricultural labor force.

The second set of technological changes relates to increased production per unit of land including increased use of fertilizers, pesticides, and crop management. Future developments in bio-engineering, computerization of agriculture and other "high technology" developments all appear aimed at improving increased returns per acreage.

In a general sense, these land saving technological developments may not affect the size distribution of farms; that is to say, they are to varying degrees neutral in regard to farm scale. However, there is ample evidence (Rogers, 1983) that access to new technology occurs unequally throughout the farming sector. Those farmers who control more resources are most likely to influence the direction of technological developments, and to be in a position to take advantage of the new technology. This advantage places them in a more favorable market position, by reducing their costs per unit produced—at least until the market price reflects the production costs of the new technology.

Market Factors

The impact of technology on the structure of farming takes place through the market. Over the historical periods discussed, U.S. agriculture has greatly increased its output. During most of these periods, rapidly increasing output has occurred in markets characterized by inelastic demand. Consequently, the returns from increased agricultural production have benefited the consumer to a significant degree. Some benefits have also gone to the manufacturing of the new technologies, but only small financial benefits have been realized by agricultural producers. Returns to units of labor and land have been below a level necessary to maintain a standard of living comparable to that prevailing in the other sectors of the economy.

To deal with the threat of low incomes, farmers have followed two courses of action. Many farmers have withdrawn their labor from agriculture completely, by abandoning agriculture, or partially by seeking employment off the farm and decreasing their hours worked on the farm (and frequently by reducing their leisure hours as well). These farmers have abandoned their dependence on the farm enterprise to attempt to provide a family income comparable to incomes in the remainder of the economy.

A second strategy for raising total farm revenue has been to increase the scale of the farm operation. If one cannot increase the dollar return per acre, one can attempt to increase the volume of profit by increasing the number of acres under production. For both farmer strategies, labor saving technologies have provided the necessary means to stretching family labor and thereby maintaining family income. In the case of larger farms, it has been cheaper to divide the cost of mechanization over more acres thus providing additional incentive to enlarge the operation. For part-time farmers, it is apparent that the reduced labor demands in agriculture have been essential to allow off-farm work.

The existence of the two strategies is well illustrated in Table 5, in which farmers are classified according to the level of their farm sales (in 1973) and the magnitude of their farm income and their net total family income. Table 5 shows very clearly that for smaller farms the proportion of family income derived from the farm is quite low. For larger farms the importance of farm income to total family income increases quite consistently.

Other Factors

The combination of technology and market forces has created two complimentary forces in U.S. agriculture: the drive towards larger farms (and thus fewer farm units) and the drive towards nonfarm income or part-time farming.

Other forces have affected these developments. Governmental policies have, sometimes simultaneously, aided and impeded these developments. Inheritance and tax laws have forced

Table 5. Families With Farm Income, By Specified Values of Farm Sales, by Average Family Net Money Income, Average Net Farm Income, and Average Net Farm Income as Percent of Average Family Net Money Income

Value of Farm Sales (Dollars)	Average Family Net Money Income (Dollars)	Average Net Farm Income (Dollars)	Farm Income as Percent of Family Income (Dollars)
Under $50	8,650	-65	0
50-999	9,151	100	1.1
1,000-2,499	9,505	451	4.7
2,500-4,999	9,265	960	10.4
5,000-9,999	9,749	2,156	22.1
10,000-19,999	10,673	4,411	41.3
20,000-39,999	12,291	7,770	63.2
40,000-99,999	18,648	14,732	79.0
$100,000 or more	29,179	29,179	100

Source: Adapted from Crecink (1979:25).

farmers to sell, thus bringing land in the market that can be purchased to enlarge farms. Income maintenance programs in agriculture have usually had as their objective the provision of an adequate income for farm families from agriculture thus deferring both migration out of agriculture and the growth of part-time farming.

Business practices in the private sector generally have favored the enlargement of farm operations through credit terms and quantity discounts. The most important role of the private sector may well be in providing nonagricultural employment. Whenever off-farm employment income competes favorably with agriculture, some farmers will be encouraged to find off-farm employment. If off-farm employment cannot be found in sufficient quantity in rural areas, there will be a transfer of agricultural labor away from the farm thus further depleting the agricultural work force and stimulating the development towards a larger and fewer farms. The development of part-time farming is very much dependent on the availability of employment near the farm. To the extent that nonfarm employment is being created in rural areas, part-time farming is likely to grow.

While off-farm employment has provided many medium sized farm families with short-run opportunity to supplement their farm income, combining off-farm and farm income has proven less than optimal in many circumstances. The middle size farm places sufficiently high managerial, labor, and capital demands on the farm family to make it difficult to combine with off-farm work. For medium sized farmers, part-time farming may be a necessary state of affairs, but not one that endures over time, especially not over generations. This may contribute to the disappearance of medium sized farms over several generations. As middle sized farms decrease in numbers, larger units grow at their expense and occupy more and more of the farmland. Small-scale farms may provide another growing class of farm operators in those areas where off-farm employment is available to provide those farm families with income.

Community Well-Being and Farm Structure
In The Corn Belt

A purpose of the chapter is to understand in more detail how change in technology may affect the farm sector, and how those changes subsequently may affect agricultural communities in the Corn Belt region. For purposes of this report, the Corn

Belt includes the states of Ohio, Michigan, Indiana, Illinois, Wisconsin, Minnesota, Iowa and Missouri.

The definition of agricultural communities is difficult to establish. Because of data availability the analysis focuses on counties rather than cities or towns. In addition, the analysis is restricted to counties outside of Metropolitan Statistical Areas. In Metropolitan Statistical Areas, the economic value of the farming industry is overshadowed by the urban economic activities; changes in agricultural income or employment are not likely to have measurable impact on the community. Therefore, county data is used for the concept of community.

Even in those counties which are not part of metropolitan areas, agriculture may be of minor significance while manufacturing, tourism, mining, and educational data for the nation suggest that this is the most likely nonfarm or farm employment category. Therefore, the counties were further defined according to the importance of agriculture for the county economy. On the basis of the percent of labor and proprietor income accounted for by agriculture, the nonmetropolitan counties were grouped as follows: counties with at least 10 percent of labor and proprietary income coming from agriculture, and counties with at least 30 percent of labor proprietor income accounted for by agriculture.

Table 6 provides the distribution of the nonmetropolitan counties according to the level of dependence on agriculture. The information is arranged for the states in the Corn Belt. As can be noted quickly, the counties depending on agriculture are located in the western part of the Corn Belt. For counties depending on 10 percent or more of agricultural income, almost 75 percent are located in Illinois, Minnesota, Iowa, and Missouri. Considering only those counties that depend for 30 percent or more of their income on agriculture, we find all but 8 percent located in the four most western states of the Corn Belt.

Table 7 provides aggregate statistics on the Corn Belt region, as well as the nonmetropolitan counties and the agricultural counties of the region. The nonmetropolitan counties account for about 30 percent of the Corn Belt's population and for over three-fourths of the Corn Belt farm population, farming acreage and sales.

When the proportion of county income derived from agriculture is taken into account, it becomes apparent that the agricultural counties account for a very modest percentage of

Table 6.   Distribution of Nonmetropolitan Counties,
         by Levels of Dependence on Agriculture,
               for States in the Corn Belt

	Nonmetropolitan Counties		Dependence on Agriculture [a] At Least 10 Percent		At Least 30 Percent	
	N	%	N	%	N	%
Ohio	49	8.67	14	4.19	–	
Indiana	62	10.97	30	8.98	5	5.00
Michigan	56	9.91	9	2.69	–	
Wisconsin	57	10.09	35	10.48	3	3.00
Illinois	80	11.16	50	14.97	17	17.00
Minnesota	71	12.57	58	17.37	26	26.00
Iowa	91	16.11	76	22.75	29	29.00
Missouri	99	17.52	62	18.56	20	20.00
Total	565	100	334	100	100	100

[a] Dependence on agriculture is measured in terms of the proportion of labor and proprietary income derived from agriculture. The figures are based on the years 1975–1979.

Table 7. Characteristics of the Corn Belt Region, Nonmetropolitan Counties, and Nonmetropolitan Agricultural Counties, in the Region.

| | | Nonmetro Counties | | County Income Derived From Agriculture | | | | | |
| | | | | 10 Percent or More | | | 30 Percent or More | | |
	Region	Value	Percent of Region	Value	Percent of Region	Percent of Nonmetro	Value	Percent of Region	Percent of Nonmetro
Population 1980	53,101,523	15,446,750	29.09	6,561,206	12.35	42.48	1,277,287	2.41	8.27
Farm Population 1980	2,308,613	1,760,442	76.26	1,192,596	51.66	67.748.08	331,551	14.36	18.83
Total Farms (1978)	757,484	576,713	76.13	211,411	27.91	36.66	106,459	14.05	18.46
Acreage in Agriculture (in thousands) (1978)	182,579	146,967	80.49	63,236	34.63	43.03	33,984	18.61	23.12
Total Sales (in millions) (1978)	33,468	26,245	78.42	12,084	36.11	46.04	6,399	19.12	24.38
Number of Counties	732	565	77.19	191	26.09	33.81	100	13.66	17.70

aDependence on agriculture is measured in terms of the proportion of labor and proprietory income derived from agriculture. The figures are based on the years 1975-1979.

the population. Approximately, 12 percent of the region's population lives in counties with at least 10 percent of county income derived from agriculture (see Table 7). Those counties most dependent on agriculture account for less than 2.5 percent of the region's population. Among the nonmetropolitan population these proportions are, of course, higher but the most agriculturally dependent counties still account for well under 10 percent of the nonmetropolitan population.

Table 7 also indicates that the agricultural counties account for considerably more of the agricultural activities of the area than might be inferred from the small population share. Those counties with at least 10 percent of income derived from agriculture account for around half of farm population and the number of farms, a little over half of the acreage in agriculture and value of agricultural sales in the region. However, the regional significance of the agricultural counties diminishes rapidly when only counties with 30 percent dependence on agriculture are taken into account.

In the subsequent analysis the focus will be predominantly on the group of counties that draw at least 10 percent of their income from agriculture. Those counties are more representative of the region both in distribution and in terms of the proportion of the agricultural activity that takes place within their boundaries. However, information on those subsets of counties which are most dependent (30 percent) will be provided when feasible to allow for special observations under circumstances of more pronounced dependence on agriculture.

Types of Agricultural Counties

Change in technology will not impact agriculture uniformly. Technological change is most likely to be enterprise specific and changes in the grain industry are probably not reflected among dairy farmers. In order to be able to make separate evaluations, the counties in the study have been subdivided into "grain" counties, "dairy" counties, and the remainder called "mixed agricultural" counties, depending on the dominant type of agricultural enterprise.

The dairy counties account for a very minor portion of the region's population and agricultural activities. Large declines in the dairy industry will not have a noticeable impact in the region with the possible exception of the effects in Wisconsin where almost all dairy counties are located. The grain and

mixed counties are more numerous and under the most inclusive
definition they account each for about 5 percent of the region's
population and one-fourth of the region's agricultural activities.
Finally, the mixed agricultural counties account for about 6
percent of the region's population and around 30 percent of the
region's agricultural activities. The data indicate that major
changes in the grain and mixed agricultural counties could have
a noticeable impact in the region.

Grain Counties

Grain counties account for more than 50 percent of their
agricultural sales from the sale of grain. In the Corn Belt, grain
sales include wheat, corn and soybeans, but some minor grains
are also included in many counties. Grain counties are characterized by the relative preponderance of flat, lightly rolling
terrain. Within the Corn Belt grain farming is predominantly
carried out by family based enterprises, frequently with a
considerable input of outside finances, but with the household
providing much of the labor and management.

Table 8 indicates that the agriculturally dependent grain
counties account for about one-fifth of the agricultural acreage
and sales and about 16 percent of farm population and number
of farms if the dependence of agriculture is defined in terms of
at least 10 percent of county income. The counties more dependent on agriculture account for less of the region's agriculture,
with the most dependent counties (more than 30 percent)
accounting for less than 10 percent of the region's agriculture.

Data are presented in Table 9 which allow one to make
some inferences about community level factors associated with
scale differences in agriculture. At each level of agricultural
dependence, the grain counties have been divided into two
groups according to the percent of total agricultural sales that
can be attributed to farms with sales of more than $100,000.
The counties are classified according to the regional mean value
of the concentration of sales on the farms in the largest sales
class.

Table 9 indicates that counties with a higher concentration
of sales on the larger farms are more likely to have farms
which are both fully rented or that have some hired labor.
Farm operators are less likely to work at least 100 days off the
farm. These factors are what would be expected in rural areas
with larger farms.

Table 8. Characteristics of Grain[a] Counties in the Corn Belt According to the Percent of County Income Derived From Agriculture

| | County Income Derived From Agriculture | | | | | |
| | 10 Percent or More | | | 30 Percent or More | | |
	Value	Percent of Region	Percent of Nonmetro	Value	Percent of Region	Percent of Nonmetro
Population 1980	2,373,079	4.47	15.36	631,437	1.19	4.09
Farm Population 1980	379,074	16.42	21.53	146,563	6.35	8.33
Total Farms (1978)	122,812	16.21	21.29	47,892	6.32	8.30
Acreage in Agriculture (in thousands) (1978)	39,602	21.69	26.95	16,900	9.26	11.50
Total Sales (in millions) (1978)	7,133	21.31	27.18	3,097	9.25	11.80
Number of Counties	122	16.67	21.59	45	6.15	7.96

[a]Grain counties are nonmetropolitan counties, with more than 50 percent of agricultural sales accounted for by the sale of grains.

150

Table 9. Comparison of Corn Belt Counties With Greater and Lesser
Concentration of Sales on Farms With Sales of More Than $100,000 for
Grain Counties[a]

| Mean County Values (ca 1980) | County Income Derived From Agriculture | | | |
| | 10 Percent or More Sales Concentration | | 30 Percent or More Sales Concentration | |
	Below the Regional Mean	Above the Regional Mean	Below the Regional Mean	Above the Regional Mean
Agriculture				
Percent of Renters of Farms	15.35	25.37	18.70	27.23
Hired Labor 150+ Per Farm	.19	.32	.22	.26
Percent of Farms Hiring Some Labor	38.18	46.85	42.80	48.00
Percent of Operators Working 100+ Days Off Farm	32.57	26.14	24.26	22.59
Demographic				
Total Population	18,074	21,022	13,269	14,829
Percent of Farm Population	20.03	16.80	26.44	22.75
Percent of Urban Population	24.95	32.19	17.00	21.95
Median of Median Family Income ($)	16,706	18,665	15,844	18,221
Median of Percent Poverty	9.46	8.05	11.60	8.30
Business and Employment				
Retail Sales Per Capita ($)	2,521	2,711	2,519	2,446
Percent Employment: Manufacturing	20.93	22.04	14.78	19.36
Percent Employment: Services	18.72	18.38	18.95	18.00
Percent of Unemployed	7.94	6.96	7.43	6.14
Number of Counties	65	57	23	22

[a]Grain counties are nonmetropolitan counties, with more than 50 percent of
agricultural sales accounted for by the sales of grains.

Table 9 also indicates that the counties characterized by the greater prevalence of larger farms tend to have larger populations and are more urbanized. Median family incomes are higher and the occurrence of poverty is less frequent. In the counties with higher scale concentration, employment in manufacturing is somewhat higher and unemployment somewhat lower. On a per capita basis, more is spent on retail sales in the counties with a higher proportion of larger farms. Overall, it can be argued that for the grain counties, the greater concentration of sales on larger farms is associated with a higher level of economic well-being.

Table 9 provides an opportunity to look at the importance of scale concentration according to a county's dependence on agriculture. Although there are some differences between the groups of counties, the data indicate that the patterns associated with the higher levels of concentration are similar regardless of the level of dependence on agriculture. Higher scale concentration is associated with higher per capita income, lower levels of poverty and less unemployment. The only reversal is found for retail sales per capita but in view of other information in this report, that difference can reasonably be attributed to chance.

Dairy Counties

The dairy counties (N=28) are those counties where dairy sales account for more than 50 percent of the agricultural sales. The dairy counties are predominantly located in Wisconsin on hilly terrain that is less suited to grain production. The dairy industry tends to be characterized by modest size enterprises as well as a very low level of full-renting. Table 10 suggests that there is only a small regional significance for the dairy counties.

When the dairy counties are classified according to the percent of total sales accounted for by farms with sales exceeding $100,000, it can again be noted that the counties with higher concentration of farm sales on the larger farms are both larger and somewhat more prosperous. It is surprising to note that in the dairy counties, where the labor demands of the agricultural enterprise are high, there is a very large amount of off-farm employment (Table 11). Because of the small number of dairy counties, a comparison of the different levels of agricultural dependence among the dairy counties is not meaningful.

Table 10. Characteristics of Dairy[a] Counties in the Corn Belt Region According to the Percent of County Income Derived From Agriculture

| | County Income Derived From Agriculture | | | | | |
| | 10 Percent or More | | | 30 Percent or More | | |
	Value	Percent of Region	Percent of Nonmetro	Value	Percent of Region	Percent of Nonmetro
Population 1980	759,081	1.43	4.91	39,951	0.08	0.26
Farm Population 1980	127,455	5.52	7.24	11,991	0.52	0.68
Total Farms (1978)	39,005	5.15	6.76	3,611	0.48	0.63
Acreage in Agriculture (in thousands) (1978)	8,273	4.53	5.63	784	0.43	0.53
Total Sales (in millions) (1978)	1,388	4.15	5.29	119	0.36	0.45
Number of Counties	28	6.15	7.96	2	0.27	0.35

[a]Dairy counties are nonmetropolitan counties, with more than 50 percent of agricultural sales accounted for by the sales of dairy products.

Table 11. Comparison of Corn Belt Counties With Greater and Lesser
Concentration of Sales on Farms With Sales of More Than $100,000
for Dairy Counties[a]

Mean County Values (ca 1980)	County Income Derived From Agriculture			
	10 Percent or More Sales Concentration		30 Percent or More Sales Concentration	
	Below the Regional Mean	Above the Regional Mean	Below the Regional Mean	Above the Regional Mean
Agriculture				
Percent of Renters of Farms	4.09	5.63	8.69	6.45
Hired Labor 150+ Per Farm	0.29	0.43	0.21	0.54
Percent of Farms Hiring Some Labor	43.53	47.27	55.56	48.91
Percent of Operators Working 100+ Days Off Farm	35.20	30.39	31.25	24.76
Demographic				
Total Population	20,576	31,950	25,642	14,309
Percent of Farm Population	18.93	16.34	31.55	27.33
Percent of Urban Population	19.07	27.27	14.00	18.00
Median of Median Family Income ($)	15,790	16,996	15,703	16,996
Median of Percent Poverty	10.60	8.60	10.60	8.60
Business and Employment				
Retail Sales Per Capita ($)	2,391	2,687	1,807	1,893
Percent Employment: Manufacturing	22.54	23.40	16.00	16.00
Percent Employment: Services	18.15	18.53	19.00	18.00
Percent of Unemployed	8.62	7.47	6.00	7.00
Number of Counties	13	15	1	1

[a]Dairy counties are nonmetropolitan counties, with more than 50 percent of
agricultural sales accounted for by the sales of dairy products.

Mixed Agricultural Counties

Once the counties characterized by the grain and dairy industry have been separated, the remainder of the counties (N=181) can be characterized as "mixed" in terms of the dominant agricultural enterprises. The characteristics of these counties vary considerably, but most are in the western part of the Corn Belt and they are characterized by mixed grain and livestock enterprises. In some cases the counties contain different enterprises such as grain, livestock or dairy without any of them accounting for more than 50 percent of the agricultural sales.

Table 12 indicates that the counties characterized by mixed agriculture with at least 10 percent dependence on agriculture account for 6.5 percent of the region's population but around 30 percent of the region's farm population, acreage and agricultural sales. When examining the 53 mixed agricultural counties most dependent on agriculture, it is clear that their significance is relatively small: they account for about 1 percent of the region's population and less than 10 percent of the agricultural activities.

Mixed agricultural counties with greater dependence on agriculture are somewhat different from counties with lesser dependence on agriculture (Table 13). Farms in the most dependent counties are slightly more likely to be fully rented and to hire some labor. In those counties, the farm operator is less likely to work more than a hundred days off the farm. The counties tend to contain lower population, and higher percentage of farm population, lower median incomes and higher levels of poverty, while retail sales and manufacturing employment levels are lower. To some extent, these differences can also be observed among the grain and dairy counties. Counties more dependent on agriculture turn out to be somewhat less prosperous.

Table 13 also indicates that the mixed agricultural counties with greater concentration of sales on larger farms have a higher frequency of tenancy, more hired labor, and less incidence of substantial off-farm employment by the farm operator. These counties are also more likely to have more people, to be more urbanized, and to be more prosperous (with lower levels of unemployment and a smaller percentage of the population below the poverty line). In other words, these counties have more farm concentration and higher levels of social well-being.

Table 12. Characteristics of Mixed[a] Counties in the Corn Belt According to the Percent of County Income Derived From Agriculture

| | County Income Derived From Agriculture | | | | | |
| | 10 Percent or More | | | 30 Percent or More | | |
	Value	Percent of Region	Percent of Nonmetro	Value	Percent of Region	Percent of Nonmetro
Population 1980	3,429,046	6.46	22.20	605,899	1.14	3.92
Farm Population 1980	686,067	29.72	38.97	172,997	7.49	9.83
Total Farms (1978)	216,668	28.60	37.57	54,956	7.26	9.53
Acreage in Agriculture (in thousands) (1978)	55,570	30.44	37.81	16,300	8.93	11.09
Total Sales (in millions) (1978)	10,874	32.49	41.43	3,183	9.51	12.13
Number of Counties	181	24.73	32.04	53	7.24	9.38

[a]Mixed counties are nonmetropolitan counties, with neither dairy nor grain accounting for more than 50 percent of agricultural sales.

Table 13. Comparison of Corn Belt Counties With Greater and Lesser Concentration of Sales on Farms With Sales of More Than $100,000 for Counties Dominated by Mixed Agriculture[a]

Mean County Values (ca 1980)	County Income Derived From Agriculture			
	10 Percent or More Sales Concentration		30 Percent or More Sales Concentration	
	Below the Regional Mean	Above the Regional Mean	Below the Regional Mean	Above the Regional Mean
Agriculture				
Percent of Renters of Farms	9.90	19.34	13.30	22.85
Hired Labor 150+ Per Farm	0.18	0.26	0.17	0.25
Percent of Farms Hiring Some Labor	36.85	43.87	38.35	47.03
Percent of Operators Working 100+ Days Off Farm	36.34	27.65	29.15	21.85
Demographic				
Total Population	16,776	21,874	10,213	13,290
Percent of Farm Population	22.93	21.62	39.54	27.52
Percent of Urban Population	18.82	30.01	8.97	21.29
Median of Median Family Income ($)	15,363	18,184	14,729	17,070
Median of Percent Poverty	11.63	8.68	13.50	10.33
Business and Employment				
Retail Sales Per Capita ($)	2,300	2,699	2,197	2,398
Percent Employment: Manufacturing	20.16	19.72	13.97	15.81
Percent Employment: Services	17.95	18.40	18.21	18.10
Percent of Unemployed	7.18	5.53	6.03	4.76
Number of Counties	109	72	32	21

[a]Mixed agricultural counties are nonmetropolitan counties, with neither dairy nor grain accounting for more than 50 percent of agricultural sales.

Change in Agricultural Counties

Regression analyses are used to determine the association of farm structure with changes in community viability. The dependent variables measuring community well-being are: 1) percent population change, 1970-80; 2) percent change in median family income, 1970-80; and 3) change in the percent of families below the poverty level 1970-80.

The determinants of change in the measures of community well-being are grouped into state variables and change variables. Inclusion of state variables is necessary to account for beginning-of-period nonagricultural conditions that, in addition to changes in agricultural characteristics, may impact change in population, incomes and poverty levels. The general model of change in the community characteristics estimated with county level data from selected Corn Belt counties is:

Change in County Well-Being=f(State Var.,Farm Structure Var.)

In order to adjust for the nonfarm environment, so as to isolate the impact of changes in the structure of the farm sector, the 1970 median family income, percent manufacturing employment, and percent service employment, are included as state variables. Communities with relatively higher incomes, and more diversified employment structures, as evidenced by the proportion of manufacturing and service employment, are expected to experience different population, income and poverty status changes than areas with lower incomes and less diverse economies.

In addition to the nonfarm state factors, the percent of farmland classified as cropland in 1970 was used to adjust for variation in the quality of the agricultural resource base of the community. As suggested by Kessler and Greenberg (1981), 1970 observations on the dependent variable were also included as state variables. The measures of change in the structure of agriculture used to analyze the relationship between changes in farming and community well-being are the percent change in the operators working 100 or more days off-farm, the percent change in the number of full and part farm owners, and the percent of total sales of agricultural products accounted for by farms selling over $100,000 annually. In addition, the percent change in farm population is also included. Data availability limited the sales measure to the percent reported in 1978.

Structural changes in the farming sector can be expected to affect county population both directly and indirectly. The direct impact is through farm numbers. A shift to a more concentrated, large-size farm structure is expected to negatively impact population growth as the decline in farm families reduces the number of people in the community. One study reported that a large-farm structure would require almost 40 percent less direct on-farm labor than a small farm organized agriculture (Sonka and Heady 1974).

The indirect impact on population is through those sectors which supply inputs and personal services to production agriculture. With a shift to larger farms, fewer inputs would be required, resulting in lower levels of off-farm activities. A structure of large farms has been estimated to generate about 25 percent less local off-farm economic activity compared to a structure of small farms (Sonka and Heady 1974).

The indirect effects of reductions in economic activity caused by a shift toward to a large-farm structure would include severe consequences for rural communities most dependent on farming. Employment multipliers for larger (above 20,000 in total population) rural counties have been estimated at 3.06 while comparable multipliers for smaller rural counties have been reported at 2.40 (Braschler and Kuehn 1976; also see Marousek 1979; Fass et al. 1981).

There is strong evidence that, while a decline in farm numbers would negatively affect rural community employment, the remaining farm families may experience substantial improvements in their net per farm operating income. Sonka and Heady (1974) report per farm returns in a farm system with large farm structures 300 percent greater than those in a farm system dominated by small farms; the major problem associated with a small farm agriculture is farm returns at poverty income levels. This accounts for the heavier reliance by Corn Belt farmers on off-farm income in communities with a smaller-scale farm sector.

While a concentrated farm structure may negatively impact population change, indicators of community income can be positively related to the degree of concentration in agriculture. Such a relationship is expected to be stronger in counties with small populations and in counties with more dependence on farming for basic economic activities. However, a counter to the positive income effects of farm concentration from the farm level are potential negative income effects at the community level. Income generated in an area from farming is comprised of: 1) the income received by the producers; 2) the income associated with the activity of agribusiness firms, both input suppliers and output handlers and processors; and 3) the income resulting from sales of consumer goods to farmers and individuals involved in agribusiness. While the income of producers may be lower for a small-farm structure, the level of input usage and off-farm economic activity can be higher. Consequently, the expected outcome of these conditions for median family community income is to be higher in areas with a smaller scaled farming sector.

While the descriptive data presented previously suggests the opposite, the work by Goldschmidt (1978) suggests a negative relation between farm concentration and community income. Heady and Sonka (1975) also report an "income generation" value 17 percent higher in the major Corn Belt states and 21 percent higher in the three Great Lakes states for a small farm agriculture, compared to the typical mixed farm structure. The values were about 30 percent higher when a small farm structure was compared to a large farm structure. The "income generation" value is the amount total income will change because of a one dollar change in the value of farm production.

However, a portion of the impact of changes in farm structure on community income reported by Heady and Sonka (1975) were the result of relatively higher farm output prices simulated under their small farm agriculture alternative. For example, feed grain prices were 35 percent higher under the small farm alternative compared to the large farm alternative. This accounts for some of the higher average incomes reported for the small farm alternative. In a cross-sectional analysis all output prices are approximately the same. Any observed relationship between farm structure and community income will reflect only the impacts of greater off-farm agricultural related economic activity and subsequent rounds of consumption spending.

Ownership of the land resource is a dimension of farm structure that is often argued to influence the community in ways not captured directly by employment or income indicators. At issue is whether farming communities characterized by owner-operated farms are substantially different and possibly better-off than similar areas dominated by tenant operated farms. For a farm operator to earn a given amount of income, fully owned land should give a higher return per acre, thereby

Table 14. Determinants of County Population Change
For Corn Belt Counties 10 Percent Dependent on Agriculture[a]

| | Type of County | | | | | |
| | Grain | | Dairy | | Mixed | |
Variable	Coefficient	Beta	Coefficient	Beta	Coefficient	Beta
MFGEMP70	.4234* (4.86)	.4741	-.1838 (0.77)	-.1552	.3126* (3.28)	.2618
SEREMP70	.8648 (1.29)	.1067	4.0258* (2.58)	.4129	1.7532* (3.45)	.1988
CRPLND70	-.3679* (3.59)	-.3246	.2984** (1.90)	.4127	-.2764* (3.72)	-.3354
POP70	-.9601 (1.46)	-.1179	-.0000 (0.04)	-.0067	-.00004 (0.46)	.0342
INCOM70	.0009 (1.30)	.1353	-.0005 (0.25)	-.0564	.0001 (1.52)	.1486
CHNGOWN	-.1102 (1.10)	.1222	-.8608** (2.93)	.7105	-.3616* (3.17)	-.3061
CHNG100+	.0465 (0.91)	.0801	.1594** (1.92)	.3040	.1430* (2.52)	.2067
CHNGFRMPOP	-.0364 (0.73)	.0547	.0017 (0.12)	.0021	.1597* (2.46)	.1447
LRGFRMSLS	-.0479 (0.65)	-.0578	.0780 (0.43)	.0862	-.0512 (0.72)	-.0636
Constant	14.34*		-38.71*		-1.23	
Sum of Squares	4329		537		12174	
F-Ratio	11.62		4.75		16.42	
R (Adjusted)	.44		.56		.44	
n	122		28		181	

[a]Dependent variable is percent population change 1970-80. Absolute t statistics are in parentheses.

*Significant at .05 level; **Significant at .10 level.

requiring fewer acres under production than if the land were rented. It is estimated that for Illinois grain farms, 300 acres of debt free land will provide an acceptable income for a farm family. A tenant farm family would need to operate 700-800 acres to earn a comparable income. This suggests that increased tenant farming or reductions in the number of fully owner operated farms may be associated with lower population growth, other things being equal.

The results of the model using ordinary least squares regression to analyze the determinants of change in population, median family income and poverty level are presented in Tables 14 through 16. The model was estimated using observations from grain counties, dairy counties and the mixed agricultural counties for counties with 10 percent of income derived from farming.

As expected, manufacturing employment in 1970 (MFGEMP70) and service employment in 1970 (SEREMPO70) were generally positively related to population change as seen in Table 14. The population in 1970 (POP70) was not significantly related to population growth in any of the estimates. Percent farmland in crops (CRPLND70) is negatively related to population change in the grain and mixed farming counties but positively related to population change in the dairy counties. The former relationship may reflect the more attractive amenity factors associated with a diverse landscape not dominated by cropland as a living environment.

The negative significant coefficient for the percent change in the number of operators that are full or part owners (CHNGOWN) gives some support to the expectation that increased tenant farming places a drag on population growth. This relationship is statistically significant in the dairy and mixed farming counties. The change in the number of farmers working 100 or more days off-farm (CHNG100+) is positively related to population change. The coefficient on this variable is not statistically different from zero in the grain counties' model. The coefficient on the percent of total farm sales accounted for by farms with over $100,000 in sales (LRGFRMSLS), is not statistically different from zero for any of the type of counties. Interestingly, farm population change (CHNGFRMPOP) is only significantly related only to overall population change.

Data not presented here indicate that the determinants of county population change for Corn Belt counties with at least 20 percent and 30 percent of their income coming from farm-

Table 15. Determinants of Change in Family Income for
Counties 10 Percent Dependent on Agriculture[a]

	Type of County					
	Grain		Dairy		Mixed	
Variable	Coefficient	Beta	Coefficient	Beta	Coefficient	Beta
MFGEMP70	.0209 (0.13)	.0139	.3509 (0.89)	.2125	.3362* (2.10)	.1759
SEREMP70	-3.7675* (3.41)	-.2759	4.1608 (1.34)	.3060	.0026 (.003)	.0002
CRPLND70	.3429** (1.87)	.1797	.3678* (1.26)	.3646	.3595* (2.81)	.2724
INCOM70	-.0098* (8.23)	-.8220	-.0080* (2.40)	-.6291	-.0120* (9.05)	-.8584
CHNGOWN	.2587 (1.52)	.1705	.4559 (0.78)	.2898	-.1110 (0.56)	-05861
CHNG100+	-.0196 (0.22)	-.0200	.3751* (2.44)	.5130	.3148* (3.29)	.2842
CHNGPOP	.4494* (2.80)	.2669	-.4532 (1.13)	-.3249	.0925 (0.73)	.05774
CHNGFRMPOP	.1264 (1.50)	.1127	-.3058 (1.25)	-.2814	-.1404 (1.28)	-.0794
LRGFRMSLS	.3645* (2.88)	.2610	-.1360 (0.45)	-.1078	.3199* (2.72)	.2480
Constant	182.84		140.53		160.10	
Sum of Square	12,716		1,551		33,613	
F-Ratio	10.79*		2.55*		13.90*	
R (Adjusted)	.42		.34		.39	
n	122		28		181	

[a]Dependent variable is percent change in median family income, 1970-80. Absolute t statistics are in parentheses.

*Significant at .05 level; **Significant at .10 level.

Table 16. Determinants of Change in Poverty Status for
Counties 10 Percent Dependent on Agriculture[a]

| | Type of County | | | | | |
| | Grain | | Dairy | | Mixed | |
Variable	Coefficient	Beta	Coefficient	Beta	Coefficient	Beta
MFGEMP70	-.3477** (1.69)	-.1112	-.0696 (0.28)	-.1926	-.0550* (2.64)	-.1549
SEREMP70	.1311 (0.83)	.0462	.1089 (0.28)	.0366	-.0368 (0.31)	-.0147
CRPLND70	-.0375 (1.46)	-.0944	-.0189 (0.49)	-.0833	-.0024 (0.13)	-.0099
PURTY70	-.4607* (15.66)	-.9249	-.6981* (7.65)	1.0595	-.5310* (12.51)	-.8977
CHNGOWN	-.0055 (0.24)	-.0175	-.0485 (0.68)	-.1311	.0387 (1.40)	.1101
CHNG100+	-.0193 (1.58)	.0948	-.0111 (0.58)	-.0695	-.0265* (1.29)	-.1287
CHNGFRMPOP	-.0273* (2.32)	-.1173	.0140 (0.47)	.0588	.0343* (2.17)	.1045
CHNGPOP	-.0319 (1.43)	-.0910	.0196 (0.39)	.0641	-.0231 (1.28)	-.0777
LRGFRMSLS	.0023 (0.13)	.0078	.0024 (0.06)	.0087	-.0538* (3.17)	-.2247
Constant	4.83		6.11		10.02	
Sum of Squares	247		24		693	
F-Ratio	39.25		12.33		36.03	
R (Adjusted)	.74		.79		.64	
n	122		28		181	

[a]Dependent variable is difference in percent of families below poverty level, 1970-80. Absolute t statistics are in parentheses.

*Significant at .05 level; **Significant at .10 level.

ing generally reinforce the findings of the model estimated with counties having 10 percent of more farm income.

Generally, the estimates do not provide strong support for a relationship between the measures of farm structure and county population change for the 1970s. A shortcoming of analyses at this general level are measurement and data problems. This could account for the general absence of more robust results. The small number of dairy counties is also problematic for that model.

The farm structure variables associated with change in median family income are the percent change in the number of farmers working 100 or more days off-farm (CHNG100+) and the percent of total farm sales accounted for by farms with over $100,000 in sales (LRGFRMSLS). The estimates for these models are presented in Table 15. The coefficient on CHNG100+ is positive and significant in the dairy county and mixed farming county models. The coefficients on LRGFRMSLS is positive and significant in the grain county and mixed county estimate. These results support the earlier descriptive evidence suggesting that the more concentrated agriculture is, the more likely median family income will be higher. Again, in data not shown here, the positive relationship between farm concentration and growth in median family income between 1970 and 1980 held for estimates using counties with 20 percent and 30 percent of their income from farming.

Attempts to explain change in poverty status (Table 16) met with limited success. Except for the mixed farming county estimates, the measures of farm structure were generally not statistically related to the change in the percent of families under the poverty level. For the mixed farming county estimate, the coefficient on percent of farm sales accounted for by farms with over $100,000 in sales (LRGFRMSLS) was negative and statistically significant. This indicates that in those counties not dominated by grain or dairy enterprises, the more concentrated the farm sector the less change in the percent of families in poverty. An unambiguous evaluation of this result is difficult, however, these findings indicate that if a low percent of families were below the poverty level in 1970, a low percent of families below poverty would be found in 1980. The opposite would also hold: if a large percent of families were in poverty in 1970, a large percent would be expected in this income class in 1980 for mixed farming counties that have a concentrated farming sector.

The fact that the data on poverty status are found not to be related to the measures of agricultural structure, but the median income data are found to be related, raises an interesting question. The findings are compatible with the notion that poverty in rural areas of the cornbelt is predominantly found among persons who have only tenuous links to the agricultural economy. For example, during the decade of the seventies, when commodity prices were high and incomes in rural areas rose, community poverty remained relatively unaffected by those developments, while being greatly affected by changes in governmental programs.

The difficulties inherent in accurately measuring farm structure and change in community well-being likely contribute to generally weak empirical findings. The shortcomings of the general analysis in confirming expected relations between changes in farm structure and community characteristics do not necessarily suggest these relations do not exist, but the preliminary analysis also does not demonstrate strong linkages between agriculture and the economic structure of the rural communities serving and served by production agriculture in the Corn Belt. The most robust results were the determinants of income change. Here a more concentrated farming sector was positively related to median family income growth in the 1970s. The small number of dairy counties severely limited the general analysis of Midwest dairy communities.

Summary of Findings

Corn Belt agriculture has been characterized by the same changes that have characterized agriculture nationwide: declining numbers of farms with concomitant increases in farm size. Technological change has played an important role in bringing about this transformation. While the process of change continues in the Corn Belt, the major change appears to have taken place two or three decades ago.

The impact of farm structure changes at the community level are difficult to isolate from other societal changes that may take place simultaneously. For example, agricultural counties (those receiving at least 10 percent of their income from farming) in the nonmetropolitan Corn Belt experienced differential population change and a sharp increase in unemployment during the 1970s, neither one of which can be attributed to structural changes within agriculture.

Comparisons within homogeneous groups (grain, dairy and mixed farming) of agricultural counties show that those counties with a relatively more concentrated presence of larger farms tend to be somewhat better off than those counties where concentration in agriculture is less. The data used here do not provide evidence of negative county level consequences associated with the historical direction of change in farm structure in the Corn Belt. However, the counties with more concentrated agriculture also contain, on the average, more people and are more urbanized, with more manufacturing and service employment. Moreover, the period analyzed, was a good period in terms of net farm income. Since it is difficult to isolate the implications of the urbanizing forces from the farm size forces for overall community well-being, these results should be interpreted with caution.

Attempts to develop an analytic understanding of the process of change in the agricultural communities during the 1970s met largely with frustration. The variables used in the analysis were selected on the basis of their expected impact on community population change and quality of life measurements as indicated in the literature Goldschmidt (1978). The results indicate that the changes taking place in the agricultural Corn Belt counties are not related to any large extent to changes in farm size. As indicated, much of the change in farm size and its impact on local communities had already taken place before the time period covered by the analysis. While in the micro-environment changes in agricultural structure may still be significant (a rural bank may be taken over by outsiders, an elevator may fold) the aggregate impact in the Corn Belt, even in the agricultural counties, is quite small.

Caution in interpreting these results should be exercised given the period over which data were analyzed. This may be particularly true for counties with greater dependence upon farming. The 1970s were relatively prosperous for both the farm and nonfarm sectors in the Midwest. Commodity prices were generally high due to rapidly expanding international markets, land values increased to historic highs and nonfarm economic growth occurred throughout the Midwest. However, while the prosperity of the time period under analysis may have had an impact upon certain relationships discussed above, the general findings of the analysis are expected to hold even for the contemporary Corn Belt, which, as is abundantly evident, has be characterized by great economic hardship.

Farm Structure and Rural Communities:
Scenarios for 2000

Causes of farm structure change include institutional forces such as federal farm policy, tax incentives and public investments in research and extension. Broad economic factors also cause change in the structure of agriculture. These factors include movements in the general price level, monetary policy and the behavior of international financial markets. These broader economic forces compound the structure shifts driven by factors internal to the farm sector with their impact being on the rate of change and not on the direction or eventual magnitude of changes. For example, recessionary conditions in farming that narrow margins and reduce farm incomes likely complement the other forces of change that have already substantially restructured Corn Belt farming. Boom times in farming, however, should have a positive impact on both ends of the scale. Incentives will be strong for farm size expansion, but at the same time a robust farm economy should cause farm income from smaller scale operations to be more competitive with income from other alternative occupations.

In addition, technological economies and changes of scale and size have altered the structure of farming in the Corn Belt and the entire country. The rewards for early adoption of new technologies place a premium on innovative, aggressive management behavior as technologies drive down average costs and encourage farm expansion. Labor and land substituting technologies have contributed to the continued growth in size of commercial corn and soybean grain farms in the Corn Belt during the past 40 years. In the past, expansion of the farm economy has resulted in the development of monoculture, cash grain farming in many regions of the Midwest at the expense of animal agriculture (Westgren, et al., 1983: 32-45). However, these expansions have been toward more large family farms operating 1,000-2,000 acres and not toward few large super farms relying on hired management and labor with extensive outside capital.

Changes in farm structure induced by advancing production technologies have impacted rural Corn Belt communities in different ways. The sketchy evidence from the 1970s suggests the more farm dependent areas may in fact be better off when farm sales are concentrated in larger farms. Implications of future technological advances for rural communities associated with changes in farm structure are suggestive, at best. However, the composition of the farming economy across the Corn Belt is not homogeneous. Therefore, the impact of adopting new technologies will vary with the agricultural character of the area, and importantly, with the dependence on farming as a basic economic activity.

Technology and Corn Belt Farms

Agricultural technology can be divided into three categories: 1) mechanical, 2) biochemical, and 3) informational/management. Major advancements in mechanical technologies, fueled by cheap energy prices, has released farm labor for other sectors since World War I. Labor substituting technologies have been a major force in the evolution of large family farms that dominate Corn Belt agriculture. Biological and chemical technologies substantially increased per acre production, and both categories of technologies have shaped the structure of today's Corn Belt farming. Information technologies, which improve management, have generally not been as significant in the past in terms of impacting the structure of Corn Belt agriculture.

Biotechnology

Future technological change on Corn Belt farms will primarily come from biotechnological advances and secondly from information technologies, mechanical technologies will unlikely facilitate farm concentration on the scale of the past.

Because monoculture cash grain farming characterizes much of the Corn Belt agriculture, the biotechnologies for animal agriculture will be of less significance, generally. The biotechnologies for plant agriculture are expected to bring about changes of the farm level relatively slowly (Office of Technology Assessment, 1985) For the rest of the century, farm size changes and related community effects will be evolutionary rather than revolutionary and the continuation of past trends will characterize the developments in the Corn Belt.

An exception to this characterization will be parts of the Great Lakes states, especially Wisconsin, where dairy production is a significant economic activity. Biotechnologies for dairy production are expected to significantly impact the industry in a short period of time and be in commercial use in the near future. The increased production per cow from these advances will accelerate the trends of the past, further concentrating dairy production in very large herds. As indicated, only 28 Corn Belt counties are dairy counties and most of these are in Wisconsin. Thus, changes in the rate of dairy farm growth and consolidation associated with these types of technologies will potentially impact a limited number of Corn Belt areas.

Technological advances in milk storage and transport, combined with the continued drop in fluid milk consumption, are likely to overshadow structural changes in Corn Belt dairy farming directly linked to the biotechnologies applied to milk production by the cow. Changes in storage and transport technologies suggest a decline in the relatively comparative advantage of the Corn Belt for milk production compared to the warmer climates in southern and western regions. A continued absolute decline in the dairy farms in the Corn Belt with technology accelerating the consolidation of operations is likely to characterize trends in dairy production through the end of the century.

The combined impact of biotechnologies on the crop and animal farming in the mixed counties in the Corn Belt is more difficult to discern. This is particularly the case where pork production is important as in the case in much of Iowa, and parts of Illinois and Missouri. However, the rate of productivity increase in pork production under the most optimistic environment of technological advance is not significantly off past trends. This suggests that structural changes linked to new biotechnologies may not be dramatically different from the events of the 1970s. What may well occur is just more of the type of restructuring that the hog industry has experienced to date. The impact of new technologies will likely accelerate the changes taking place.

Information Technology

It is even more difficult to assess the impact of information technologies on corn and soybean dominated Midwest agriculture. Management information from electronic animal monitoring and other advances will be less significant in its impact because of the dominance of cash grain farming. Software advances in crop oriented management systems such as pest control modeling will be more important in the Corn Belt. Accounting, production and financial management, and computer assisted marketing information systems will be as important for the financial success of the large family grain farm in the Corn Belt during the next 15 years as any other information technologies. Included among technologies will be improved weather forecasting for optimal crop production. While these advances will provide early adopters a comparative management advantage, they will not likely overshadow other more powerful forces shaping the organizational arrangement of agricultural resources in farms, particular variability in the market. The management technologies embedded in electronic information systems will be complementary to the biotechnologies of crop and animal agriculture. Effective application of these advances will require enhanced management skills demanding improved information. The information technologies will reinforce the structural impacts of biotechnologies.

Future Farm Size Distributions

The structure of farms in the United States were simulated under three different policy scenarios given the expected advances in production and management technologies. The policy scenarios represent: 1) a projection of current policies; 2) policies to speed the move to the bimodal size distribution of farms; and 3) policies to retard the trend to larger sized farms. The scenarios were reported for all farms and major farm types (i.e., grain, dairy, cattle, poultry, hog and cotton). The grain and dairy farm distributions for the U.S. are presented in Table 17.

To investigate the implications of these scenarios for agriculture in the Corn Belt and for rural communities in the region, the farm size distribution under the first policy scenario (current policies projected to 2000 under expected technological change) is compared to available information on the current size distribution of Corn Belt farms. In Table 18 the comparisons are presented for the grain counties, the dairy counties and the mixed agricultural counties in the Corn Belt that are 10 percent dependent on farm income. In general, the distribution of farms in the U.S. under scenario one is more concentrated compared to Corn Belt grain and dairy farms in 1978. This is not unexpected and can be attributed to: 1) the impact of technological change and other factors during the rest of the century; and 2) differences in grain enterprises on Corn Belt grain farms compared to all the grain farms of the nation. Midwest grain production is concentrated in corn and soybeans which is

Table 17. Three Different Scenarios, Year 2000 Size Distribution
of Grain and Dairy Farms, United States

| Dollar Sales | -------------- Size Distribution -------------- | | | | | |
| Category (annual) | Scenario 1 | | Scenario 2 | | Scenario 3 | |
	Grain	Dairy	Grain	Dairy	Grain	Dairy
	------------------- percent ---------------------					
Less than $20,000	28.6	38.0	38.2	44.4	28.6	38.0
$20,000 to $99,999	38.4	25.6	28.8	19.2	44.6	31.3
$100,000 to $499,999	24.7	22.9	12.3	11.5	20.6	20.6
$500,000 and over	8.3	13.5	20.7	24.9	6.2	10.1

Scenario 1: Markov Chain projection (current policy)
Scenario 2: Policies implemented to speed move to bi-modal size
distribution
Scenario 3: Policies implemented to slow trend to larger size
Source: Office of Technology Assessment, 1985, mimeo

Table 18. Size Distribution of Grain, Dairy, and Mixed, Farms for U.S.
in 2000 and Corn Belt in 1978*

Dollar Sales Category (annual)	Grain		Dairy		Mixed	
	U.S.	Corn Belt	U.S.	Corn Belt	U.S.	Corn Belt
	----------------------------- percent -----------------------------					
Less than $20,000	28.6	37.5	38.0	47.8	51.3	45.4
$20,000 to $99,000	38.4	46.3	25.6	46.7	29.1	42.6
$100,000 and over	33.0	16.2	36.4	5.5	19.6	12.2

*U.S. 2000 size distribution in OTA's Scenario 1, which is a markov chain
projection under current policies. The $100,000 to $499,999 sales category
is added to the $500,000 and over category because of 1978 data limitations.

generally smaller in scale than wheat and other small grain farming. The shifts in size distribution for dairy reflect the expected significant impact of biotechnologies.

The comparison of the projected national size distribution of farms under scenario one with current farm structure in the Corn Belt, suggests that the size distributions with the other two policy scenarios will exaggerate grain farm concentration in the Corn Belt. Obscured by the national dairy projection - under all scenarios - is the anticipated regional relocation of the dairy industry: the bulk of the dairy industry is expected to be relocated in the south and the west. Dairy farming will be of less importance in the Corn Belt in 2000 than today. The relatively few dairy operations remaining in the Corn Belt, will be quite large and supply the fluid milk markets in the region.

The continued concentration of grain farming in the Corn Belt is expected to be characterized by more large sized family farms with limited growth in super, industrialized farming operations on which most management and labor is not contributed by family members. The family units may include more than one generation and may be legally organized on something other than single proprietorships. Economic circumstances, historical settlement patterns and current fragmented landownership suggests capital ownership, particularly land, will become even more external to operating units with resources being controlled through lease arrangements.

The evidence from the 1970s suggests that the use of hired labor in the Corn Belt will continue to grow with farm expansion. However, the use of hired labor will generally be supplemental to family provided labor and management resources and complementary to the mechanization of crop farming in the Corn Belt. Trends in labor-substituting technology will continue, requiring human capital investments in both family and nonfamily labor. The operation and maintenance of $100,000 plus field equipment is a skilled task that will not be left to supplemental, untrained farm laborers. non-family hired labor is not expected to be significant on grain farms in the Corn Belt in the upcoming decade.

Impacts on Rural Communities

The empirical evidence presented here suggests a number of observations relative to the association between changes in the structure of farms and rural communities in the Corn Belt. The agricultural counties included in the analysis contain about half the agricultural sector in the Midwest, but only one-eighth of the population of the Corn Belt region. Even assuming that technological changes would impact the grain, dairy or mixed sectors of the industry simultaneously the impact on many subregions of the Corn Belt, especially the eastern states, would be quite modest.

The findings also provide evidence, albeit sketchy, that communities will greater concentration in farming were not found to be associated with a deterioration in community well-being.

The alternative futures represented by the three scenarios do not appear to foreshadow negative community impacts of a substantial nature in the Corn Belt. As noted, the Corn Belt appears to lag the trends at the national level towards concentration for grain and mixed farming areas, and in particular for dairy areas, when compared to both the scenarios based on the continuation of present trends (Scenarios 1 and 2). Since documentation of aggregate negative consequences of recent movements toward higher concentration in farming was not provided in the cross-sectional county level analyses, the scenarios do not appear to be associated with serious problems in the Corn Belt, especially when taking into account that farm concentration in Corn Belt counties is at lower levels than is the case in grain regions of the plains and west.

The mixed agricultural counties in the Corn Belt appear to be very similar in their historical experiences to the region's grain counties. For dairy farms both scenarios 1 and 2 foresee a very drastic change in the size distribution. These outcomes reflect the national trends in the industry rather than the current situation in the dairy counties in the Midwest. Again, on a regional basis, the changes in the dairy industry appear to be of minor consequence, but certain Wisconsin counties will likely undergo drastic restructuring. However, the analyses of secondary data also indicate that in the dairy counties of the Corn Belt other socioeconomic forces, such as population growth, have been present which will likely mitigate the consequences of substantial reductions in numbers of dairy farms.

Technological change in agriculture is endemic. It provides new opportunities for some farm operators, and causes serious hardships for others. Local communities will see the impacts of changes in agriculture, although in many instances such changes will be mitigated or exacerbated by other developments. For most of the communities in the Corn Belt and for the region as a whole, the consequences of changes in the structure of farming will be masked by larger regional, national and international developments. However, if a decrease in farm numbers, and maybe even agricultural activity, were to coincide with a cyclical downturn in the economy, local impact would be serious in selected communities.

Policy Alternatives

The limited analyses of the Corn Belt suggests that extensive negative impacts on rural communities from the continued concentration of farms into more large family farm units is not likely over the remainder of this century. This conclusion does not imply that a vibrant agriculture sector is not vital for the well-being of Midwest rural economies, but that continued reorganization of agricultural resources in more large operating units, in and of themselves, will not be economically or socially devastating, on average, to the rural regions of the Corn Belt.

Greater concentration in Midwest farming does not imply very large industrialized operating units characterized by a separation of management and labor and extensive reliance on investor capital. Industrial farming systems, now found in the Southwest and Western regions, are not expected to characterize the grain and grain-livestock agriculture in the Midwest in 2000.

The consequences of structural changes in agriculture, driven by technological, market forces, international trade, and other factors, will not be homogeneous among rural areas in the Corn Belt. For example, the implications for the more agriculturally dependent areas in the western reaches of Missouri, Iowa and Minnesota will be more serious than for the economically diverse areas of Ohio, where nonagricultural employment provides an economic base for farm and nonfarm family income, as well as the economic base of support for community services.

Overshadowing of the impact of farm structure changes on the well-being of most areas of the Corn Belt are global socioeconomic forces. This, does not imply that there are no costs associated with the historical trend toward a more concentrated Corn Belt agriculture. However, because of the relative economic role of farming in the local economy, the implications of these costs, which begin at the farm level and work through community and regional economics, will vary geographically or by commodity and farm type. National and regional economic conditions and the particulars of the agricultural economy will influence the rate of structural change in Corn Belt farming, and the severity of the adjustments associated with emerging farm structural change. Some communities, such as those areas dependent on dairy, will be most affected by expected technological changes. In general, the heavily dependent dairy communities are few and concentrated in Wisconsin. From a regional perspective, the transition of the dairy industry can be viewed as a minor event, but for particular communities substantial readjustments will be necessary. It is this type of subregional transitions that policy and policy makers must be sensitive toward. It is also a very difficult typeof policy to fashion.

The implications of these findings for public policy are varied. Price support policies of the feed grains, wheat and dairy commodity programs will help determine the rate of technology-induced structural changes in Corn Belt agriculture, but not the general trends toward concentration. Agricultural policy alternatives such as limiting benefit payments, targeting on selected farm groups, high loan rates or price supports, are instruments of income maintenance policy in agriculture but they address only indirectly the issues brought about by technological change in agriculture.

Since agriculture operates amidst the forces of the larger economy, programs attempting to ameliorate the stress resulting from structural changes in agriculture will be more effective when focussed on the individual or the household, rather than the community.

In order to deal with the problems of rural communities, a direct community development approach will be required. Interest in healthy, growing rural economies extends beyond concerns for farmers and how the resources of agriculture are organized into operating firms. There is, however, some reciprocity. A diverse rural economy with competitive, local economic alternatives softens the costs imposed by structural changes in farming for farmers and farm families.

The policy alternatives to address the implications of farm consolidation trends on rural communities should first address the human problem of transition out of farming and then the more general concern for geographically balanced economic opportunities.

Individual-Family Focused Policies

Technology induced changes in the agriculture of the Corn Belt will force farm families to leave agriculture and cause many farms not to be passed onto succeeding generations. Both individuals and families need to be provided with opportunities to achieve the most efficient transition. The exit from the farm and entrance into an alternative living and working environment can be facilitated by providing families with transition support. Programs for farmers and their families making the adjustment out of farming need to be targeted and transitional, avoiding developing long-term dependency. The character of these programs (job training, income maintenance, counseling) would basically be no different from programs targeted at the structural unemployment problems of other sectors. The geographically diverse nature of the client provides a challenge to the efficient functioning of the programs. Programs will need to be developed to rely heavily on existing local resources both in the private and in the public sector. Existing institutions such as the school system and the Cooperative Extension Service will need to be provided with the financial resources to deal with these transition problems.

Geographically Balanced Economic Opportunity

Policies aimed at encouraging equitable opportunities for economic development and diversity must recognize the inequities emanating from spatial and climatic barriers. Major contributors to the development of diversity in rural Corn Belt economies were the public investments in transportation infrastructure and other public capital assets in the 1960s and 1970s. As a prerequisite to economic change, infrastructure assets provide the opportunity for equal access to economic diversity and strength.

Overshadowing prerequisites for policies fostering geographically balanced economic development opportunities are effective, appropriate monetary and fiscal policies, restructuring of the federal tax code and international trade policies. The stress in the Corn Belt from agriculture problems is compounded by the decline in the international competitiveness of traditional "trade good" manufacturing industries that provide a significant part of the nonfarm economic base in the Midwest. Their relative international competitiveness is associated with monetary and fiscal policies of the federal government as well as the emergence of international competition from the newly industrialized counties.

If the local rural economy cannot generate employment for members of farm families who no longer derive their livelihood from agriculture, the communities will either see a noticeable rise in the number of people at or near the poverty level, or as has happened in the past, many families will leave these local communities thus alleviating local pressures and often making economic contributions elsewhere. However, migrants potentially can also contribute to employment and social problems in the areas they move to, and the migration process leaves the rural community with a smaller and sometimes demographically distorted population base.

Adjustment problems of the rural economy, based on changes in agricultural structure, will be experienced more accurately in those communities with a higher level of dependence on agriculture. For the Corn Belt this indicates that community development programs ought to be concentrated more heavily in the dairy counties and in the area of the Corn Belt west of the Mississippi.

There is evidence (Farmline, 1985) that the employment and demographic gains the rural areas experienced in the 1960s and 1970s have been reversed in the 1980s. A rural development policy which addresses the needs of all rural areas will go far in assisting rural communities in dealing specifically with the problems resulting from structural changes in agriculture.

REFERENCES

Binswanger, Hans P.
  1978   "Measured Biases of Technical Change: The United States." In H. P. Binswanger et al., eds. *Induced Innovation*, Baltimore, MD: Johns Hopkins Press.
Braschler, Curtus and John Kuehn
  1976   "Differential Employment Multipliers for Nonmetropolitan Counties." *Southern Journal of Agricultural Economics* 8:187-192.
Crecink, John C.
  1979   Families With Farm Income, Their Income, Income Distribution and Income Sources. Washington, D.C.: ESCS, USDA.

Farmline
  1985 "The Boom Has Faded, and Many Rural Areas Lag
        Behind." *Farmline* 6(3):12-13.
Fass, R. C., David Holland and Douglas Young
  1981 "Variation in Farm Size, Irrigation Technology and
        After-Tax Income: Implications for Local Economic
        Development." *Land Economics* 57:213-220.
Goldschmidt, Walter
  1978 *As You Sow.* Montclair, NJ: Allanheld, Osmun and
        Company.
Heady, Earl O. and Steven T. Sonka
  1975 Farm-Size Structure and Off-Farm Income and
        Employment Generation in the North Central Region.
        Ames, IA: North Central Regional Center for Rural
        Development, Iowa State University (February).
Kessler, Ronald C. and David F. Greenberg
  1981 *Linear Panel Analysis: Models of Quantitative Change.*
        New York, NY: Academic Press.
Lu, Yao-Chi
  1979 "Technological Change and Structure." In Structure
        Issues of American Agriculture, Washington, D.C.:
        ESCS, USDA: 121-127.
Marousek, Gerald
  1979 "Farm Size and Rural Communities: Some Economic
        Relations." *Southern Journal of Agricultural Economics*
        11:57-61.
Office of Technology Assessment (OTA)
  1985 Technology, Public Policy, and the Changing Structure
        of American Agriculture, Draft Report, Washington,
        D.C.: U.S. Congress (February).
Penn, I. B.
  1979 "The Structure of Agriculture: An Overview of the
        Issue." In Structure Issues of American Agriculture,
        Washington, D.C.: ESCS, USDA:2-23.
Rogers, Everett M.
  1983 *Diffusion of Innovations.* New York, NY: The Free
        Press.
Sonka, Steven T. and Earl O. Heady
  1974 American Farm-Size Structure in Relation to Income
        and Employment Opportunities of Farms, Rural
        Communities and Other Sectors. CARD Report 48,
        Ames, IA: Center for Agricultural and Rural
        Development, Iowa State University.

Tweeten, Luther
  1984 Causes and Consequences of Structural Change in the Farming Industry. Washington, D.C.: National Planning Association.

Westgren, Randall E., John Braden, David L. Chicoine, and Bartelt Eleveld
  1983 Structure of Illinois Food Economy: Resource Issues. Doc. No. 83/28, Springfield, IL: Illinois Department of Energy and Natural Resources.

5
Farm Structure and Rural Communities in the Northeast

Frederick H. Buttel, Mark Lancelle, and David R. Lee

This paper is devoted to reviewing the historical and contemporary literature on the relationships among technological, farm structural, and rural community change in the Northeast region. In addition, we will present the results of an empirical study of the interrelationships among changes in farm structure, agricultural technology, and rural communities during the 1970-1980 period.

The initial portion of this paper presents a historical overview of the development of agriculture and rural communities in the Northeast region. We then survey the major research literature on farm structure and rural communities in the Northeast for the period from 1970 to the present. The post-1970 period is emphasized for three major reasons. First, the years from 1970 to 1980 represent the most recent decade-long period for which change in agricultural technology, farm structure, and rural community conditions can be examined quantitatively. Second, the Northeast (and the U.S. as a whole) witnessed a new pattern of farm structural change in the 1970s. While the farm population and the number of farms in this region generally were in continuous decline from 1900 to 1970, the period from 1970 to present has generally been one of stabilization in the number of farms and, in several states in the Northeast, has involved small increases in the number of farms. Third, the Northeast and the U.S. as a whole experienced a new pattern of rural-urban population growth during the 1970s such that nonmetropolitan counties grew faster than metropolitan counties.

Among the most important points to be emphasized below are that agriculture tends to be a smaller component of the Northeast economy than of the economies of other regions such as the Great Plains or western Corn Belt and that the Northeast has had a relatively privileged nonmetropolitan-rural population for several decades. These characteristics of the Northeast agricultural economy and its rural communities have long historical roots, which are traced in some detail in the initial section of the paper. The preliminary results from an empirical study of technological, farm structural, and rural community change in the Northeast, utilizing census-type data for all nonmetropolitan counties in this region during the period from 1969/1970 to 1978/1980 is then examined. The results are used to estimate the recent impacts of change in technological and farm structure on the viability of rural communities in the Northeast.

For purposes of this paper, the Northeast region includes the states of Connecticut, Maine, Massachusetts, New Hampshire, New Jersey, New York, Pennsylvania, Rhode Island, and Vermont. This delineation of the region is coterminous with that used for reporting of Census of Agriculture data. To a large extent the data presented in this paper will be for the Northeast region as defined above. We will, however, present some data that pertain to the Northeast-Great Lakes region utilized for purposes of reporting Census of Population data (see Hines et al., 1975; Brown and Beale, 1981). The Northeast-Great Lakes region includes the nine states noted above, plus Maryland, Delaware, Ohio, Michigan, and parts of Indiana, Illinois, Wisconsin, and Minnesota.

The Northeast has a certain coherence as a region, principally on the basis of its agricultural economy. Relative to the rest of the U.S., the nine Northeastern states are characterized by farm structures that involve little industrial-type farming, small average farm sizes, a pattern of specialization of commodity production in which products tend to be destined for markets in major urban centers in the region (rather than for interregional or international markets), and a longstanding pattern of loss of land in farms (which was, however, attenuated beginning in the early 1970s). Also, the farm population as a percentage of the rural (or, in terms of the more recent measure, the nonmetropolitan) population in the Northeast has, since the turn of the century, been lower than that of the other agricultural regions of the U.S.

Despite the broad similarities among the states and substate areas in the larger Northeast region, the region is nonetheless quite diverse. There are two major sources of diversity relevant to this paper. One source of diversity is agroecological in nature. The six New England states (Connecticut, Maine, Massachusetts, New Hampshire, Rhode Island, and Vermont) generally have low-quality soils and short growing seasons, albeit with certain exceptions such as the Connecticut River Valley. The three Middle Atlantic states (New Jersey, New York and Pennsylvania) generally have more favorable agricultural conditions. The second source of diversity is socioeconomic in nature and relates to the dramatic variations in urban-metropolitan influence in the region. The contrasts are striking between the Boston to Washington, D.C. megalopolis and its densely-settled 35 or so million inhabitants on one hand, and the highly rural state of Vermont, which has no Standard Metropolitan Statistical Area (SMSA), on the other.

Historical Perspectives on Agriculture and the Rural Community in the Northeast Region

Settlement Patterns And Forms Of Agrarian Organization In The Seventeenth And Eighteenth Centuries

The Northeast, although it encompasses only about 6 percent of the total U.S. land surface (Schertz, 1979:259), was settled over an extended, two-century-long period from roughly 1630 to 1830. The brief analysis that follows can hardly do justice to the changing conditions and nature of settlement over such a long period of time. Nevertheless, it is useful to consider the formative period of settlement and agrarian organization in the Northeast colonies, since the patterns that emerged at that early stage have had lasting impacts on farm and rural community structure up to the current era.

During the first century of settlement in the Northeast, there were two major forms of settlement patterns: the village settlement and the dispersed farmstead (isolated farmstead or open country) patterns. The village settlement pattern involved the clustering of farmers' homes to form a village or hamlet, leaving the pastures, fields, and forest lands in the surrounding areas devoid of dwellings. Barns and other farm buildings were generally clustered toward the village core as well. The dispersed farmstead pattern, by contrast, involved farm dwellings and other buildings being located on the farming plot. Hence, farm residences would tend to be relatively isolated or scattered from one another. With regard to the village form of settlement, there was, in a sense, a clear unity of farm and community structure. The agricultural community consisted, in large part, of the farm families who had their residences and other buildings at the community core. The allotments of land made to settlers, in fact, tended not to be individually fenced, but rather, the entire village community—both the village core and the outlying lands—was surrounded by a common fence. With regard to the dispersed farmstead system, settlers typically did not enjoy the presence of a hamlet or trade center; several years—often even a decade or more—would pass before there would appear a population concentration such as a hamlet (MacLeisch and Young, 1942:11).

Both the village and dispersed farmstead forms of settlement during the first century of colonization involved manorial (or estate) and nonmanorial subtypes. One of the major mechanisms of distributing land in the colonies was for the King of England to make large grants of land to his friends or supporters. Proprietors of these land grants were expected to colonize the land. The King, for example, made land grants to Lord Baltimore to found the colony of Maryland and to William Penn to found the colony of Pennsylvania. Many such proprietors receiving land grants attempted to create manorial estates with a system of hereditary nobles and peasants. These attempts were most common in Maryland and the Carolinas. Most attempts to establish manorial forms of agricultural organization involved transplanting the English village system to the colonies. There were, however, Dutch-colonial analogs of the manorial system that emerged in areas, such as the Hudson and Mohawk valleys of New York State, where there was extensive land speculation and a general absence of the village settlement pattern (Ebling, 1979:25). Here the Rensselaers, Livingstons, Schuylers, and other families became aristocratic landlords who lived off the labors of their many tenants (Gates, 1960:36). The manorial-patroon system established by the Dutch in New York State was largely adopted by the British after Holland conceded the colony to England in 1664. This system would remain largely intact until the Revolutionary War, and remnants would persist until the mid-nineteenth century (Herman, 1979).

Attempts to establish manorial or semiservile forms of agricultural organization, based either on village or dispersed farmstead settlement patterns, tended to be short-lived. To be sure, landlordism and tenancy were still flourishing in parts of New York State and Pennsylvania well into the late 1840s. Yet the general abundance of land tended to undermine manorial schemes. Would-be feudal lords in Maryland and elsewhere for obvious reasons found themselves unable to attract settlers, and many were forced to distribute their lands as gifts or sell land for nominal prices in order to encourage settlement.

In New England, virtually all the early settlements took the village form. These village settlements were very similar to English villages. Village settlements spread throughout most of southern New England and, to some degree, into New York, New Jersey, and Pennsylvania. Until 1725, when the village system was experiencing a demise, land speculation was essentially unknown, and there tended to be a relatively small degree of social class inequality among farmers (Main, 1965). As the village system evolved, however, population growth in conjunction with destructive farming techniques tended to result in increasing landlessness, land fragmentation, and conflicts within the corporate group over taxation, property qualifications for voting, and the responsibility of the wealthy to the poor. Outlying sections of the village typically sought to separate from the village, while the village centers resisted these demands (Lockridge, 1970:Chapter 3). Increasingly after 1750 the propertyless, the poor, and the young and strong from southern New England villages began to look north and west for land to settle. Socioeconomic conditions in southern New England—particularly Massachusetts—deteriorated even further after the Revolutionary War. State and local debts were high, leading to heavy and inequitable taxation. Land was becoming crowded, expensive, and worn out. The Massachusetts ruling class and the Congregational Church were felt to be unfair to the poor. Migration from southern New England toward northern New England and the western areas accelerated after the war.

New settlements after the early 1700s were largely of the dispersed farmstead type. The settlement of northern New England, which began around 1765 and accelerated after the Revolutionary War, was virtually all of the dispersed farmstead type. In New York, where the original settlers were Dutch, the Dutch authorities placed considerable pressure on settlers to adopt the village form (Herman, 1979:38). These efforts were successful only to a minor degree, and the bulk of the state was settled with dispersed farmsteads. The dispersed farmstead

settlement pattern that was to prevail in New York has generally been credited with diffusing the scattered-farmsteads form
of settlement westward (Smith and Zopf, 1970:123; Gates,
1960:Chapter 2). The colony of Pennsylvania had both village
and dispersed farmstead settlement patterns from the beginning;
most of the colony, however, was settled in the dispersed-
farmsteads pattern, especially after the Revolutionary War.

There were a number of reasons why the village pattern of
settlement, which was nearly universal at the outset of colonization, would ultimately yield to the isolated farmstead and
complementary trade center pattern. First, the dispersed
homestead form was most compatible with livestock production.
Second, as responsibility for the dispersal of land shifted from a
governmental to a proprietorial basis, there was less control over
settlers' location of housing and other buildings, especially since
settlers attempted to choose plots that had the highest quality
land. Third, squatting became relatively prevalent on lands in
northern New England and the West, and the only means by
which a squatter could hope to hold the land which he occu-
pied extra-legally was to establish himself and family directly
on the farm. Fourth, the rapidly deteriorating socioeconomic
conditions of the village settlements in southern New England
no doubt motivated settlers to avoid the organizational conditions that might lead to tyranny and inequality in their new
regions of residence. Nevertheless, by 1800 the isolated
farmstead and complementary trade center had become the predominant pattern of agricultural and rural community organization in the North.

The agricultural structures of the Northern colonies (and,
after the Revolutionary War, the "Northern" states) generally
involved relatively egalitarian landholding systems. At the time
of the Revolutionary War, most farming communities were
largely self-sufficient; relatively little wealth was accumulated,
and accordingly there were few farmers of great wealth (Main,
1965). Relative equality of landholdings was generally the case
in the frontier areas, especially outside of the areas of New
York and western Pennsylvania where land speculation was
prevalent.

There were two major exceptions to the pattern of relative
equality of landholdings. The first exception was that of
communities, generally in southern New England or New Jersey
proximate to cities or navigable rivers, where agriculture had
become commercialized by the time of the Revolutionary War

(Main, 1965; Lockridge, 1970). These farming areas, which produced foodstuffs for the growing urban populations, exhibited high degrees of concentration of land and income. It was typical, for example, in commercial farming areas of Massachusetts in the mid-eighteenth century for 50 percent of the income to be accounted for by the most affluent 10 percent of the population (Lockridge, 1970:142). Main (1965:28ff.), in his study of the class structure of America at the time of the Revolutionary War, found that commercial farm communities tended, by comparison with subsistence communities, to have greater land concentration, relatively few small farmers, a larger proportion of propertyless laborers, and a larger proportion of artisans and professionals.

The second exception to the pattern of relative equality of landholdings in the Northern states was, as noted earlier, certain regions of New York, Pennsylvania, and New Jersey where land was originally controlled by "landed aristocrats," as in the Hudson and Mohawk valleys of New York and portions of New Jersey, or where there was extensive land speculation, as in western Pennsylvania and parts of central and western New York. In the last decade of the eighteenth century, for example, one man in Penn Yan, New York, owned 25,000 acres that were rented to tenants, and eighteen individuals and partnerships held 4.2 million acres in western Pennsylvania in the early 1930s (Gates, 1960:31, 41).

Despite these staggering instances of land concentration in the western frontier, there were strong tendencies as the nineteenth century unfolded for large landholdings and landlordism to disappear. In New York, Tory landholdings were confiscated after the Revolutionary War and sold to speculators and small farmers (Herman, 1979:47). Freeholding was given an additional post-Revolutionary War boost when the state of New York granted large areas in central New York as homesteads to soldiers who served in the militia (Hedrick, 1933:63; Herman, 1979). Further, if tenant-settlers had no hope of obtaining ownership of their lands, they would be able to sell out or abandon their possessions and move west to new frontier areas. Landlords thus came to have to deal leniently with their tenants, lest they risk the wholesale abandonment of their properties by disgruntled tenants. Large landholdings also tended to be liquidated over time as a result of tax burdens, slow returns from marginal lands, and the availability of nonfarm investment outlets. Other estates were divided upon inheritance or through foreclosure (Gates, 1960:Chapter 2). Monopolistic landlordism in New York was dealt its final blow by the Anti-Rent Movement from the 1830s through the 1850s, which carried out violent resistance against landlord patroons during the early years of the movement and which would later elect Anti-Rent candidates to local and state offices (Herman, 1979:48, Hedrick, 1933:57-61).

Farm Structure And Rural Communities
In The Nineteenth Century

Although many frontier areas tended to exhibit self-sufficient subsistence agriculture, by the end of the second decade of the nineteenth century agriculture in the Northeast had become strongly commercial (Gates, 1960:Chapter 19). Commercialization was stimulated at the farm level by indebtedness and taxation and at the macro level by urbanization, industrialization, and transportation-infrastructural development—especially steamboat- and canal-based commerce in the 1820s and 1830s and extensive railroad development from 1830 to 1860 (Cochrane, 1979:Chapter 11). Commercialization, however, was a mixed blessing for many farmers in the Northeast. On one hand, urban-market-led commercialization in the Northeast enabled many farmers to service their debts and avoid foreclosure, but agriculture in this region generally fared poorly in the competition with that of the West, which was opened up by post-1830 transportation improvements.

The history of Northeastern agriculture during the nineteenth century was one of slow decline and relatively rapid adjustment. Numbers of farms and farmers in southern New England began to level off and decline after the turn of the century. Farm numbers in northern New England reached their apogee from 1840 to 1880, and farm numbers in the Middle Atlantic states were at their peak during the 1880s (Fitchen, 1981:Chapter 3; Edwards, 1940; Shannon, 1945:Chapter 11). Farm numbers in the region as a whole began a steady decline after 1880 (Tostlebe, 1957:50).

Agricultural decline in the Northeast was caused by several factors. First, and most important, was the deepening of commercial agriculture on an interregional basis, which subjected Northeastern farmers to the competition of their counterparts in Ohio, Indiana, and later, the western prairie states (Edwards, 1940:204-5). At the same time, Northeastern farmers' competitive position was weakened by their general tendency to use primitive technologies—what Edwards (1940:205) referred to as being essentially "medieval" practices—which, in conjunction with land resources that were generally inferior to those of the West, galvanized agricultural decline in the Northeast.

It should be stressed, however, that the agricultural decline of the Northeast was highly uneven and that significant adjustments were made that, by and large, persist up to the present time. As late as 1840, Pennsylvania was America's leading wheat-producing state (Ebling, 1979:78), and Pennsylvania, New York, and New Jersey at that time were the nation's "bread states" (Edwards, 1940:205). There were several other prosperous areas of commercial agriculture in the Northeast at mid century—especially the Connecticut Valley, the Narragansett country of Rhode Island, and the western counties of Massachusetts. But, in general, Northeastern agriculture from 1840 to the turn of the century underwent a progressive decline because of unfavorable agroecological conditions and western competition. By 1850, there were 7,000 miles of railroad in the country, and flour made from Western wheat was generally used by New England residents, even by farmers (Edwards, 1940:207). From 1840 to 1850, sheep raising in Southern New England declined by nearly 50 percent and by an additional 35 percent from 1850 to 1860 (Edwards, 1940:207; see also Gates, 1960:Chapter 19; Shannon, 1945:Chapter 11).

Beginning after 1810, the Northeast region, especially southern New England, began to experience three parallel trends—rapid population growth, urbanization, and industrialization—that would leave a lasting imprint on agriculture and community in the region. From 1810 to 1840, the population of the New England and Middle Atlantic states doubled, with much of this population increase concentrated in urban areas and derived from immigration. "The population of the Eastern States increased from 3,487,000 in [1810] to 6,761,000 in 1840; urban centers of over 8,000 inhabitants increased from 3 in 1790 to 33 in 1840; while in southern New England all but 50 of the 479 townships had at least one manufacturing village clustering around a textile mill, an iron furnace, or some other industry" (Edwards, 1940:206).

These changes in the population morphology of the Northeastern states, in conjunction with western competition, would have three major impacts on agriculture in the region. First, there developed a substantial home market, which deepened the commercialization of Northeastern agriculture. Second, Northeastern agriculture shifted from general farming to commodity specialization; each subregion between 1810 and 1840 came to concentrate on a small number of commodities for which the agroecological conditions were best suited. These commodities, because of their perishability or bulk, tended to escape western competition. Third, commercialization and specialization stimulated technological change such as use of the grain cradle, the steel plow, and horsedrawn machinery (Edwards, 1940; Shannon, 1945:Chapter 11).

The Northeast region thus became progressively more specialized in producing milk, butter, cheese, poultry, vegetables, and fruits for the growing urban markets. Market gardening and dairying developed in the close proximity of major urban areas, particularly in New York, Philadelphia, Boston, Providence, and Newport. Production of fluid milk became more prevalent close to cities, while butter and cheese production increased rapidly in upstate New York, especially after completion of the Erie Canal. Areas more distant from urban centers became specialized in cattle and sheep production while other areas emphasized producing horses or hay for city and town stables.

The restructuring of Northeastern agriculture to the conditions of western competition and creation of an urban home market was, nonetheless, an uneven process. The tendency toward specialization was earliest and strongest close to major urban centers. Credit was typically scarce, and many farmers found it difficult to secure the financing to alter their farm infrastructure in line with the new market imperatives (Gates, 1960: Chapter 19). Also, as Edwards (1940:207) noted, the impulse toward land speculation tended to cause many farmers with sufficient capital to divert this capital into the purchase of more real estate rather than to use it to update their farm enterprises. Nonetheless, there was a steady trend across the region toward specialization of commodity production—a process that was substantially completed by 1850 (Cochrane, 1979:Chapter 4).

Equally significant for Northeastern agriculture and Northeastern society as a whole was the emergent articulation between farm and community structure based on backward and forward linkages between agriculture and industry. Virtually all manufacturing industry in the U.S. at mid century was located in the Northeast. This industry was not, however, concentrated solely in large urban centers. Textile mills, grist mills, and other factories were quite dispersed spatially, as indicated in a previous quote from Edwards (1940). Edwards (1940:207) discussed the relationships between agriculture and community in the Northeast as follows:

> Now that the farmer received a cash income he turned to factories to supply him with the clothes, tools, and furniture he had formerly made for himself. The decline of household industries had as revolutionary an influence on rural life as the growth of industrialization had on the formation of a wage-earning class. As self-sufficient farming waned, long-established habits and traditions in thinking and living were uprooted. The family as an economic unit became less important, with all that implied for rural mores; farmers' sons and daughters began migrating to the mill towns to take up a new way of life. Those who remained behind developed a taste for urban standards of living.

Thus the articulation between agriculture and nonfarm industry, much of it located in relatively rural places, played a major role not only in the restructuring of the Northeastern agriculture, but also in contributing to the industrialization of the region during the nineteenth century (Gates, 1960:Chapter 2).

This articulation between agriculture and industry in the Northeast was, however, on less favorable terms for the former than for the latter. Northeast industry generally prospered during the latter decades of the nineteenth century, while Northeastern agriculture, relative to the other agricultural regions of the U.S., tended to stagnate. The average number of acres per farm in the Northeast region declined from 104 in 1870 to 95 in 1890; it would not be until 1950 that the average number of acres per farm in the Northeast would reach its 1870 level (Tostlebe, 1957:87)! Similarly, the average level of physical farm assets per farm increased by only 7 percent (in constant prices) from 1870 to 1900, in comparison with a 104 percent increase for the U.S. as a whole. The Northeast region was the only U.S. region that exhibited a decline in the value of physical farm assets per farm from 1900 to 1920. For the entirety of the 1870-1920 period, the Northeast exhibited the slowest rate of increase in physical farm assets on the basis of both aggregate and per farm comparisons (Tostlebe,

1957:Chapter 4). Gross farm income in the region increased by only about 30 percent from 1869 to 1899 (in constant prices), while the next most stagnant agricultural region—the Appalachian region—exhibited an increase of more than 100 percent during the same time period (Tostlebe, 1957:215). From 1890 to 1900, the Northeast began to experience an absolute decline in the number of persons engaged in agriculture (Tostlebe, 1957:48), while all other U.S. regions during the decade exhibited increases in the number of persons in agriculture. This decline in the number of persons in agriculture in the Northeast would continue more or less unabated until the 1970s.

Two further aspects of agricultural change in the Northeast should be noted. First, by the end of the nineteenth century virtually all estate type holdings—except for the Wadsworth holdings in Genesee County, New York—had disappeared (Hedrick, 19 33:62-3). By 1880, the Northeast in general and New York in particular had tenancy rates well below the U.S. average (Shannon, 1945:418). Second, beginning in the 1880s there emerged a trend toward the decline of land in farms that, with the except ion of the Depression years, was not stemmed until 1945. From 1880 to 1940, land in Northeastern farms declined from 68 to 47 million acres, and improved land from 46.4 to 26.6 million acres (Tostlebe, 1957:50). The bulk of this land reverted to forests.

Concomitant with the agricultural decline of the Northeast at the end of the nineteenth century were the beginnings of rural community dislocations. For example, Fitchen (1981) in her study of an upstate New York farm community, noted that the period from 1870 to 1920 was one of slow decline of agriculture and of shifts in the relationships between farm families and the trade center/hamlet (see also Smith and Zopf, 1970:Chapter 3). Most farms were small and combined subsistence and commercial farming. There was a steady turnover of the farm population as farmers left agriculture for jobs in towns, farm children left the farm for education or employment, and new farm operators came in to buy up the hill farms when others left. Nevertheless, the farm population slowly but steadily declined, and the most marginal farmland was abandoned for forest. Farming remained the predominant economic base of the community, but this base was unhealthy. Fitchen noted in her historical research that the increased rate of turnover in the ownership and operation of farms tended to reduce the cohesion of the hamlet community, while the dimin-

ishing farm population caused a contraction in the volume and
diversity of retail trade. Further, the region as a whole was
experiencing growth in large villages and cities, and Fitchen
found that farm families and residents of the trade center
community began to turn to larger outlying villages and cities
for more and more of their retail purchases. Fitchen argues,
nonetheless, that the hamlet, though experiencing decline from
1870 to 1920, remained a viable, active community. But this
community ultimately was to experience disintegration in the
period from 1920 to 1950 as the two forces that emerged earlier—agricultural decline and the rising importance of larger
villages and cities—became intensified after World War I. This
trend would become quite widespread in the areas of the Northeast that had low-quality agricultural resources and were a
long distance from major urban centers.

Structural Change in Northeast Agriculture, 1900-1970

The distinctiveness of the Northeast region can be gauged
by the fact that the region's farm population began to decline
significantly after 1900 and, with the exception of the decade
of the Great Depression, declined steadily until 1969. The
Northeast's farm population decreased from 3.36 million in 1900
to 0.74 million in 1969, a 78 percent decline, while the U.S.
farm population declined by about 58 percent during this same
period. Moreover, the U.S. farm population did not begin to
decline appreciably until the early 1940s. The farm population
in the six New England states declined at a more rapid rate
than did that of the three Middle Atlantic states. In 1969,
roughly 81 percent of the Northeast region's farm population
was in the three Middle Atlantic states (U.S. Bureau of the
Census, 1976).

Farm numbers in the region began a long-term pattern of
decline after 1900, interrupted only by World War II. Farm
numbers in the U.S. as a whole did not begin to decline until
after 1920, and the rate of decline was quite slow until the
post-World War II period. Within the Northeast region, the rate
of decrease in farm numbers was consistently more rapid in the
New England states than in the Middle Atlantic states (see
Stanton and Plimpton, 1979). The post-war loss of farms in
both the U.S. and the Northeast was most pronounced among
relatively small farms (Schertz, 1979; Stanton, 1984; Stanton and
Plimpton, 1979).

Total acres of cropland in the Northeast region peaked around 1880 and declined thereafter. After rising again during the Depression and World War II years to a level of 21 million acres in 1944, the region's cropland acres reached a post-World War II low of 12 million acres in 1969. The rate of decline in cropland acres in the Northeast after World War II was far sharper than in the U.S. as a whole. Moreover, while the Northeast followed the general national trend in the 1960s toward increases in cropland acres, the increase in cropland in the Northeast began later—in 1969, as opposed to 1962 for the U.S. as a whole—and was relatively smaller—8 percent in the Northeast compared to 13 percent for the U.S. (Schertz, 1979:259-60).

The Northeast has long had relatively small farm operations by comparison with the U.S. as a whole. Average acreage per farm in the Northeast was virtually constant from the late 1800s to the end of World War II, averaging roughly 100 acres per farm during the 65 years from 1880 to 1945. By comparison, average acreage per farm in the U.S. after 1880 rose steadily, with the exception of a slight decline in average acreage during the first half-decade of the Great Depression. Following the end of World War II, average acreage per farm in the Northeast began to increase, from 98 acres per farm in 1945 to 169 acres in 1969, a 72 percent increase. This rate of increase, however, was smaller than for the U.S. as a whole (from 195 acres per farm in 1945 to 390 acres in 1969, a 100 percent increase). Average acreage in farms in the New England subregion increased more rapidly than in the Middle Atlantic subregion during the post-World War II period. In 1969, New England farms averaged 195 acres, while Middle Atlantic farms averaged 163 acres (U.S. Bureau of the Census, 1976).

The average value of all farm property per farm in the Northeast was substantially above the national average until the turn of the century. After 1900, however, the value of farm property per farm in the Northeast was generally lower than that of the U.S. as whole, with the exception of the Great Depression decade. Moreover, these disparities have generally increased so that, by 1969, Northeast farms averaged $59,426 in farm property while U.S. farms averaged $75,725 (U.S. Bureau of the Census, 1976).

At the onset of the Great Depression, farmers in the nine Northeastern states accounted for roughly 10 percent of the value of total U.S. farm products sold (978 and 9.610 million, respectively). With the exception of the Great Depression decade, the Northeast has experienced a slow decline in its relative share of farm products sold. By 1969, the value of farm products sold by farmers in the Northeast was about $2.8 billion, which represented slightly over 6 percent of the $45.6 billion of farm products sold by U.S. farmers in that year. Within the Northeast region, the Middle Atlantic states, especially New York and Pennsylvania, have been far more dynamic in terms of aggregate gross farm sales than have the New England states. The Middle Atlantic states accounted for 76 percent of the region's sales of farm products in 1969 and exhibited a 100.1 percent increase in farm products sold from 1945 to 1969 compared with the 89.3 percent increase for the New England subregion. In addition, the total value of farm products sold in New England declined from 1964 to 1969, making New England the only one of the nine U.S. Census of Agriculture subregions to exhibit a decrease in farm product sales during this period (U.S. Bureau of the Census, 1976).

Rural Communities And The Rural Population
In The Northeast, 1900-1970

The character of our current knowledge on rural communities has changed dramatically since the period from the 1920s to the 1950s when detailed community case studies—many of them done on a national basis—were quite common. As Larson (1981:147) has noted, "Comprehensive information about rural communities and recent social change in American rural society does not equal that available in the 1920s, 1930s, and 1940s, aside from demographic and similar census-type data, [since] systematic nationwide studies that would provide this information have been discontinued." While the data on rural communities over the past two decades have been derived largely from census statistics, the data that are the basis of this section of the paper were largely generated from "social surveys" of communities. The advantages of census-type data are their regular availability and suitability for statistical analyses using areal units (e.g., counties) as the units of analysis. The key advantage of the older method of community analysis was its richness of detail about the nature of social relationships and subcommunity processes. The very richness of these data, however, does not lend them to a brief summary for purposes such as those of this paper. Fortunately, however, we will be able to make use of several useful summaries by Taylor et al. (1949), Kolb and Brunner (1952), Brunner and Kolb (1933), Richardson and Larson (1976), and others.

From the outset of the twentieth century, the Northeast has been the most highly urbanized region in the nation. As early as 1920, the Northeast region's population was in excess of 75 percent urban, while the U.S. population as a whole was only 51.4 percent urban (Brunner and Kolb, 1933:16). In that year about two-thirds of the Northeast's rural population was nonfarm, while for the U.S. as a whole fewer than four out of ten rural residents were nonfarm (Brunner and Kolb, 1933:17).

The most comprehensive data on rural communities in the Northeast during the early twentieth century can be found in Brunner and Kolb's (1933) compilation of impressively detailed information on 140 rural villages across the U.S. for 1920 and 1930. Brunner and Kolb's comparative regional analyses of rural social trends generally underscored the influences of urbanization and industrialization on one hand, and agricultural stagnation on the other, in shaping the character of rural communities in the Northeast. They (1933:88) noted, for example, the fact that in the Northeast a large proportion of rural village and open country residents was employed in nonagricultural pursuits and that "[in] some of the New England states, supplementary work has grown to such an extent that it has become the more important source of income for many farmers who might be better characterized as part-time farmers than as farmers doing part-time work" (Brunner and Kolb, 1933:50).

The data reported by Brunner and Kolb for villages in the Middle Atlantic states (the authors generally did not report data for the New England states) have a dual character. On one hand, incorporated—in general, relatively large—places in the Middle Atlantic region tended to show rates of population growth well in excess of the national average from 1910 to 1930. The trend toward vibrant growth was particularly the case for relatively large Middle Atlantic incorporated places. Of the villages in the Northeast with 1,750 or more residents in 1910, 53.3 percent exhibited population growth in excess of 20 percent from 1910 to 1930, while 42.1 percent did so in the U.S. as a whole (Brunner and Kolb, 1933:75). However, Brunner and Kolb (1933:69) also reported data showing that agricultural neighborhoods in the Middle Atlantic region were disintegrating at a more rapid pace than in the entire U.S., and much of their data on the socioeconomic conditions of agricultural hamlets and small villages in the various regions of the U.S. suggested a pattern of agricultural community decline in the Northeast. Overall, the data indicated that the growing industrialization and spread of urban influence in the Northeast were tending to benefit relatively large, incorporated villages in urban areas of the region, while smaller hamlets and villages in peripheral areas of the region were tending to experience declines related to the lack of dynamism in the agricultural sector (see MacLeisch and Young, 1942, for a corroborating case study of a community in New Hampshire).

The Brunner and Kolb (1933) data generally showed that rural villages in the Middle Atlantic region had less advantageous socioeconomic conditions than villages in the Midwest and Far West, with only the Southern region having poorer socioeconomic conditions than the Middle Atlantic area. This observation was the case for per capita retail sales (p. 163), retail stores per village (p. 146), average expenditures for village schools (p. 178), tax revenues per capita (p. 294), and other village characteristics.

Brunner and Kolb's observations about the socioeconomic conditions of rural communities in the Middle Atlantic area were repeated two decades later by Kolb and Brunner (1952). Kolb and Brunner (1952:190-1) reported that from 1940 to 1950, nonsuburban villages (with populations of 1,000-2,500) in the Middle Atlantic area had, along with the West North Central region, the slowest rate of population growth in the U.S.

The foregoing observations about rural communities in the Northeast before mid century can be supplemented by the data collected by Carl C. Taylor and his associates (1949) in the Division of Farm Population and Rural Life of USDA's Bureau of Agricultural Economics. Taylor et al. identified seven major farming area types in the U.S. (the Cotton Belt, the Corn Belt, the wheat areas, the range-livestock areas, dairy areas, Western specialty-crop areas, and the general and self-sufficing areas) and argued that the commodity in which an area specialized would shape the character of local community life and of town-country relationships. In terms of the seven farming region types identified by Taylor et al., their observations on the dairy and the general and self-sufficing areas are most germane for our purposes.

The dairy area identified by Taylor et al. (1949) encompassed the bulk of the counties in upstate New York; most of

Vermont; portions of southern New Hampshire, Massachusetts, Connecticut, and New Jersey; and several counties in the eastern, western, and southeastern fringes of Pennsylvania. Raper (1949a) argue that the nature of dairying—the types of inputs purchased and the need to market milk to a local creamery, cheese factory, or other processing plant—tended to result in a close relationship between farm families and their local hamlet or village trade center. Raper noted, however, that there was a different configuration of farm-trade center relations in New England than in the rest of the dairy areas. In New England, social and political activity has long tended to revolve around the town, rather than the county, and accordingly New England dairy farmers were more likely to identify with and trade within small town centers than were non-New England dairy farmers; village trade centers located west of New England, where counties were more important than townships, tended to be larger than those in New England and tended to offer a more complete range of commercial services. Raper emphasized as well the fact that the nature of dairying—especially its year-around character and location in agroecological areas unsuited for large-scale grain or livestock farming—tended to lead to relatively small farm operations with little hired labor. Further, because dairy areas tended to have a high level of urbanization and industrialization, these areas had a relatively high prevalence of part-time farming. Raper also detected a trend toward recreational development in dairy areas, especially those in the Northeast. He noted (1949a:432) that recreational development was leading to an "influx of urban people, many of whom are wealthier and better educated than the resident farm families" and that this influx was "affecting local leadership, local organizations and institutions, market outlets for dairy and other farm products, and other aspects of farm and community life."

At the time that Raper wrote about rural communities in the dairy areas, the presence of a creamery or cheese factory in a local village was nearly universal, and he placed great stress on the marketing nexus in the cohesion of dairy communities. Since that time, of course, one of the major trends in the U.S. dairy industry as a whole has been the shift to Grade A fluid milk production, with most milk sold to large plants in large villages and cities (Jacobson, 1980). Accordingly, in a more recent period, Richardson and Larson (1976) observed a strong trend among New York farming villages of a decline in agriculturally-related industries and a concomitant rise in nonagricultural industries. Thus, the character of dairy-based farm communities in the Northeast has changed substantially since Raper's (1949a) study—with the decline of the village creamery and cheese factory spearheading the increased orientation of farm families' input and retail purchases and marketing decisions away from smaller villages.

The "general and self-sufficing areas" in the Northeast region, as defined by Raper (1949b), were primarily located in New York's southern tier; in southern Maine and New Hampshire; in parts of Massachusetts, Connecticut, Rhode Island, and New Jersey; and in the central three-quarters of Pennsylvania. The principal defining characteristics of these areas were their low-quality agricultural lands, small farm operations, lack of commodity specialization, low farm incomes, tendency toward part-time farming, and, in some areas, the persistence of small-scale self-sufficient farming. Raper emphasized that the general and self-sufficing areas had an extraordinarily high degree of interaction between farm households and villages. Given the lack of commodity specialization, many farm products were marketed directly to residents of the village. Also, given the typical rough terrain, social interaction and retail purchases tended to be sharply delineated by village. The life of the village was typically organized around the school and the church. Raper (1949b) noted that, similar to the dairy areas, farm-village relationships tended to vary between New England and the remainder of the general/self-sufficing areas; in New England, retail purchases and social interactions tended to be focused around the center of town (township) government, while larger county-seat villages and cities tended to be more important outside of New England.

The only significant quantitative empirical study of the relationships between farm and rural community structure during the pre-1970 period in the Northeast has been that of Swanson (1982). Swanson's study was oriented toward investigating the "Goldschmidt thesis" (see Goldschmidt, 1978; Buttel, 1982a, 1983a) in Pennsylvania. More specifically, Swanson's concern was with whether rates of decline in farming numbers and of the increase in average farm size were associated with declines in farm trade center populations during the 1930-1960 period, which represented hypotheses consistent with the Goldschmidt thesis. Swanson examined 520 agricultural trade centers in 30 Pennsylvania counties over the 30-year period, and his results were generally inconsistent with Goldschmidt. In particular, there was no association between declining farm numbers and changes in the population of Pennsylvania agricultural trade centers, and there was a positive association between average farm size (measured as total acres harvested per farm) and trade center population over the 30-year period. It should be noted, however, as Swanson did, that average farm size in the 30 Pennsylvania counties increased very little (an average of 16 acres) over the period, implying that there was little dramatic farm structural change of the sort that Goldschmidt (1978) referred to in his study. The small increases in average farm size in Swanson's Pennsylvania study area, moreover, were from a relatively small base in 1930 (an average of 40.5 harvested acres per farm), and family farmers were quite readily able to absorb increased harvested acreages into their farms with modest use of mechanization and with little or no hired labor. Overall, total harvested acres per rural community declined by 21 percent from 1930 to 1960, consistent with the pattern noted above for the Northeast region as a whole.

Swanson's study suggests two other findings of importance to the relationships between agriculture and community in the Northeast. First, Swanson found that the principal predictor of population change in Pennsylvania agricultural trade centers was change in the proportion of the population employed in manufacturing and tertiary industries, with increases in the former associated with increases in the latter. Average distance to the nearest urban place and to the nearest metropolitan center were generally not associated with population change in farm trade centers, except for a negative relationship between distance to the nearest metropolitan center and trade center population change in the agriculturally-rich, highly urbanized southeastern region of Pennsylvania. Second, there was evidence that regional economic changes had affected not only trade center population change, but also farm structure. Swanson argued that expansion of trade center populations tended to encroach upon villages' farm land bases, accelerating the rate of loss in land in farms. He also suggested that regional economic change in the form of expanded employment opportunities in manufacturing and services tended to stabilize farm numbers through the availability of the part-time farming option.

More recently, Ali (1973) studied the 13 villages in New York State which were among the 140 villages studied by Brunner and his colleagues (1927, 1933, 1937) in the 1920s and

1930s. Ali focused on changes over the 1920-1970 period, particularly with regard to village population growth. He found that the five villages with high rates of growth were all located within or adjacent to (1970) SMSA counties, while both declining communities were distant from SMSAs. Ali (1973) also examined trends in the number of business services in the 13 communities. He found that there were very high correlations between population size and the number of business services (r = .70 or larger in 1924, 1930, and 1936, and .91 in 1970). In addition, the number of business services was closely associated with proximity to an SMSA county; of the eight communities in or adjacent to an SMSA, seven exhibited increases in the number of business services and one stayed the same over the 50-year period. However, for five villages distant from an SMSA, four experienced declines in the number of business services and one stayed the same.

In the early 1970s, Richardson and Larson (1976) restudied the same villages examined by Ali and by Brunner and associates in the 1920s and 1930s. Richardson and Larson noted that while most of the 13 New York villages had been relatively stable over time, there was strong evidence of increased socioeconomic differentiation among these villages. Moreover, their stability was stronger in noneconomic terms—for example, in the persistence of neighborhood and social functions—than in the economic sphere. Overall, Richardson and Larson (1976:57) detected a pattern of differentiation among the 13 communities based on the ability "to compensate for the major adjustments in the farming part of their communities." The communities that were able to compensate were those located in or proximate to SMSAs in which "vanishing farmers are being replaced, or more than replaced, by nonfarmers" (p. 57). Villages located far from SMSAs had been generally unable to compensate for the decline in farm operators and the farm population. This latter pattern is consistent with Fitchen's (1981) analysis of a declining rural hamlet in a nonmetropolitan region of New York. Finally, Richardson and Larson (1976:57), relying on the data collected by Ali (1973), noted that "increasingly, town (township) rate of population growth has been outstripping that of the population center."

Richardson and Larson's observation about the relatively vibrant growth of the hinterlands of the 13 New York agricultural villages parallels the findings of Brown and Beale (1981:29-31) about regional patterns of population growth and decline of nonmetro counties in the 1960s and 1970s. Brown and Beale's data show that the nonmetro population "turnaround," which began in the U.S. in the beginning of the 1970s, began far earlier in the Northeast-Great Lakes region. Over 75 percent of nonmetro counties in the Northeast-Great Lakes area exhibited population growth during the 1960s, compared to 47.5 percent of nonmetro counties in the U.S. Nearly 71 percent of Northeast-Great Lakes nonmetro counties grew in population during both the 1 960s and 1970s. In contrast, only 44.3 percent of U.S. nonmetro counties experienced population growth during both decades. Further, 18 percent of U.S. nonmetro counties exhibited population declines in both decades, compared to only 3.5 percent of Northeast-Great Lakes nonmetro counties.

The data reported by Brown and Beale underscore the high degree of influence of the urban-industrial economy in the Northeast, similar to the configuration revealed by Swanson (1982). Thus, the Northeast, which experienced disproportionately rapid declines in the farm population and in the number of farm operators during the post-War period up to 1970, was the region of the country with the most favorable pattern of nonmetro population growth during the 1960s and 1970s. Clearly, the rapid decline in farm numbers in the Northeast in the 1960s did not, in the main, lead to deterioration of the nonmetro social fabric in the region because of its strongly urban-industrial character. It should be kept in mind, however, that despite the pervasiveness of urban-industrial forces in the Northeast region, there remain a significant number of nonmetro counties that lie outside the orbit of these forces (see Eberts, 1984). The two declining New York village communities studied by Richardson and Larson (1976), the New York hamlet studied by Fitchen (1981), and Shover's (1976) case study of Bedford, Pennsylvania, are examples of this latter pattern.

Further perspective can be gained on the character of the Northeast's nonmetro population at the end of the first seven decades of the twentieth century from the research of Hines et al. (1975). Hines et al. reported data on the socioeconomic characteristics of the population of metro and nonmetro counties for 1970 disaggregated by region. The following are among the observations made by Hines et al. about the characteristics of the Northeast nonmetro population relative to the North Central, South, and West regions.

The Northeast's nonmetro population in 1970 was distinctive in that it had the lowest proportion (5.2 percent) of residents of the four major regions in extractive industries (agriculture, forestry, fisheries, and mining), while the U.S. nonmetro average was 11.1 percent. Likewise, the Northeast nonmetro counties had the highest proportion of employment in manufacturing (29.2 percent) and the second highest proportion in the service industries (28.4 percent), compared to the U.S. averages of 2 4.3 and 27.2 percent, respectively. But while the Northeast nonmetro population had a strongly "urban" labor force profile, Hines et al. (1975:36) reported that the Northeast region as a whole was the only one to have exhibited a decline from 1960 t o 1970 in the number of workers in manufacturing (-6.9 percent), while the nonmetro counties in the Northeast had the second lowest rate of increase (6.2 percent) in the number of manufacturing workers among the four major regions. The nonmetro population of the Northeast, however, showed substantial growth in employment in the service sector (32.8 percent) from 1960 to 1970, which was slightly above the average for the U.S. nonmetro counties as a whole (28.6 percent). Thus, while the Northeast's nonmetro counties did experience the growth in rural industrialization that became prevalent throughout the U.S. in the 1960s and 1970s (Campbell, 1975; Summers et al., 1976), the region's nonmetro counties were already highly industrial in 1960 and exhibited little increase in manufacturing employment during the decade. The Northeast's growing nonmetro population tended more strongly to take service sector jobs from 1960 to 1970.

Data reported by Hines et al. (1975:41) on median 1970 earnings for residents of nonmetropolitan counties showed that the Northeast was well above the U.S. nonmetro average ($6,970 and $6,236 for males, and $3,363 and $3,052 for females, respectively). Earnings of Northeast nonmetro males were the second highest of the four regions, while Northeast nonmetro females' earnings were the highest in the country. These high nonfarm wage rates encouraged farmers in the Northeast to leave agriculture in the post-World War II period (Schertz, 1979:274). But while earnings of Northeast nonmetro residents were above the national average in 1970, the nonmetro Northeast's median family income grew somewhat more slowly (68.3 percent) from 1959 to 196 9 than it did in U.S. nonmetro counties as a whole (69.4 percent; Hines et al., 1975:46).

The pattern that emerged from the Hines et al. data was of a Northeast nonmetro population that was relatively privileged in 1970, but that was tending to decline in its socioeconomic advantages relative to the U.S. nonmetro population as a whole. The relatively slow pace of nonmetro industrial growth in the region, which paralleled the decline of Northeast industry that began in the 1960s (Young, 1984), apparently contributed substantially to this phenomenon. The Northeast nonmetro counties also experienced a decline in employment in the extractive industries (-36 percent) during the 1960-1970 decade that was above the national nonmetro average (-34 percent) (Hines et al., 1975:36). The decline of the Northeast's extractive industries' employment probably contributed to some degree to the worsening of the region's relative socioeconomic status among the nation's nonmetro counties, especially in the region's highly rural areas such as northern New England and the north country of New York State.

**Interrelations Between Farm Structure and
Rural Community Well-Being in the Northeast,
1970 to the Present**

Recent Farm Structure Changes In The Northeast

Virtually all analyses of farm structural change in the Northeast during the first seven decades of the twentieth century have emphasized that declines in farm numbers and in the size of the farm population accelerated after World War II and that these declines were most pronounced among small farm households (see, for example, Schertz, 1979; Stanton and Plimpton, 1979). But it is now widely recognized that there emerged a distinctly new pattern of farm structural change in the Northeast and the U.S. during the 1970s; the trend of farm structural change in the 1970s was toward "dualism," in which there were increases in the relative numbers of both very large and very small farms, along with a "disappearing middle" of medium-sized, full-time family farms (Tweeten and Huffman, 1980; Buttel, 1983b, 1984). Concomitant with the 1970s trend away from rapid loss of smaller farms was the stabilization of farm numbers.

Table 1 reports data on numbers of farms by selected characteristics for the Northeast region and the U.S. for 1974 and 1982. These data show that the Northeast generally followed the larger U.S. trend toward a more dualistic farm structure during this period of time. For both the Northeast and the

TABLE 1. NUMBERS OF FARMS BY SELECTED CHARACTERISTICS 1974 and 1982, AND PERCENT CHANGE, 1974-82, NINE NORTHEASTERN STATES AND U.S.

Farm Structure Characteristics	Northeast Region 1974	Northeast Region 1982	Percent Change, 1974-82	U.S. 1974	U.S. 1982	Percent Change, 1974-82
Number of Farms	127,531	131,991	3.5	2,314,013	2,241,124	-0.3
Land in Farms (acres)	23,359,889	23,061,163	-1.3	1,017,030,357	984,755,115	-0.3
Aver. Size of Farm	183	175	-4.4	440	439	-0.1
Value of Land & Bldgs.						
Aver. per Farm	121,227	214,623	77.0	147,838	347,974	135.2
Aver. per Acre	662	1,236	86.7	336	791	135.4
Farms by Size						
Less than 10 Acres	7,689	10,599	37.8	128,254	187,699	46.3
10-49 Acres	19,416	26,421	36.1	379,543	449,301	18.3
50-179 Acres	54,901	51,866	-5.5	827,884	711,701	-14.0
180-499 Acres	37,864	34,533	-8.8	616,098	526,566	-14.5
500-999 Acres	6,421	7,070	10.1	207,297	203,936	-1.6
1,000-1,999	1,046	1,282	22.5	92,712	97,396	5.1
≥2,000 Acres	194	220	13.4	62,225	64,525	3.7
Land Use						
Total Cropland	13,851,473	13,972,802	0.8	440,039,087	445,527,557	1.2
Woodland	5,809,958	5,899,750	1.5	92,527,627	87,133,026	-5.8
Agricultural Products Sold						
Market Value ($1,000)	4,291,380	7,179,543	67.3	81,526,124	131,810,903	61.6
Aver. per Farm	33,650	54,394	61.6	35,231	58,815	66.9
Crops	1,440,397	2,181,303	51.4	41,790,360	62,274,394	49.0
Livestock	2,216,436	4,998,240	125.5	33,301,560	69,536,509	108.8
Poultry	616,094	844,395	37.1	6,202,291	9,732,222	56.9
Farms by Type of Organization						
Individual or Family	82,142**	115,713	40.9	1,517,573**	1,945,724	28.2
Corporation	2,615**	4,098	56.7	28,656**	59,788	108.6
Tenure of Operator						
Full Owner	83,389	82,043	-1.6	1,423,953	1,325,931	-6.9
Part Owner	36,112	40,005	10.8	628,224	656,219	4.5
Tenant	8,030	9,943	23.8	261,836	258,974	-1.1
Principal Occupation						
Farming	78,144	75,111	-3.8	1,427,368	1,234,858	-13.4
Nonfarming	46,390	56,442	21.5	851,902	1,006,266	18.1
Operators Reporting Any Days of Work Off Farm						
Any	56,670	67,751	19.6	1,011,476	1,187,490	17.4
≥100 Days	46,691	56,048	20.0	814,555	963,728	18.3
Selected Production Expenses ($1,000)						
Commercial Fertilizer	207,433	309,769	49.3	5,137,361	7,689,577	49.7
Other Agric. Chemicals	74,225	140,301	89.0	1,757,776	4,282,795	143.6
Hired Labor	401,846	712,383	77.3	4,652,074	8,434,399	81.3
Workers Working						
≥150 Days: Farms	21,775**	29,242	34.3	223,093**	312,621	40.1
Numbers of Workers*	66,149	88,547	33.9	712,715**	950,112	33.3
Machinery and Equipment						
Estimated Value ($1,000)	2,879,414	5,337,081	85.4	48,402,626	93,686,308	93.6
Average per Farm	23,470	40,435	72.3	22,303	41,930	88.0

*Computed from the preliminary reports for the nine Northeast states.
**Among farms with sales ≥$2,500.

Sources: 1974 data: 1978 Census of Agriculture Preliminary Report (Northeast Region and United States) (Washington, D.C.: Bureau of the Census, U.S. Department of Commerce, 1980); 1982 data: 1982 Census of Agriculture: Preliminary Report (nine Northeastern states and United States) (Washington, D.C.: Bureau of th Census, U.S. Department of Commerce, 1983).

U.S., farm numbers and the average size of farms in acres were relatively unchanged over the eight-year period. The Northeast exhibited a 3.5 percent increase in the number of farms from 1974 to 1982 along with a 4.4 percent decrease in the average size of farm, indicating that the bulk of the gain in farms was concentrated among the smallest farm sizes. U.S. farms decreased in number by 0.3 percent during the period.

The data in Table 1 on farm numbers by size of farms in acres underscore the dualistic trajectory of structural change in both the Northeast and U.S.; farms with less than 50 acres exhibited significant increases, farms from 50 to 499 acres declined, and farms with 1,000 or more acres increased in numbers. The Northeast region differed from national trends only in its substantial growth in farms with 500 to 999 acres, a 10.1 percent increase, compared to a 1.6 percent decrease for the U.S., and in its more rapid increases in the numbers of farms with 1,000 or more acres than was the case for the U.S. as a whole.

The data in Table 1 suggest that there has been a stabilization of the position of Northeast agriculture in the U.S. agricultural structure during the 1970s and early 1980s. The value of agricultural products sold in the Northeast increased more rapidly from 1974 to 1982 (67.3 percent) than was the case in the U.S. (61.6 percent), although average sales per farm grew somewhat more slowly in the Northeast than in the U.S. (61.6 and 66.9 percent, respectively). The value of land and buildings, measured either on a per farm or per acre basis, increased somewhat more slowly in the Northeast than in the U.S. The average value of land and buildings per acre in the Northeast, however, remained substantially above the U.S. average in 1982 ($1,236 and $791, respectively). Increases in the overall inventory of machinery and equipment and in the value of machinery and equipment per farm in the Northeast lagged slightly behind the U.S. averages. Finally, the Northeast continued its long trend toward decline in land in farms (a 1.3 percent decrease from 1974 to 1982, compared to the U.S. figure of -0.3 percent) and exhibited a slower rate of increase in total cropland during the 1974 to 1982 period than did the U.S. (0.8 and 1.2 percent, respectively).

The farm structure of the Northeast during the 1970s and early 1980s showed increased strength in its small-farm, part-time farming component. The number of farm operators whose principal occupation was nonfarming, who worked any days off the farm, and who worked 100 or more days off the farm increased more rapidly in the Northeast than in the U.S. The Northeast also exhibited a larger increase in the number of individual or family farms than did the U.S., which, given the fact that small, part-time farms tend to be family- or individual-type farms (Buttel, 1982b; Buttel and Gertler, 1982), underscores the growing importance of the small-scale, part-time farming sector in Northeast agriculture.

It was noted earlier that the Northeast registered greater increases in the number of farms with 1,000 or more acres than did the U.S. as a whole. This relatively rapid growth of farms with large acreages apparently did not, however, tend to take the form of industrial-type, capital-intensive farming. The dollar value of hired labor increased less rapidly in the Northeast than it did for the U.S. as a whole (77.3 and 81.3 percent, respectively), as was the case for the number of farms with hired workers working 150 or more days per year (see Table 1). The rate of increase in the use of chemical fertilizers and other agricultural chemicals in the Northeast was also lower than for the U.S. Also, as noted earlier, the value of the Northeast's machinery and equipment inventory increased less rapidly than did that of the U.S. Finally, while the Northeast exhibited a 56.7 percent increase in the number of corporation farms, this increase was substantially lower than the 108.6 percent increase for the U.S.

As noted earlier, the Northeast has long had a low rate of tenancy. During the 1974 to 1982 period, however, the number of tenant farms in the Northeast increased considerably (23.8 percent, versus the U.S. average of -1.1 percent). This may be the case because many of the persons entering agriculture in the Northeast as small farm operators did so on rented land. Nevertheless, the proportion of tenants in Northeast agriculture remains substantially lower than the U.S. average (7.5 and 11.6 percent, respectively; see Table 2).

Table 2 reports comparable farm structure data for the Northeast and the U.S. for 1982; however, instead of reporting the numbers of farms and percent changes by selected characteristics for 1974 and 1982, Table 2 shows percent distributions and other standardized measures of farm structure for the Northeast and U.S. for the most recent (1982) Census of Agriculture. The dominant feature of Table 2 is the similarity between the farm structure of the Northeast and that of the U.S. Although North east farms tend to be considerably smaller than U.S. farms in average acreage and average value of land and buildings, average gross sales per farm in the Northeast and the U.S. and distributions of farms by value of gross sales are quite similar. Likewise there is considerable similarity in the distributions of farms by type of organization, tenure of operator, principal occupation of the farm operator, and prevalence of off-farm employment. It should be noted, however, that these gross indicators of farm structure may conceal important differences; for example, legally incorporated farms in the Northeast average only about 400 acres per farm, whereas legally incorporated farms in the U.S. (both family and nonfamily) average approximately 2,000 acres each. Thus, legal incorporation of farms has a substantially different character in the Northeast than in much of the rest of the U.S., where many corporation farms are industrial-type farms that are characterized by absentee ownership, hired management, and hired labor (Rodefeld, 1980).

Table 2 indicates that farms in the Northeast, while typically small in acreage relative to national standards, tend to be farmed relatively intensively. Northeast farmers tend to use higher levels of commercial fertilizers and other agricultural chemicals per acre than do U.S. farmers. Northeast farmers in 1982 derived 44.0 percent of their gross farm sales from sales of dairy products, a relatively labor- and capital-intensive commodity (Forste and Frick, 1979), compared to 12.4 percent for U.S. farmers as a whole. While U.S. farmers derived a larger proportion of their gross sales from crops than did those in the Northeast in 1982, Northeast farmers tended to devote a high proportion of their cropland to labor- and capital-intensive fruit and vegetable commodities (Schertz, 1979). Finally, despite the relatively low prevalence of industrial-type farming in the Northeast (as gauged by low proportions of corporation farms and of farms with high levels of gross sales and large acreages), the Northeast region is characterized by a high level of use of hired labor. Table 2 shows that in 1982, hired labor expenses as a percent of agricultural products sold were higher in the Northeast than in the U.S., and a substantially larger proportion of Northeast farmers hired full-time agricultural laborers (150 or more days of work) than did U.S. farmers (22.2 and 13.9 percent, respectively).

The pattern that emerges from these data on farm structure in the Northeast and the U.S. is that the Northeast region has achieved parity with the rest of U.S. agriculture—and accord-

Table 2. Farm Structure Indicators: Northeast Region and United States, 1982

Farm Structure Indicators	Northeast	U.S.
Average Size of Farm (Acres)	175	439
Average Value of Land and Buildings per Farm	$214,623	$347,974
Average Value of Land and Buildings per Acre	1,236	791
Percent Distribution of Farms by Acreage		
<10	8.0%	8.4%
10-49	20.0	20.0
50-179	39.3	31.8
180-499	26.2	23.5
500-999	5.4	9.1
1,000-1,999	1.0	4.3
≥2,000	0.2	2.9
Percent Distribution of Farm by Type of Organization		
Individual or Family	87.7%	86.8%
Corporation		
Family-held	2.7	2.3
Other Than Family Held	0.4	0.3
Percent Distribution of Farms by Tenure of Operator		
Full Owner	62.2%	59.2%
Part Owner	30.3	29.3
Tenant	7.5	11.6
Percent Distribution of Farms by Principal Occupation of Operator		
Farming	56.9%	55.1%
Nonfarming	42.8	44.9
Percent of Farm Operators Reporting Any Days of Work Off Farm	51.3%	53.0%
Percent of Farm Operators Reporting ≥10 Days of Work Off Farm	42.5%	43.0%
Average Market Value of Agricultural Products Sold per Farm ($)	$54,394	$58,815
Percent Distribution of Farms by Value of Sales		
>$250,000	3.6%	3.9%
$100,000-249,999	11.2	9.6
$40,000-99,999	16.9	14.9
$20,000-39,999	8.9	11.1
$10,000-19,999	9.1	11.6
5,000-9,999	1.2	12.6
<$5,000	39.1	36.4
$ Commercial Fertilizer/Acre of Cropland	$22.2	$17.25
$ Other Agricultural Chemicals/Acre of Cropland	$10.0	$9.6
$ Hired Labor as Percent of Cultural Products Sold	9.9%	6.4%
Percent of Farms With Workers Working ≥150 Days	22.2	13.9
Workers/Farm	3.03	3.04
Estimated Value of Machinery and Equipment/Farm	$40,435	$41,930
Sales of Crops as Percent of Market Value of Agricultural Products Sold	30.4%	47.2%
Sales of Livestock as Percent of Market Value of Agricultural Products Sold	69.6	52.8
Sales of Dairy Products as Percent of Market Value of Agricultural Products Sold	44.0	12.4
Sales of Poultry as Percent of Market Value of Agricultural Products Sold	11.8	7.4

ingly, a comparable pattern of farm structure—and has done so by continuing and deepening its longstanding pattern of special-ization in dairy products, poultry, and fruits and vegetables. The position of Northeast agriculture in the U.S. agricultural structure has become stabilized now that thousands of marginal acres have been shifted out of agricultural production. This is not to say that the farm structures in the Northeast and the U.S. are identical; the Northeast has somewhat larger proportions of very small, "subfamily" farms, lower levels of large-scale industrial farming, and a greater prevalence of medium-sized farms (i.e., with sales of $40,000-99,999) than does the U.S. Nevertheless, farm structure in the Northeast appears to have converged with that of the nation over the past several decades. Moreover, the Northeast and the rest of the U.S. exhibited comparable trends in the 1970s and early 1980s toward a more dualistic pattern of farm structure.

Social Forces Affecting Rural Communities
In The Northeast: The Case Of New York State

To our knowledge there have been no quantitative empirical studies, such as that of Swanson (1982) for Pennsylvania counties from 1930 to 1960, of the relationships between farm structure and rural community characteristics in the Northeast pertaining to the post-1970 period. Neither has there been a continuation of the rural community studies of the sort done by Brunner and associates (1927, 1933, 1937) into the 1970s and 1980s. There is a certain irony in the fact that as our ability to generate and analyze social data has grown, we now know less about the relationships between farm and community structures than we did 50 years ago (Larson, 1981). Lacking current information in this area, we will proceed in two ways. First, we will review some available data on trends in the changing characteristics of the nonmetropolitan population in one Northeast state, New York State. The present section is devoted to this task. Second, in the succeeding section of the paper we will present selected data from an empirical study of nonmetro-politan counties in the Northeast conducted by the authors.

The major source of data on recent trends in Northeast rural communities is a study by Eberts (1984) on **Socioeconomic Trends in Rural New York State** prepared for the New York State Legislative Commission on Rural Resources. Eberts' study reports data for New York counties grouped into six categories—two categories of metro counties and four categories of nonmetro counties. The two metro categories consist of "downstate" (New York City area) and "upstate" metropolitan counties. The four nonmetro categories consist of those with extensive, considerable, moderate, and limited urban influence.

Eberts' New York State data suggest several tentative observations relevant to the contemporary relationships between farm structural and technological change and the socioeconomic condition of rural communities in the Northeast region. First, his data demonstrate that agriculture in New York State is by no means confined to highly rural counties (see Schertz, 1979, for a similar observation with respect to the Northeast region as a whole). Moreover, in terms of the value of agricultural products sold, the most dynamic agricultural counties in New York State have tended to be rural counties with extensive urban influence; this county type was the only one to have exhibited an increase in the value of agricultural products sold from 1970 to 1980 (in constant 1980 dollars). Rural counties with limited urban influence exhibited a significant decline in the value of agricultural products sold from 1970 to 1980. Thus, to the degree that the more rural and agricultural regions of New York are experiencing major changes in their farm sectors, these changes appear to be related more to the overall decline of the farm sector due to low-quality agricultural resources than to the dynamism of technological change, concentration of agricultural assets, and the replacement of family-type farms by larger than-family or industrial-type farms.

Second, the nonmetropolitan population in New York State and in the Northeast in general (Schertz, 1979; Hines et al., 1975) has for several decades had a relatively "urban" economic and labor force structure. For example, in 1970, U.S. nonmetropolitan counties had 24.3 and 27.2 percent of their labor forces in manufacturing and service employment, respectively (Hines et al., 1975:35). In 1970 all rural county types in New York State had in excess of 63 percent of their labor forces in the service sector, while all rural county types except the rural counties with limited urban influence had proportions of the labor force in manufacturing above the U.S. nonmetro county average. The combined services and manufacturing shares of the New York State rural county labor force in 1970 were all in excess of 90 percent, compared to 51.5 percent for U.S. nonmetro counties as a whole. Put somewhat differently, the data reviewed above demonstrate that rural counties in New York State (and the

Northeast) have a significantly lower share of their labor forces in agricultural and other extractive industries than do the other major regions (especially the North Central and West regions; Hines et al., 1975:35). The major implication of these data is that New York State (and presumably the Northeast) counties have, by national standards, a relatively low dependence on agriculture, and, given their already highly "urban" economic bases and labor force profiles, there are likely to be relatively few counties in the Northeast that will be highly affected by technological and structural changes in the farm sector.

Third, the data reviewed above do not suggest the existence of any striking patterns of socioeconomic decline among the nonmetro population that might be attributable to adverse impacts of farm structural change on rural communities. There remain relatively modest metropolitan-nonmetropolitan disparities in median family income as well as modest income disparities among the four rural county types in New York State. Poverty rates among the rural county types remained virtually unchanged from 1970 to 1980. The only indicator of deterioration of the socioeconomic condition of the New York State nonmetro population was the sharp rise in nonmetro/rural unemployment rates from 1970 to 1980. These increases in unemployment rates, of course, paralleled national trends during the 1970s. There was, however, some evidence of a widening of metro-nonmetro disparities in unemployment rates in New York State during the 1970s; moreover, the highest unemployment rates in New York State were observed among the rural counties with limited urban influence. Nevertheless, the overall character of the data on the nonmetropolitan population in New York does not indicate that there has occurred any dramatic relative or absolute deterioration of the socioeconomic well-being of the rural population that might be attributable to adverse impacts of farm structural change on rural communities.

Toward a Model of Technological, Farm Structural, and Rural Community Change in The Northeast

Preliminary Considerations

There has emerged over the past 10 years a significant empirical literature on the impacts of farm structural changes on rural communities in the U.S. (see, for example, the reviews and summaries in Harris and Gilbert, 1982; Heffernan, 1982; Buttel, 1983a). This literature, most of which has been inspired by the "rediscovery" and reissue of Goldschmidt's (1978) **As You Sow**, has generally confirmed the fact that a cluster of changes that have occurred in the U.S. farm sector during the post-World War II period—technological change, the trend toward fewer and larger farms, the disproportionate decline of "family farms," the rise of industrial-type farming, decline of the farm population, and so forth—have tended to have adverse impacts on rural communities. It has been argued, however, that the "Goldschmidt thesis" probably does not hold uniformly across the farming regions of the U.S. and that this approach has significant theoretical and methodological limitations (see, for example, Buttel, 1982a; Hayes and Olmstead, 1984). Indeed, the bulk of the empirical research that has provided support for the Goldschmidt thesis has been conducted in states and regions in which there is a high dependence on agriculture (e.g., Flora and Conboy, 1977) and/or in areas in which highly concentrated, industrial-type farming is much more prevalent than in the nation as a whole (e.g., MacCannell and White, 1984). Most importantly for our purposes, there has been only one such study in the Northeast region which has been conducted in the general methodological tradition of the "Goldschmidt-thesis" literature—that of Swanson (1982), reviewed at some length above—and this study was concerned with farm structural and rural community changes (in Pennsylvania) for the 1930-1960 period. Thus, our intention in this section of the paper will be to develop an empirical model that estimates the applicability of "Goldschmidt-type" hypotheses to the experience of the Northeast's nonmetropolitan counties during the past decade.[2]

Development of the Model:
Theoretical and Methodological Considerations

The model of farm structural and rural community change that will be estimated below can be said to be largely in the Goldschmidt tradition, at least insofar as research stimulated by Goldschmidt's **As You Sow** has primarily tended to emphasize areal ("ecological") data based on indicators derived from the Censuses of Population and Agriculture. Moreover, there is a relatively close correspondence of the model that will be examined below and the implicit model structure developed in **As You Sow** and in subsequent literature (bearing in mind that

Goldschmidt's [1978] study had only two cases and was largely qualitative in nature).

The adoption of the major elements of the Goldschmidt-type model is not to ignore some of its major theoretical and methodological limitations. For instance, this model (and our elaboration of the model) ignores the reciprocal impacts between farm structure and rural communities—for example, how community territorial expansion, property taxation, and provision of services affect its farming hinterland. Aside from some danger of misspecification of the model, we do not, however, feel that this limitation of the model is a major problem for our purposes, especially because our major interest is in the impacts of farm sector changes on rural communities (and not vice versa). There are, moreover, certain limitations of the original and many subsequent applications of the Goldschmidt model that can be rectified within the context of the approach taken here. For example, unlike Goldschmidt's original formulation, we will be able to: (1) include measures of two dimensions of technological change (mechanization and use of biochemical inputs), (2) utilize measures of farm structure that reflect recent trends toward dualism, and (3) consider dependence on agriculture and influence of urban-industrial context as contextual and control variables, respectively (see Swanson, 1982).

The model we outline below has three principal theoretical methodological assumptions. First, we assume that the properties that we will measure—ranging from indicators of technological and farm structural change to change in the size of the farm and rural populations and in the socioeconomic characteristics of rural areal aggregates—are, indeed, variable properties. That this is the case is implicitly supported by the fact that previous studies have been successful in identifying and explaining such variations and is supported more explicitly by the data reviewed above and by other studies (Gregor, 1982; Dorner, 1983).

A second, and more problematic, assumption is that these variables can be usefully measured at the county level. There is, of course, an obvious disparity between the conceptual language that we have employed—rural communities or places and their farming hinterlands—and that which is implicated in the use of county-level data; counties contain a large number of communities that typically exhibit a high degree of variation in the population sizes, economic bases, and other characteristics. There are also certain within-county variations in agricultural structure, although given the general tendency in U.S. agriculture for regions or subregions to have a fairly high degree of homogeneity in farm structure (Cochrane, 1979; Gregor, 1982) this should not be a major problem. Nevertheless, the heterogeneity of community conditions within any particular county is a significant issue and a potential limitation of the present study. We would argue that this limitation can be approached in two ways. One is to urge caution that these results should not be used to infer directly how farm structure affects rural communities in the Northeast; if such impacts are detected in the model, it would be prudent to assume that the strengths of relationships are likely to be substantially variable across rural communities, depending upon their characteristics. A second approach to the limitation of a high level of ecological aggregation is to note that one of the theoretical premises of the model that is developed below—that farm structural impacts on rural communities are likely to be confined to communities that are highly dependent on agriculture—will cause us to limit our population to a set of counties that contain relatively little variation in the size of places. We will focus our analysis on a subset of nonmetropolitan counties in the Northeast and, further, will give principal emphasis to nonmetro counties in which 5 percent or more of county income is derived from agriculture. Restricting ourselves to nonmetropolitan counties eliminates counties with places larger than 50,000 inhabitants (and, as well, eliminates counties in which a large number of persons commute to an adjacent metropolitan county for work). Further, eliminating those nonmetro counties with low proportions of income derived from agriculture should, in general, result in a deletion of counties with a high degree of spatial (community-level) and socioeconomic diversity. Thus the theoretical logic of this study serves to reduce the problem of within-county community heterogeneity that would otherwise reduce the generalizability of the results.

The third broad assumption of the study is that recursive equations will be adequate for estimating the relationships among technological, farm structural, and rural community variables. This assumption of recursivity involves the notion that the relationships between variables are not, in the main, of two-way causality or, put somewhat differently, that the effects are largely if not entirely unidirectional. This assumption would appear to be warranted for two reasons. First, the logic of recursive equations has been applied successfully in previous research on this issue. Second, there is no existing research at the county level, to the best of our knowledge, which has demonstrated that the effects of rural community structure on farm structure approach the strengths of relationships found in analyses postulating causality in the opposite direction.

Our model, which is presented in greater detail in Buttel et al. (1986), is intended to set forth the general nature of relationships that would be expected based on existing literature. As emphasized earlier, however, the relationships, especially those involving community socioeconomic conditions, are not expected to be large. The model consists of five clusters of independent variables and one cluster of dependent variables. The dependent variables are measures of change in community socioeconomic conditions. These dependent variables consist of differences (over a 10-year span) in: (1) the proportion of families in poverty, (2) median family income, (3) retail sales per capita, (4) per capita property tax revenues, (5) the unemployment rate, and (6) the percent of housing built before 1940. Measurement details and a complete presentation of the empirical results are given in Buttel et al. (1986).

The majority of the independent variables—the technological change, farm structural change, farm population change, and rural population change clusters—reflect a postulated causal logic, which is discussed below, involving the ways that change in the farm sector affects rural communities. The fifth cluster of independent variables reflects characteristics of the regional socioeconomic context of farm structure and rural communities and consists of measures of the proportion of the labor force in manufacturing and service sector employment, percent of the population living in urban places (i.e., with 2,500 or more inhabitants), and a dichotomous indicator of the proportion of income derived from agriculture (5 percent or more and less than 5 percent).

The logic of farm technological and structural change and its possible impacts on rural community socioeconomic conditions is as follows. Two measures of technological change—change in the value of machinery and equipment per farm and change in the ratio of fertilizers and other agricultural chemicals to gross sales—are included as exogenous variables which reflect major causes of farm structural change through, respectively, labor displacement and increased capital-intensity. Changes in these two aspects of technology are seen, along with the regional socioeconomic context (percent urban, 1970; percent of labor force in manufacturing and services, 1970), to affect change in farm structure. Four dimensions of change in farm structure are included: (1) a measure of the prevalence of family ownership of agricultural resources (change in percent of farms with sales of $2,500 or more for which the operator is the full owner of the land, 1969-1978), (2) a measure of the prevalence of corporate operation of farms (change in percent of legally incorporated farms, 1969-1978), (3) a measure of the prevalence of part-time farming (change in percent of farms for which the operator worked 100 or more days off the farm, 1969-1978), and (4) a measure of change in the composition of the farm labor force (change in number of regularly employed, hired farm workers per farm reporting hired labor expenditures, 1969-1978).

Further, technological change and farm structural change are hypothesized to affect change in the structure of the farm population. Variables reflecting change in the farm population include indicators of: (1) change in the size of the farm population, and (2) change in the number of agricultural laborers employed for 150 or more days. Technological, farm structural, and farm population change are postulated to affect change in the size of the rural population. Finally, the five clusters of independent variables are hypothesized to affect the five indicators of change in community socioeconomic well-being.

Results

The results of the analysis are discussed in the following four subsections. The first discusses the relationships between technological inputs and change in the structure of farming in the Northeast. Second, the impact of change in the farm sector on change in population size and composition is considered. Third, the effects of change in farm sector and population characteristics on changes in indicators of community well-being are discussed. A final subsection offers our summary and conclusions.

There are 217 counties in the Northeast region, of which 107 are nonmetropolitan. The Census of Agriculture did not report figures for two of the nonmetropolitan counties because the number of farms in each was too small to avoid disclosure problems. The remaining 105 counties provide the basis for our analysis. We considered it important to distinguish a subset of counties that were judged to be the most dependent on the agricultural economy. Therefore we selected those counties in which five percent or more of the total income in the county was derived from agriculture. Each phase of the analysis was conducted for both the total number of nonmetropolitan counties and the subset of counties which we have labeled "agricultural." Thirty counties (29 percent of all the nonmetropolitan counties) fall into this latter category.

With four exceptions, the variables used in the following analyses are measured as simple gain scores (the absolute value of change) over a nine to ten-year period of time. The two variables which measure regional socioeconomic context—percentage of the labor force in services and manufacturing and percent urban population—are measures of 1970 characteristics. A third exception is change in gross farm sales, which is measured as a percentage change between 1969 and 1978. The fourth exception applies to time-one measures of the dependent variables in the analytical models. These are included to control the effect that initial size differences on a dependent variable exert on differences in the gain scores associated with that variable.

There are several methods of modeling change analysis in a panel design. The approach employed in the following analyses is one which emphasizes the relationships between contemporaneous changes in the independent and dependent variables, after differences in the initial sizes of dependent variables are statistically controlled. Coefficients for our independent variables do not refer to effects on percentage changes in the dependent variables over time, but rather to effects on differences between values of the dependent variables at time-one and time-two of changes in the characteristics of nonmetropolitan Northeast counties.

The Impact of Technological Inputs
On Changes In Farm Structure

Among all nonmetropolitan counties, change in the value of machinery and equipment per farm was found to be negatively associated with change in full-owned and part-time farms. In other words, where the value of machinery and equipment has increased most, the percentages of full-owned and part-time farms have declined or increased least. However, it should be noted that the proportion of explained variance for each of these two models was quite low. The coefficients for the machinery variable in predicting change in the percentage of corporate farms and change in the number of workers per farm were relatively small and insignificant compared to other variables in the models. Change in chemical inputs was negatively related to changes in the percentage of corporate farms and the number of workers per farm and was positively related to change in the percentage of part-time farms.

The models which apply to the more agriculturally dependent counties reveal some differences in the patterns of association. Change in the per farm value of machinery and equipment was found to be related to change in the farm structure indicators in essentially the same ways as it was for all nonmetropolitan counties; the coefficients, however, were relatively small. Change in the use of agrochemical technology was positively associated with change in full ownership, but was relatively insignificant in the model. The coefficient for the impact of the agrochemical technology variable on change in part-time farming indicated that this variable was the single best predictor of change in the model. Yet the total variance explained in three of the four farm structure models applied to the more agricultural counties was quite low, the exception being the model for workers per farm, in which change in gross sales provides a significant predictor of change in this indicator of farm labor force composition.

The Impact Of Change In Technology And Farm Structure On Change in Population Size and Composition

We expected that change in the size and composition of the population in nonmetropolitan counties between 1970 and 1980 would not be closely related to changes in farm sector variables over that time period. The relatively high level of rural-urban, farm-nonfarm integration in the Northeast region suggests that change in the population variables has been due more to changes in the nonfarm sector than to changes in the farm sector. However, change in the number of hired farm workers in the labor force was expected to be related to changes in the structure of farming, and changes in farm sales and the percentage of incorporated farms were considered likely to be associated with change in the reliance on hired labor.

Change in the percentage of incorporated farms, which can be considered an indicator of the changing scale of farm operations,[3] was not found to be highly related to change in the number of workers, contrary to expectation. Increases in the number of hired workers are apparently occurring across farms of varying sizes, though increases in the number of hired workers were greatest in counties where production had become more mechanized and where gross farm sales had increased most rapidly. However, in the more agriculturally dependent counties, where the mean increase in number of hired workers is greater, mechanization was less strongly related to changing numbers of workers than in the larger group of nonmetro countries.

Change in the size of the farm population was also found to be positively associated with mechanization and sales, although to a lesser extent. Changes in farm structure were not found to be highly related to changes in farm population size, with one exception: The extent of full ownership within the farm sector was positively associated with farm population change in the more agricultural counties. Nonfarm employment was positively associated with change in the size of the farm population, even though change in the percentage of part-time farms was not.

None of the farm sector or contextual variables was found to be related to change in the size of the rural populations of the total sample of nonmetropolitan counties to any significant extent. There was, however, more evidence of such a relationship within the agricultural segment of counties. Changes in sales and mechanization were negatively related to change in the size of the rural population. The substantial negative coefficient for the effect of change in the number of full-time hired workers on change in the size of the rural population among the more agricultural counties suggests that the increasing scale of farm operations is associated with rural population decline or less rapid growth. Change in the rural populations of the most agriculturally dependent counties has been more closely related to changes in the farm sector than it has been for nonmetropolitan counties generally.

To summarize, changes in the general state of the agricultural economy and in mechanization were found to be positively but modestly associated with change in the farm population and in the regularly employed hired worker segment of the labor force. Change in the total rural population has generally not been associated with changes in the farm sector, although the relationships are stronger in agricultural counties. Full ownership was found to be positively related to farm population change, and within the agricultural counties corporate farming was negatively related to farm population change. With these exceptions, changes in the organizational structure of farming (incorporation, full ownership, part-time farming, and workers per farm) are generally not associated with population and labor force changes.

The Impact of Changes in Technology, Farm Structure
And Population Characteristics on Change in
Community Socioeconomic Well-Being

The extent of association between change in the farm sector and community changes is examined below in three ways. First-order and third-order correlation coefficients are reported in Tables 3 and 4, respectively. The first-order coefficients control the effect of initial size on the change score variable, and the third-order coefficients control the effects of the initial size and the two nonfarm contextual variables. In Table 5, the results of regression analyses are presented in the form of unstandardized coefficients. The full model is fit for all nonmetropolitan counties. For the agricultural subset of counties, a step-wise regression technique was used to identify the best four variable model for each of the community well-being variables. Preliminary regression analysis led to decisions to eliminate certain variables from the analysis. The technology variables did not have appreciable direct effects on indicators of community well-being when other factors were taken into account, and they were eliminated from the list of independent variables. The model for change in the unemployment rate explained less than 10 percent of the variations in this indicator, and it was therefore omitted from the analysis as well.

An interesting pattern emerges when considering the poverty and income models together. Change in the proportion of the farm population, change in the proportion of fully-owned farms, and change in the vitality of the local farm economy are all associated with improved community well-being. The coefficients and the direction of the relationships suggest that when the farm population declines as a proportion of county population, when the proportion of fully-owned farms declines, or when total farm sales in a county remain relatively stagnant or decline, poverty rates tend to increase. The effect of corporate farming appears to be negative. Change in this variable is positively associated with the poverty rate and negatively associated with median family income, especially in the agricul-

222

TABLE 3. FIRST-ORDER AND THIRD-ORDER PARTIAL CORRELATION COEFFICIENTS FOR THE REGRESSION OF CHANGE IN COMMUNITY WELL-BEING ON SELECTED VARIABLES, ALL NONMETROPOLITAN COUNTIES (N=105)[1]

Farm Sector and Control Variables[2]	Community Characteristics									
	POVERTY		INCOME		RETAIL		HOUSING		TAXES	
RURALPOP%	.02	(.07)	.05	(-.01)	-.05	(-.10)	.16	(.03)	-.14	(-.07)
FARMPOP%	-.21	(-.17)	.20	(.14)	.39	(.32)	.06	(-.10)	-.08	(.01)
CORPORATE	.02	(.03)	-.03	(-.05)	.03	(.00)	-.14	(-.21)	.05	(.06)
FULLOWN	-.25	(-.21)	.22	(.17)	.20	(.15)	.12	(.00)	-.06	(-.01)
PART-TIME	-.14	(-.15)	.24	(.26)	.26	(.27)	.06	(.10)	.14	(.12)
WORKFARM	-.08	(-.05)	.05	(.02)	.00	(-.03)	.09	(-.01)	-.13	(-.10)
SALES	-.08	(-.06)	.16	(.13)	-.04	(-.05)	.23	(.17)	-.23	(-.19)
NFEMPLOY	-.10	--	.14	--	.09	--	.38	--	-.26	--
URBAN	-.08	--	.12	--	.14	--	.25	--	-.12	--

[1]First-order partials are reported in each column. They represent the correlation between a community change score and a farm sector change score or contextual variable, controlling the initial size of the community variable. Third-order partials, which control the influence of the urban and nonfarm employment contectual variables in addition to initial size, are reported in parentheses.

[2]The definitions of the variables in Tables 3-5 are as follows:

RURALPOP% = change in the size of the total rural population, 1970-1980.

FARMPOP% = change in the size of the farm population, 1970-1980.

CORPORATE = change in the percent of all farms operated under an incorporation form of ownership, 1969-1978.

FULLOWN = change in percent of farms with sales of $2500 or more per year which are fully owned by the operating entity, 1969-1978.

PART-TIME = change in percent of farm operators who reported 100 or more days of off-farm employment, 1969-1978.

WORKFARM = change in the number of regularly employed hired workers per farm reporting hired labor expenditures, 1969-1978.

SALES = change in total gross farm sales, 1969-1978.

NFEMPLOY = percent of employment in manufacturing and services, 1970.

URBAN = percent of total population in urban places, 1970.

POVERTY = change in percent of all families which had below-poverty level incomes, 1970-1980.

INCOME = difference in median family income, 1970-1980.

RETAIL = change in retail sales per capita, 1967-1977.

HOUSING = change in percent of housing units in buildings built before 1940, 1970-1980.

TAXES = change in the average per capita property taxes paid, 1967-1977.

TABLE 4. FIRST-ORDER AND THIRD-ORDER PARTIAL CORRELATION COEFFICIENTS FOR THE REGRESSION OF CHANGE IN COMMUNITY WELL-BEING ON SELECTED VARIABLES, ALL NONMETROPOLITAN COUNTIES (N=30)[1]

Farm Sector and Control Variables	Community Characteristics									
	POVERTY		INCOME		RETAIL		HOUSING		TAXES	
RURALPOP%	.12	(.00)	.00	(-.04)	.01	(-.08)	.45	(.13)	.02	(.08)
FARMPOP%	-.10	(-.21)	.39	(.36)	.48	(.40)	.24	(-.07)	.14	(.11)
CORPORATE	.24	(.18)	-.25	(-.14)	.18	(.22)	-.33	(-.45)	.03	(.05)
FULLOWN	-.27	(-.29)	.33	(.35)	.03	(.03)	.13	(.13)	-.04	(-.07)
PART-TIME	-.16	(-.16)	-.01	(.03)	.40	(.42)	-.29	(-.31)	.19	(.12)
WORKFARM	-.43	(-.44)	.40	(.36)	.34	(.32)	.08	(.03)	.20	(.24)
SALES	-.41	(-.40)	.55	(.48)	.38	(.34)	.04	(-.01)	.06	(.10)
NFEMPLOY	.06	--	.24	--	.17	--	.39	--	-.23	--
URBAN	.22	--	-.07	--	.08	--	.50	--	.05	--

[1]First-order partials are reported in each column. They represent the correlation between a community change score and a farm sector change score or contextual variable, controlling the initial size of the community variable. Third-order partials, which control the influence of the urban and nonfarm employment contectual variables in addition to initial size, are reported in parentheses.

TABLE 5. UNSTANDARDIZED REGRESSION COEFFICIENTS FOR MODELS PREDICTING CHANGE IN SELECTED COMMUNITY CHARACTERISTICS, 1970-1980, FOR ALL NONMETROPOLITAN AND FOR AGRICULTURAL COUNTIES IN THE NORTHEAST

Dependent Variables

Independent Variables[1]	POVERTY All Nonmetro	POVERTY Agricultural	INCOME All Nonmetro	INCOME Agricultural	RETAIL All Nonmetro	RETAIL Agricultural	HOUSING All Nonmetro	HOUSING Agricultural	TAXES All Nonmetro	TAXES Agricultural
Time 1 Control	-.41*	-.36	.77*	.42	.75*	.39*	-.19*	-.22	.94*	.94
RURALPOP%	1.41	--	-262.07	--	37.22	--	3.11	--	-49.12	--
FARMPOP%	-9.42	--	2530.62	11503.17	8417.93*	6544.20*	-1.69	--	132.57	--
CORPORATE	.12	--	-86.34	-179.90	-3.20	-14.25	.07	-1.38*	1.62	--
FULLOWN	-.07*	-.08	60.1*	--	4.94	--	-.01	--	-.46	--
PART-TIME	-.02	--	32.98	--	15.34	18.12*	-.02	-.14	.54	--
WORKFARM	-.13	-1.18*	-375.21	--	24.25	--	-.58	--	4.73	48.96
SALES	-.13	--	585.46	580.32*	-59.09	--	.84	--	-26.61	-26.01
NFEMPLOY	-.01	--	15.67	--	.28	--	.19*	--	-1.58*	-1.97
URBAN	.00	.03	6.14	--	-2.00	--	.03	.17*	-.34	--
Intercept	3.02	2.89	1630.70	4509.67	665.82	701.02	-8.48	.13	109.82	82.96
R-Squared	.37	.40	.33	.41	.40	.61	.22	.63	.52	.69

[1] Each dependent variable is measured as a simple gain score over a ten-year period, therefore a time-one control variable is introduced in each model. The poverty level in 1970 is included in the POVERTY model. Median family income in 1969 is included in the INCOME model. Per-capita retail sales in 1967 is included in the RETAIL model. The percentage of housing units built before 1940 which existed in 1970 is included in the HOUSING model. Per capita property taxes in 1967 is included in the TAXES model.

* $p < .05$

tural counties. Changes in full ownership and part-time farmer percentages are positively associated with improved poverty rates and median family incomes, with full-ownership being the most significant contributor to explaining change in these community variables.

Retail sales are related positively to changes in the farm proportion of the population. The strength of the association across both types of counties indicates that where the farm population has declined, retail sales per capita has also tended to decline. Interestingly, the rate of change in farm sales appears negatively related to retail sales change, as does corporate farming, although both are statistically insignificant in the regression models. These relationships suggest that a dynamic agricultural economy does not necessarily contribute to local retail sales. Alternatively, change in part-time farming is significantly and positively related to change in retail sales within the agricultural segment of counties.

Change in housing quality (percent of housing built before 1940) appears to depend more on nonfarm influences than on the farm sector variables. Nonfarm employment is associated with poorer housing across all nonmetropolitan counties, and percent urban population is related to housing in the same way for agricultural counties. The overall quality of housing does not appear to have been affected by change in the farm sector, although there is some indication that where the farm percentage of the population has declined, housing conditions have not improved as much as elsewhere.

Beyond the contributions of variables measuring the initial scores on the dependent variables, change in the percentage of fully-owned farms was the most important variable affecting changes in the poverty rates and median incomes. Where proportions of fully-owned farms have declined, incomes and poverty rates have tended not to improve as much as elsewhere. Part-time farming is associated with incomes and poverty in the same ways.

Farm structure variables have significance in other respects. The most important variables explaining change in per capita retail sales were change in the farm population and change in the percentage of part-time farms. Each of the models indicates that change in the farm structure variables is relatively important to explaining changes in indicators of community well-being, but the goodness-of-fit statistics cause us to introduce a note of caution. Much of the variation among nonmetropolitan counties in the Northeast remains unexplained by the models which we have introduced in this analysis.

Summary

Our hypotheses have generally been confirmed by the results of our analysis. We did not expect the technology variables to be strongly related to changes in farm structure, nor did we expect significant relationships between the agricultural variables and changes in the sizes of farm and rural populations. Our models assessing the impact of technological inputs on farm structure account for little of the variance in the dependent variables after the effects of initial size are considered. The directions of the relationships between mechanization and farm structure variables are as expected, and the negative relationships between mechanization and full ownership and part-time farming are statistically significant. Chemical inputs are negatively related to indicators of changes in farm scale (percent of farms legally incorporated and the number of full-time hired farm workers), contrary to expectations. Perhaps large-scale farms already existing in 1969 relied heavily on chemical inputs and thus increased their use of these inputs least over the ten-year period. Given the poor fit of the models, we have little evidence to suggest that changes in technological inputs over the ten-year period covered in this study have had a major impact on changes in farm structure. This period may not have been a time of major structural change in Northeast farming, and limiting our analysis to this period may result in an underestimation of the influence of technological change on farm structure.

In our models of farm and rural population change, we see little evidence of impacts due to change in other farm sector variables. The strongest evidence is for the impact of change in fully-owned farms, which is positively associated with farm population change, especially in the most agriculturally dependent counties. Where part-time farming is increasing there is no evidence that this trend contributes to growth or stability in the farm and rural populations of these counties. Generally the farm sector variables contribute little to explaining variation in measures of farm and rural population change.

The models for predicting change in community well-being do, nonetheless, reveal some surprisingly consistent patterns of association between changes in the farm sector and other

socioeconomic changes in nonmetropolitan areas. The relationships between change in full-ownership and in poverty and
income suggest that this aspect of farm structure is an important correlate of economic well-being, particularly in the most
agriculturally dependent counties. Change in part-time farming
is also associated with indicators of economic well-being and
appears to contribute significantly to retail trade activity in
agricultural counties.

These patterns suggest that even in the Northeast, where
urban and other nonfarm influences on the farm sector have
been substantial for some time, we can still identify relationships between indicators of farm structure and indicators of
well-being in the general community. Yet we do not have con-
clusive evidence regarding the significance of the changing
composition of the farm sector; in particular, a trend toward
large-scale production units in agriculture does not necessarily
imply detrimental consequences for rural communities in the
Northeast. Corporate farming does not appear to be a significant
independent influence on community well being. But the trend
toward decline in the proportion of fully-owned farms would
imply negative consequences based on our analysis. Our data
offer little evidence that changes in the scale of farming or the
form of legal ownership have had important impacts on the
quality of life in rural areas of the Northeast. However, tenure
and the relative size of the farm population do appear to have
important impacts on overall community well-being.

Summary and Conclusions

The literature review and results of the empirical study in
the preceding sections of this paper provide the overall context
for evaluating future agricultural policies and their impacts on
the nonmetropolitan population and rural communities in the
Northeast. The major conclusions that we have drawn about
technology, farm structure, and rural communities in the
Northeast are as follows.

First, historical and contemporary data underscore the fact
that the nonmetropolitan population in the Northeast region is,
in absolute terms and relative to the nonmetro populations of
other regions, relatively privileged in terms of having high
income levels, low levels of poverty, and favorable access to
public services. Second, the Northeast region has relatively few
counties that, by national standards, could be considered

"agricultural counties." Late-1970s data show that only one county in the Northeast had in excess of 20 percent of labor-proprietor income derived from agriculture—the criterion that is generally used by USDA and other researchers to identify agricultural counties in the U.S. Of the 217 counties in the Northeast, 107 were considered nonmetropolitan in 1980, and only 30 of these nonmetropolitan counties had 5 percent of more of labor proprietor income derived from agriculture in the late 1970s. Thus, to reiterate, nonmetropolitan counties in the Northeast generally now have a relatively low dependence on agriculture.

Third, we found that technological change—mechanization and use of purchased soil amendments and other agricultural chemicals—had relatively little impact on change in farm structure in the Northeast during the 1970s, at least insofar as spatial variations in technological change were not associated with spatial variations in farm structural change. This empirical observation is likely accounted for by several factors:

> **Technological change** in the Northeast was not rapid during the 1970s by comparison with national trends. In part, this may be due to the fact that new technologies adopted in the 1970s were primarily applicable to commodities largely produced elsewhere in the country.

> **Farm structural change** in the Northeast appears to be caused more by the character of agricultural resources in the region (the prevalence of low-quality soils, short growing seasons, and other factors that limit agricultural productivity) and by nonfarm factors. In particular, it appears that the central factor affecting Northeast farm structure is the tendency toward the marginalization and disappearance of farms with low-quality agricultural resources.

Two important qualifications of this conclusion must be noted, however. One is the fact that the farm structure impacts of technological change in the Northeast during the 1970s were relatively moderate does not lessen the importance of prior technological and structural changes in the 1950s and 1960s. As noted previously, the post-World War II era in general has witnessed an extraordinary degree of change in agricultural production technology and in farm numbers, size, and structure throughout the U.S., including the Northeast. Also, the predominance of dairying in the Northeast farm economy, the likelihood of rapid—perhaps unprecedented—technological change in this industry over the next 10 to 15 years, and the inevitability of changes in national dairy policy all suggest that future changes in farm structure in the Northeast will likely be significant. There is growing evidence that several emerging technologies in dairying—bovine growth hormone, ultrafiltration and reverse osmosis—will have dramatic socioeconomic impacts on the dairy sector over the next 10 to 15 years (Boynton et al., 1984; Buttel, 1986; Kalter et al. 1984).

Our fourth and final conclusion was that during the 1970s there was only modest evidence of impacts of farm structural change on rural communities, even in the most agricultural counties in the region. Moreover, technological change did not appear to have major direct or indirect effects on the socioeconomic character of agricultural counties and rural communities in the Northeast. To be sure, among the relative handful of Northeast counties with 5 percent or more of labor-proprietor income derived from agriculture there were some modest associations between farm structure and work force variables and indicators of rural community well-being. But, on the whole, the nonmetropolitan social fabric in the Northeast region has generally been only modestly affected by agricultural technology and farm structure changes over the past decade. Again, though, it is virtually certain that there will be a major wave of technological change in Northeast dairying over the next decade or two. This pattern of technological change will clearly have major impacts on the farms and nonfarm agribusinesses in the region and, more than likely, will have some significant effects on small agricultural trade centers in the more agricultural, dairy-dominated nonmetro counties.

The available evidence suggests, however, that future technological change in Northeast agriculture will affect individual farm households and the nonfarm agribusiness sector far more than it will affect the nonmetropolitan population or small rural communities in the region. Thus, there would appear to be little rationale to design farm policies with the goal of enhancing the well-being of Northeast nonmetro communities as population aggregates, though such a rationale probably exists in some of the more agriculturally dominated regions of the country. And given the general lack of targetability and efficiency of farm commodity policy, macroeconomic policy, and regulatory, research, and related policies in providing specific solutions to these problems, it is appropriate to ask if directly addressing the problems of employment creation, income enhancement, rural infrastructure development, etc., might not be the most constructive policy approach.

There are several important reasons why a comprehensive rural development policy approach directed toward these goals might be constructive. First, there is evidence that from the late 1960s to the end of the 1970s aspects of such a program in fact worked. Prior to the 1960s there were major regional disparities, with rural/nonmetro places and counties exhibiting lower incomes and access to services than their urban/metro counterparts. But beginning in the late 1960s and continuing through the 1970s, there emerged a distinct pattern of convergence in the socioeconomic characteristics of metro and nonmetro counties. While many factors were no doubt involved in this pattern of convergence, there is agreement that the deepening of the social welfare apparatus—transfer payments, service subsidies, extension of protective labor legislation, regional commissions, economic development programs, revenue sharing, small business loan programs, and so forth—played a major role.

Second, a comprehensive rural development program would be fair; it would benefit the nonmetro counties and communities of the U.S. in a relatively equal manner, regardless of their dependence or lack of dependence on agriculture. Third, there has long been evidence that the majority of Americans would prefer to live in small places rather than in large cities if they had the opportunity; thus, a program of this sort could be justified on the grounds that it would provide residential (and, indirectly, employment) options that are of interest to a large proportion of the U.S. population. Fourth, such a policy would have the greatest likelihood of effectively meliorating future adverse changes in farm technology and structure, since it would enhance the ability of those displaced in this process to find alternative employment in their community or region of residence. The existence of additional employment opportunities is, after all, probably the major challenge for public policy in dealing with these technology and structure-induced changes. Finally, one might add that a sustained program of rural development would likely cost less than farm commodity programs currently do and that it could provide the long-term institution building that would help to insulate rural places from adverse farm technology and structure changes that extend into the next century.

NOTES

[1] This is an abridged version of a paper (Buttel et al., 1986) originally prepared as a report for the Task Force on Technology, Farm Structure, and Rural Communities of the assessment on "Technology, Public Policy, and the Changing Structure of American Agriculture," Food and Renewable Resources Program. Office of Technology Assessment, Congress of the United States. The authors would like to thank Robert Boynton, Ann Gerken, Craig K. Harris, Steven E. Hastings, Brian How, Robert Kalter, Lillian Kirk, Olaf F. Larson, Robert Milligan, Andrew Novakovic, Michael Phillips, Louis Swanson, and Nancy Strang for their assistance in the preparation of this manuscript.

[2] The choice of 1969/70 to 1978/80 as the time frame for the empirical analysis has one major advantage but also a key disadvantage. The advantage is that this is the most recent decade-long period for which data are available, giving us greater confidence that the empirical patterns that are discovered are generalizable to the current structure of the Northeast's agricultural and rural economies. But it should also be recognized, as noted above, that the decade of the 1970s was not one of rapid technological change in Northeast agriculture. Thus, our results will be limited to some degree in the inferences that might be drawn regarding the socioeconomic impacts of rapid technological change in Northeast agriculture over the next 15 to 20 years.

[3] As noted earlier, legally incorporated farms in the Northeast in 1982 averaged approximately 400 acres per farm, about 2.3 times larger than the average for all census farms in the region. The percentage of incorporated farms is, to be sure, a less-than-ideal measure of the degree to which agricultural production is concentrated in large farm units, but we feel that this measure is preferable to others available in both the 1969 and 1978 Censuses of Agriculture. Gross farm sales in particular, is a frequently employed indicator of farm scale. There are, however, several major problems in utilizing gross farm sales categories from the 1969 and 1978 censuses as the basis for an indicator of the changing scale of agricultural production. First, due to inflation, gross farm sales categories are not comparable

over time. Second, the upper bound for gross farm sales in the
1969 Census of Agriculture was $40,000 or more, which could
be said to represent a category of somewhat larger than average
commercial-size farms. An indicator based on farm acreage
would also be inappropriate for the Northeast region because of
its highly variable soil resources. Thus we have chosen the
percentage of incorporated farms as an indicator of the scale of
agricultural production in preference to alternative indicators
based on gross farm sales and acreage categories.

REFERENCES

Ali, Y. A.
 1973 "Social Changes in Thirteen New York Rural
       Communities: 1920-1970." M.S. Thesis, Cornell
       University.
Boynton, R. D., A. M. Novakovic, and R. D. Aplin
 1984 "Economic Opportunities for the Dairy Industry." New
       York State Agriculture 2000 Project, November.
Brown, D. L., and C. L. Beale
 1981 "Diversity in Post-1970 Population Trends." Pp. 27-71
       in A. H. Hawley and S. M. Mazie (eds.),
       Nonmetropolitan America in Transition. Chapel Hill:
       University of North Carolina Press.
Brunner, E. deS., G. S. Hughes, and M. Patten
 1927 *American Agricultural Villages.* New York: George H.
       Duran Co.
Brunner, E. deS., and J. H. Kolb
 1933 *Rural Social Trends.* New York: McGraw-Hill.
Brunner, E. deS., and I. Lorge
 1937 *Rural Trends in Depression Years.* New York: Columbia
       University Press.
Buttel, F. H.
 1982a "Farm Structure and Rural Development." Pp. 213-35
        in W. P. Browne and D. F. Hadwiger (eds.), *Rural
        Policy Problems. Lexington, Mass.: Lexington Books.*
 1982b "The Political Economy of Part-Time Farming."
        GeoJournal 6:293-300.
 1983a "Farm Structure and the Quality of Life in Agricultural
        Communities: A Review of Literature and a Look

Toward the Future." Pp. 150-173 in Agricultural Communities: The Interrelationship of Agriculture, Business, Industry, and Government in the Rural Economy. Committee Print prepared by the Congressional Research Service, Library of Congress, for the Committee on Agriculture, U.S. House of Representatives, 98th Congress, 1st Session. Washington, D.C.: U.S. Government Printing Office.

1983b "Beyond the Family Farm." Pp. 87-107 in G. F. Summers (ed.), *Technology and Social Change in Rural Areas.* Boulder, Colo.: Westview Press.

1984 "Agricultural Land Reform in America." Pp. 55-72 in C. C. Geisler and F. R. Popper (eds.), *Land Reform, American Style. Totowa, N.J.: Rowman and Allanheld.*

1986 "The Crisis and Opportunity of Northeast Agriculture." Paper presented at the Conference on Sunrise Agriculture, University of Maine, October.

Buttel, F. H., and M. E. Gertler
1982 "Small Farm Businesses: A Typology of Farm, Operator, and Family Characteristics With Implications for Public Research and Extension Policy." *Journal of the Northeastern Agricultural Economics Council* 11:35-44.

Buttel, F. H., M. Lancelle, and D. R. Lee
1986 "Emerging Agricultural Technologies, Farm Structural Change, Public Policy, and Rural Communities in the Northeast." Pp. i-B2 in Office of Technology Assessment, Technology, Public Policy, and the Changing Structure of American Agriculture, Volume II—Background Papers. Springfield, VA: National Technical Information Service.

Campbell, R. R.
1975 "Beyond the Suburbs: The Changing Rural Scene." Pp. 93-122 in A. H. Hawley and V. P. Rock (eds.), *Metropolitan America in Contemporary Perspective.* Beverly Hills, Calif.: Sage Publications.

Cochrane, W. W.
1979 *The Development of American Agriculture.* Minneapolis: University of Minnesota Press. Dorner, P.

1983 "Technology and U.S. Agriculture." Pp. 73-86 in G. F. Summers (ed.), *Technology and Social Change in Rural Areas.* Boulder, Colo.: Westview Press.

Eberts, P. R.
1984 Socioeconomic Trends in Rural New York State.

Albany: New York State Legislative Commission on Rural Resources.

Ebling, W.
1979 *The Fruited Plain: The Story of American Agriculture.* Berkeley: University of California Press.

Edwards, E. E.
1940 "American Agriculture—The First 300 Years." Pp. 171-276 in Farmers in a Changing World: Yearbook of Agriculture, 1940. Washington, D.C.: U.S. Department of Agriculture.

Fitchen, J. M.
1981 *Poverty in Rural America.* Boulder, Colo.: Westview Press.

Flora, J. L., and J. L. Conboy
1977 "Impact of Type of Agriculture on Class Structure, Social Well-Being, and Inequities." Paper presented at the annual meeting of the Rural Sociological Society, Madison, Wisconsin.

Forste, R. H., and G. E. Frick
1979 "Dairy." Pp. 119-147 in L. Schertz et al. (eds.), *Another Revolution in U.S. Farming?* Washington, D.C.:U.S. Department of Agriculture.

Gates, P. W.
1960 *The Farmer's Age: Agriculture, 1815-1860.* New York: Holt, Rinehart, and Winston.

Goldschmidt, Walter
1978 *As You Sow.* Montclair, N.J.: Allanheld, Osmun & Co.

Gregor, H. F.
1982 *Industrialization of U.S. Agriculture.* Boulder, Colo.: Westview Press.

Harris, C. K., and J. Gilbert
1982 "Large-scale Farming, Rural Income, and Goldschmidt's Agrarian Thesis." *Rural Sociology* 47:449-458.

Hayes, M. N., and A. L. Olmstead
1984 "Farm Size and Community Quality: Arvin and Dinuba Revisited." *American Journal of Agricultural Economics* 66:430-436.

Hedrick, U. P.
1933 *A History of Agriculture in the State of New York.* Albany: J. B. Lyon.

Heffernan, W. D.
1982 "Structure of Agriculture and the Quality of Life in Rural Communities." Pp. 337-346 in D. A. Dillman and

D. J. Hobbs (eds.), *Rural Society in the U.S.* Boulder, Colo.: Westview Press.

Herman, C.
1979 "Regionalism and Development: A Socio-History of New York, 1835-1875." Ph.D. Dissertation, Cornell University.

Hines, F. K., D. L. Brown, and J. M. Zimmer
1975 Social and Economic Characteristics of the Population in Metropolitan and Nonmetropolitan Counties, 1970. Agricultural Economic Report 272. Washington, D.C.: Economic Research Service, U.S. Department of Agriculture.

Jacobson, R. E.
1980 "Changing Structure of Dairy Farming in the United States: 1940-79." Pp. 127-156 in Farm Structure: A Historical Perspective on Changes in the Number and Size of Farms.Committee Print, Committee on Agriculture, Nutrition, and Forestry, U.S . Senate, 96th Congress, 2d Session. Washington, D.C.: U.S. Government Printing Office.

Kalter, R. J., et al.
1984 "Biotechnology and the Dairy Industry: Production Costs and Commercial Potential of the Bovine Growth Hormone." A. E. Research 84-22, December.

Kolb, J. H., and E. deS. Brunner
1952 *A Study of Rural Society. Fourth Edition.* Boston: Houghton Mifflin.

Larson, 0. F.
1981 "Agriculture and the Community." Pp. 147-193 in A. H. Hawley and S. M. Mazie (eds.), *Nonmetropolitan America in Transition.* Chapel Hill: University of North Carolina Press.

Lockridge, K. A.
1970 *A New England Town: The First Hundred Years.* New York: W. W. Norton.

MacCannell, D., and J. White
1984 "The Social Costs of Large-Scale Agriculture: The Prospects of Land Reform in California." Pp. 35-54 in C. C. Geisler and F. R. Popper (eds.), *Land Reform, American Style.* Totowa, N.J.: Rowman and Allanheld.

MacLeisch, K., and K. Young
1942 Culture of a Contemporary Rural Community: Landaff, New Hampshire. Rural Life Studies No. 3. Washington,

D.C.: Bureau of Agricultural Economics, U.S.
Department of Agriculture.

Main, J. T.
1965 *The Social Structure of Revolutionary America.*
Princeton, N.J.: Princeton University Press.

Raper, A. F
1949a "The Dairy Areas." Pp. 413-433 in C. C. Taylor et al.
(eds.), *Rural Life in the United States.* New York:
Knopf.
1949b "The General and Self-Sufficing Areas." Pp. 446-463
in C. C. Taylor et al. (eds.), *Rural Life in the United
States. New York: Knopf.*

Richardson, J.L., and 0. F. Larson
1976 "Small Community Trends: A 50-Year Perspective on
Social Economic Change in 13 New York
Communities." *Rural Sociology* 41:45-59.

Rodefeld, R. D.
1980 "Farm Structural Characteristics: Recent Trends, Causes,
Implications, and Research Needs—Exerpts." Part III in
L. Tweeten et al. (eds.), Structure of Agriculture and
Information Needs Regarding Small Farms.Washington,
D.C.: National Rural Center.

Schertz, L. P.
1979 "The Northeast." Pp. 257-276 in L. P. Schertz et al.
(eds.), *Another Revolution in U.S. Farming?*
Washington, D.C.: U.S. Department of Agriculture.

Schertz, L. P., and Others
1979 *Another Revolution in U.S. Farming?* Washington,
D.C.: U.S. Department of Agriculture.

Shannon, F. A.
1945 *The Farmer's Last Frontier: Agriculture, 1860-1897.*
New York: Holt, Rinehart, and Winston.

Shover, J. L.
1976 *First Majority—Last Minority.* DeKalb: Northern Illinois
University Press.

Smith, T. L., and P. E. Zopf, Jr.
1970 *Principles of Inductive Rural-Urban Sociology.*
Philadelphia: F. A. Davis Co.

Stanton, B. F.
1984 "Changes in Farm Structure: The United States and
New York, 1930-1982." Cornell Agricultural Economics
Staff Paper No.84-23, Department of Agricultural
Economics, Cornell University, September.

Stanton, B. F., and L. M. Plimpton
  1979 "People, Land, and Farms: 125 Years of Change in the Northeast." Ithaca, N.Y.: Department of Agricultural Economics, Cornell University.
Summers, G. F. et al.
  1976 *Industrial Invasion of Nonmetropolitan America.* New York: Praeger.
Swanson, L. E., Jr.
  1982 "Farm and Trade Center Transition in an Industrial Society: Pennsylvania, 1930-1960." Ph.D. Dissertation, Pennsylvania State University.
Taylor, C. C. et al.
  1949 *Rural Life in the United States.* New York: Knopf.
Tostlebe, A. S.
  1957 *Capital in Agriculture: Its Formation and Financing Since 1870.* Princeton, N.J.: Princeton University Press.
Tweeten, L., and W. Huffman
  1980 "Structural Change." Part I in L. Tweeten et al. (eds.), Structure of Agriculture and Information Needs Regarding Small Farms. Washington, D.C.:National Rural Center.
U.S. Bureau of the Census
  1976 Historical Statistics of the United States. Washington, D.C.: U.S. Government Printing Office.
Young, R. C.
  1984 "Industrial Location and Regional Change in New York State." Unpublished manuscript, Department of Rural Sociology, Cornell University.

6
Farm Structure and Rural Well-Being in the South

Jerry R. Skees and Louis E. Swanson

This report deals with the enormous subject of farming and community well-being in the nonmetropolitan South, *and*, how these two highly complex and interrelated dimensions of Southern life and work may be transformed by the advent of new agricultural technology. A detailed treatment of this subject is clearly beyond the scope of this chapter. Instead, we examine this subject in a general manner. For the most part unique characteristics of Southern agriculture and rural community organization are not considered in great detail, nor are the many different subregions given special attention. Rather, the region is treated as a whole, focusing upon general indicators of technology, farming and rural community economic and social well-being.

A centerpiece of this report is the role of technology in societal change. The development and use of technology is generally and erroneously conceived of in a deterministic manner. That is, technology seems to develop independently of particular economic or social conditions and exerts an autonomous causal influence upon society. This is often the case for agricultural technologies. For instance, the popular notion that the mechanization of agriculture, particularly the "coming of tractors," caused U.S. farm numbers to decline and average farm size to increase. A more complex and substantively meaningful way of comprehending the role of technology as a force of economic and social change is as a tool that is a product of social and economic organization.

While this report has among its principal foci the influence of new technologies upon farm structure, and, in turn, the association of subsequent changes in farm structure with community well-being, technology is considered only to have an indirect association with community well-being. As a consequence, we will treat the role of technology apart from our discussion of farm and rural community change.

Our primary focus is upon farm change and community well-being in the nonmetropolitan South. Despite the nonmetropolitan South's immense diversity and the inherent difficulty of giving each aspect its proper due, the rewards of a general overview remain substantial. In particular, the South's agricultural sector offers a storied, and at times villainous, history of social organization and change. Investigation of this past demands careful attention to the myriad economic, social, and political forces that have shaped the options and molded the opportunities of millions of individuals and thereby helped create current conditions. Consequently, the articulation of the relationship of technology to various socioeconomic conditions, government policies, and the ways in which they act upon one another, is critical for both interpreting the past and making educated guesses about the future. We offer a condensed version of our understanding of these complicated relationships relative to the experiences of the South.

Historical Conditions

The economic and social history of the South is characterized by radical economic and social upheaval. The legacy of the antebellum period still persists in subtle forms, particularly in the structure of agriculture and rural community social organization. It is impossible to discuss future changes in farming and community well-being without first assessing how the South's unique history has contributed the present situation. In the century after the Civil War, the South's agricultural and rural nonfarm industries increasingly have been shaped by the same forces of rationalization that have produced the phenomena of the industrial revolution and urbanization. Consequently, the rural South today reflects both the legacy of the antebellum period and the social and economic organization of an advanced capitalist society.

Three types of social formations dominated Southern agricultural production during the antebellum period: (1) slavery and the plantation system, (2) commercial family farming, and (3) subsistence family farming. Each of these agricultural systems had a distinctive association with production technologies, the quality and structure of local society, and market orientation. Any discussion of the present relationships among agricultural technology, farm structure, and rural communities must necessarily include the character and transitions of these historical conditions.

Southern society has been characterized by a dependency upon agricultural production. However, the types of commodities produced, the variety of social and economic relationships used to produce agricultural commodities, and their distinctive market structures have been associated with relatively unique types of local societies. All three types of agricultural production systems of the antebellum period have left their impression on the present structure of Southern rural society. The social and economic character of each of these systems is briefly reviewed in order to place the present structure of Southern rural society within a historical framework.

Slavery and the Plantation System

The plantation system and the coercive bondage of slave labor is rooted in the colonial period when land was abundant and labor scarce. Large agricultural production units found more security in using slave or bonded labor than freeman hired labor that could leave at any time. Given the labor intensive requirements of the agricultural commodities being produced, control over the labor force was seen as essential to the persistence of large scale production units. Plantations, while producing some commodities for their own consumption, were primarily oriented toward commercial production. Moreover, the plantation system, then, was a highly stratified social and economic institution that was totally dependent upon slave labor and world markets.

The use of slave labor had many irrational tendencies that inhibited the economic development of the South and undermined social stability (Genovese, 1965:16) Genovese (1965), Weber (1947), and other scholars who have examined slavery identify at least four important irrational features that eventually undermined its economic viability and social legitimacy. First, plantation owners could not easily alter the size of their captive labor forces in order to adjust to changing market conditions. Consequently, economic efficiency could not be attained by frequent reorganization of the labor force. Second, "the capital outlay [was] much greater and riskier for slave labor than for free labor (Genovese, 1965:16). Third, "the domination of society by a planter class [increased] the risk of political influence in the market" (Genovese, 1965:16). Fourth, cheap labor was often scarce or unavailable. As a result, at a certain economic threshold, slave labor became very expensive (Genovese, 1965:Chapter 1; Weber, 1947).

Furthermore, unlike the emerging capitalist economy which demonstrated a remarkable ability to react to the pressures of competitive markets, plantation owners could not react effectively to changing market conditions and tended not to reinvest a greater part of their profits in their production systems. The customs and status roles of the plantation class were characterized by high consumption of non-production goods. Such consumption provided a visible confirmation of the plantation class's economic and social domination, but had the contradictory effect of diverting scarce capital from the production process.

The plantation system was also characterized by an under-utilization of efficient production technologies. In particular, the crude production technologies that were used were of poor quality. Three factors contributed to this poor performance in adjusting to technological change. First, because significant proportions of the profits were diverted to non-production commodities there often was not enough capital left over to invest in production technologies. Second, the slaves often showed their resistance to their social position by deliberately destroying or disabling tools. Third, because of the low demand for high quality labor-saving technologies, and because of the low demand for such production technologies by commercial family farmers (given their relative low accumulation of capital to invest), the South did not develop an economically viable manufacturing sector that could supply such technologies.

This last factor is of particular significance for the slow industrialization, and therfore modernization, of the South (see Genovese, 1965: Part Three). The inability to develop "home" or "regional" markets for manufactured goods is considered to have contributed to the South's loss of the Civil War, since prior to the war the antebellum South was dependent upon the North and Europe for cheap and quality manufactured goods, and consequently could not produce the manufactured implements of war. This dependence was directly associated with the irrational characteristics of the plantation system.

The North rose on the rapid expansion of the rural market, whereas the South remained dominated by slave plantations until the [North], interested in a new system of rural exploitation imposed a reorganization from without. An adequate home market could not grow in the antebellum South and has evolved slowly and painfully during the last century (Genovese, 1965:159).

Prior to the Civil War in the North and Midwest, commercial family farmers provided a large market for labor-saving production technologies that accelerated both agricultural and industrial development. Manufacturing in the North increased on the basis of this almost insatiable demand. In the South, the internal market for manufactured goods "consisted primarily of plantations, which bought foodstuffs from the West and manufactured goods from the East" (Genovese, 1965:165). Furthermore, the Plantation class was not eager to see the rise of a capitalist class or of commercial family farms, which it correctly perceived to pose a threat to its economic, political, and social domination (Genovese, 1965:Part Three; Hahn, 1983).

While it was not in the Plantation class's interest to encourage the emergence of potential economic competitors, the long-term effect was to place the South at a distinct disadvantage once it entered the industrial revolution. The antebellum South on the one hand provided one of many markets for Northern and European manufacturers, yet, on the other hand, did not have enough internal demand to adequately support an indigenous manufacturing sector. As the antislavery Kentuckian Cassius M. Clay remarked "A home market cannot exist in a slave state" (Genovese, 1965:173).

The plantation system, then, was based upon slave labor which restricted its ability to adjust to changing market conditions, and was characterized by a plantation elite who, rather than plowing most of their profits into production, chose the path of conspicuous consumption as a symbol of their domination. The destruction of the plantation system after the Civil War created a large group of landless black laborers, which was critical to the emergence of a new farm structure based upon racial social relations and economic dependency -sharecropping (Mandle, 1978). But, perhaps the most important legacies of the antebellum period for current circumstances were the plantation class's ability (1) to retard the development of internal markets, (2) restrict the rise of a capitalist class and a skilled industrial labor force, and (3) thwart the expansion of commercial family farms.

Commercial and Subsistence Family Farms During the Antebellum Period

Commercial and subsistence family farms formed the remainder of the agricultural sector during the antebellum period. Their total population greatly exceed the plantation population, including slaves. Yet, together these two farm structures had little in the way of economic and political power (Billings, 1979; Hahn 1983). Both of these farm production systems were dependent upon family labor supported by community cooperation. Most of these yeoman farms did not fit neatly into these ideal categories, but were situated somewhere in between, following the logic of both subsistence and commercial farming systems. The principle differences were in the ways in which each organized the family labor process, employed the powers of technology, and depended upon the market for their persistence.

Subsistence family farms primarily produced for local consumption. The persistence of these farm families, and their local societies, depended upon the ability to produce a wide variety of commodities other than commercial agricultural goods. Family labor, then, was organized to produce multiple commodities. The technologies that were employed tended to be made locally from available resources. The most common form of tillage system was a wooden plow pulled by a team of oxen.

Commercial family farm labor was organized to produce only a few agricultural commodities, relying upon their earnings in the marketplace to purchase most of their nonagricultural commodity needs. These farms tended to rely upon labor-saving technologies that permitted them to work a greater number of acres. Unlike subsistence family farms, commercial family farms were more likely to use an iron-tipped or steel plow pulled by draft horses. Furthermore, commercial family farms were dependent upon their performance in the marketplace.

Family farms often were characterized by both subsistence and commercial farming strategies, depending upon their proximity to non-local markets, and their capital and labor resources. The world of the Southern yeoman farm family "was one in which production and consumption focused on the household, in which kinship rather than the marketplace mediated most productive relations, in which general farming prevailed and family self-sufficiency provided the fundamental concern, and in which networks of exchange proliferated" (Hahn, 1983:20).

These farm families were characterized by considerable but by no means rigid internal stratification based upon property ownership, gender, and age. The men primarily were responsible for field work, though the women often joined in the labors of the harvest. "Complementing the labors of the men, women played a pivotal role in assuring that the household produced much of what was consumed" (Hahn 1983:30). Relationships among family members were mediated by the dominant male (Hahn, 1983:31)

Local societies tended to involve a significant community-help network, from which the notion of "community" has emerged. Such community efforts, though, were not based upon innate altruism, but upon the necessities of survival under conditions of both labor and resource scarcity. Consequently, instead of an egalitarian society, these local societies tended to reflect household social stratification. Community power rested in the hands of older white males with property. Free blacks and slaves, while not ostracized, were none-the-less segregated. Blacks lived in separate buildings on family farms, and generally formed subcommunities within local society. Consequently, black economic dependency and social segregation was the norm in both the plantation "Black Belt" and the yeoman farm society. This legacy of racial segregation along economic, social, and political lines continues to shape rural Southern Society.

The economic and social subordination of family farmers to the plantation system in great part was due to their inability to accumulate enough wealth to establish regional markets and political power on their own. The economic logic of these farming systems did not involve an entrepreneurial spirit as it is conceived of today (Henretta, 1978). The development of economic ties with regional markets primarily was seen as the responsibility of the state.

The Rural South's Transition to a Modern Society

The Civil War wrecked internal communications and transportation facilities and radically altered the agricultural structure. Furthermore, the emergence of an industrial economy was very uneven. In agriculture, two transitions stand out: (1) the replacement of the plantation system by sharecropping, and eventually large-scale industrial-type farms, and (2) the eclipse of subsistence family farming and the rise of tenant and full-owner commercial family farms and eventually larger-than-family farms.

The Civil War did not end the economic and political domination of the former plantation class.

> Plantations do not reflect the entire Southern rural experience, ante- or postbellum; but they have ever been the focus of economic power and the vanguard of change. Twentieth-century planters, probably more so than their predecessors, were landlords, bosses, and creditors to many times their numbers. They organized and dominated much of the flatland and hill South (Kirby, 1983: 257).

The cotton plantations of the South tended to be subdivided into small holdings on which recently emancipated black laborers and some poor white laborers worked the land. However, these black families did not own the land, used production technologies supplied by the landlords, did not make either annual or daily management decisions, and were paid on the basis of a share of the crop (Mann, 1984). Furthermore, these black families were securely tied to the credit systems established by the landlords (see Pryor, 1982).

In contrast to the cotton plantations, the sugar cane plantations remained relatively in tact through the use of labor gangs. Shlomowitz (1984) has attributed these two historically divergent responses to the demise of the antebellum period in terms of each crop's unique production and market characteristics. Shlomowitz (1984:14) argues that:

> the primary advantage that the plantation mode of organization had in the farming of sugar cane were in reducing the transaction costs in the coordination of harvesting and milling, in reducing the costs of measuring the sucrose supplies of cut cane to be milled. The primary advantages that the smallholding mode of organization had in the farming of cotton were in the making fuller use of the labor of women and children and allowing for the close personal attention that only the small holder would have an incentive to give.

However, the great majority of plantations produced cotton, and as a result, sharecropping become the primary social formation to emerge in cotton production.

Sharecropping as the primary type of farm organization producing cotton lasted only for three-quarters of a century. The demise of sharecropping had a considerable influence on the rural South's old Black Belt (Kirby, 1983; Vandiver, 1978).

> When planters decided to alter fundamentally their mode of production - as they did most dramatically during the 1930s and 1940s - much of the region was convulsed. Millions of people were dispersed to cities. Sharecropping shrank to insignificance. And mules, symbols and factotums of traditional farm life, became rare. The Southern landscape was depopulated and enclosed; agriculture at last became capital intensive (Kirby, 1983: 257).

Sargen (1979), in a comparative study of the mechanization of American agriculture between the turn of the twentieth century and World War II, notes that the economic rationale for the adoption of tractors was more evident in the North and Midwest than it was in the South. He proposes, in fact, that on the eve of World War II the very cheap labor requirements of the sharecropping system continued to make it more economically efficient for planters to continue that system rather than to consolidate the land parcels via the adoption of labor-saving technologies such as tractors and self-propelled harvesters. Vandiver (1978) proposes that the mechanization of cotton production was as much a response to the perceived unreliability of sharecropper labor due to labor organizing efforts during the 1930s as it was to market incentives. By the end of World War II, sharecropping was being eclipsed by large-scale farms that often relied upon hired managers and hired laborers. These new farm types were clearly industrial in character, and not commercial family farms.

The Ascendency and Decline of Commercial Family Farms

The economic and social upheaval caused by the Civil War and the introduction of regional market structures facilitated the emergence of commercial family farms and tenant family farms. However, the ascendency of these two types of family-labor farm structures was not without social and economic hardship.

The economic and social viability of family farming was now
dependent upon survival in a highly competitive marketplace.
The difficulties of family farms in all regions of the nation
during this period were evident in the rise of the landless
family farms in the form of tenancy and the populist movement.

Commercial family farmers found that the terms of trade
not equal, and argued for political and economic reforms to
address these inequalities. Their vision of society was a mixture
of antebellum values of independence and community coupled
with the desire to participate in the economic benefits of the
industrial revolution. Genovese (1965: 162) argues that the
antiindustrialism and anti-urbanism of the South was particularly
virulent:

> An agrarianism uncompromisingly hostile to industry and
> urbanization - to "manufacturing as a system" - existed
> only in the South and cannot be separated from the ideo-
> logical leadership of the slaveholding planters.

By the Great Depression the populist movement had lost its
political clout as the American population became more urbanized. However, many of its proposed agricultural policies were
reflected in the farm programs of the New Deal.

The high water mark of family farming in the South,
including both tenant and full owner farms, was the Great
Depression. Since that period, both types of farms have declined
in numbers and in their contribution to total agricultural
production in the South. Perhaps the latter measure is the best
indicator of the decline in the importance of family farming
since World War II. While family farms presently are the
numerically dominant farm type in the South, with a few
exceptions, they no longer produce the majority of agricultural
products. The most important exception is the production of
tobacco where New Deal production control programs have
facilitated the persistence of small scale family farming (Mann,
1975).

Farm Structure in the New South

Since World War II, the economic and social forces shaping
the structure of American agriculture have also been central to
Southern agricultural production. However, the South, unlike

many other regions, is not easy to categorize in terms of farm structure. In the deep South where the plantation system was strongest and both cotton and sugar cane are still raised, there is a greater preponderance of industrial-type farms and larger-than-family farms. But, these two commodities have never been raised by family farms. On the other hand, both Kentucky and North Carolina are centers for tobacco production and are characterized by a proportionately larger number of small family farms. Consequently, current farm structure in the South reflects both the historical legacies of the antebellum period and the early years of the South's industrial revolution, and the labor, capital, and biological requirements of particular commodities.

The Industrialization of the Postbellum Rural South

Throughout the antebellum period, local societies differed according to the differential influence of the farming structures within their hinterlands. Agricultural trade centers for cotton, sugar cane, and tobacco had a particularly agrarian economic and social texture, and were politically and economically controlled by the plantation class. The rural backlands of the South, on the other hand, were very much influenced by the economy and society of yeoman family farms.

The anti-industrial policies of the plantation class subverted the emergence of even a textile industry. In 1860, New England alone had three times as many textile factories as the entire South with a total capital investment for each factory twice that of the South (Genovese, 1965:165). Consequently, there were few industrial centers in the antebellum urban South and rural industrialization was almost nonexistent.

Agricultural trade centers that serviced a yeoman farm hinterland were generally untouched by the plantation class (Hahn, 1983). Their primary function was to provide local markets for locally produced commodities, with some ties to urban trade centers (Hahn, 1983). As a result, during the antebellum period and the decades following the Civil War, Southern agricultural trade centers were dependent upon their farming hinterlands. Their limits to growth were determined by the productivity of their agrarian sectors.

The rapid rationalization of the American economy has been pervasive but uneven, especially within regions that were late in undergoing the process. Emblematic of the emerging advanced capitalist society has been the redistribution of the population around trade and manufacturing centers—the twin processes of urbanization and industrialization. The growth of urban areas and manufacturing required a source of wage labor, increased agricultural production to feed the industrial work force, and a source of raw materials for industry. Each of these were available in the rural South. Consequently, the rural South was a necessary partner in the modernization of Southern society, but not an equal partner in sharing the wealth generated.

The rate of modernization between urban and rural areas has been uneven since nonfarm, indeed nonrural, capital first penetrated the hinterland and established the necessary internal markets, that the rural economy could not have done as quickly on its own. As the agricultural trade centers and their farming hinterland entered long-distance trade with the emerging industrial centers, their social and economic functions began to reflect the requirements for facilitating and reproducing the new trade and industrial relations. Previous social formations, such as autonomous rural churches or one-room six-grades schoolhouse, whose function was the persistence of yeoman family farming gave way to the demands of external trade. Horizontal ties that facilitated local production and consumption were subordinated to the economic realities of emerging vertical ties with distant economic and social institutions (c.f., Warren, 1978; Bender, 1978). Eventually, a trade center's persistence became less dependent upon internal exchange and more dependent upon its position within the new regional and national market structure.

The requirements for capital accumulation of the new industries included a geographical spatial organization that facilitated the speedy circulation of capital, access to new sources of industrial labor, and the establishment of public and private institutions that prepared and supplied an industrial labor force (e.g., standardized public schools, public health, concentrated retail firms, etc.). Once autonomous communities were pulled into the regional market and a hierarchy of central places emerged. Christaller (1966) has used central place theory to describe the structural and spatial distribution of a regional market and social network in terms of the "spatial arrangements of various sized central places and the functions they provide to their surrounding area" (Forsht and Jansma, 1975).

The penetration of internal markets and the resulting spatial organization also facilitated the development of commercial nonfarm industries within the rural hinterland. These internal markets tended to open the way for manufacturing firms to locate in rural areas. These firms were generally peripheral in character, often looking for new sources of cheap labor. Billings (1979) has examined the industrialization of rural and urban areas of North Carolina following the Civil War. He found that both planter capital and new bourgeois capital (most notably the Duke's of Durham) employed both white and black labor. Small agricultural trade centers such as Durham, North Carolina rapidly expanded both their industries and population. In 1865, Durham Station had a population of less than 500, yet by the turn of the century, it boasted a population of almost 70,000. However, the racial segregation that characterized both the plantation and yeoman societies persisted in the expanding industrial labor force.

The availability of indigenous capital after the Civil War appears to have varied by region. While Billings (1979) provides evidence that former plantation owners and wealthy farmers invested heavily in new manufacturing enterprises, especially textile mills, in North Carolina, Mann (1984) proposes that among the Gulf states, such heavy investment was not common. Therefore, capital scarcity was a major problem for some areas of the South during the late 1800s, and this scarcity contributed to the uneven development of industry during the past century.

The introduction of manufacturing into the hinterland provided a source of nonfarm employment that could compete for labor and capital with the farm sector. Furthermore, the locally generated income tended to increase the area's consuming ability. The introduction of manufacturing led to a decline in the dominance of farm production as the principle economic activity in the hinterland, and, therefore, provided an important influence on trade center persistence and change.

The expansion of industrial production into the hinterland fundamentally reorganized the formerly independent rural society. The new division of labor among these trade centers within the regional economy did not necessarily include all of the former trade centers. Those agricultural trade centers not strategically positioned in the regional economy at best remained stable, continuing to be dependent upon farm production. However, this dependence made them vulnerable to changes under way in their farming sector.

Therefore, both farm change and trade center change have been independently influenced by the ascendency of an advanced industrial economy. Farming has lost much of its mystique as a unique way of life, and gained a new image as a way of business. The farm sector has become more concentrated as marginal farms go out of production and the remaining farms wither expand production or seek off-farm employment to supplement sagging farm income. Once isolated trade centers are now members of the regional economy's hierarchy of places. as manufacturing and tertiary industries expand their influence, these trade centers gradually cease to be bucolic country villages and become industrial-based communities. Most have lost their functions associated with the yeoman family farm or plantation system, and, if centrally located, gained new functions associated with the requirements of an industrial society.

The rationalization of the Southern economy and society, then, has been pervasive but uneven. The rate of rationalization between urban and rural areas has been especially uneven. The emerging regional market structure required a spatial organization that facilitated the accumulation of capital, the circulation of capital, easy access to necessary labor, and efficient utilization of public institutions that educated, supplied, and kept healthy an industrial labor force. This spatial organization has greatly influenced which trade centers persist and which are left behind. Those communities that remained primarily dependent upon their farming hinterland are thought to be the most likely to experience a decline in their populations, quality of services, and in their retail establishments (see Whiting, 1974).

Southern rural society presently is influenced by a myriad of economic and social conditions, both endogenous and exogenous to their territorial boundaries. Their ecological characteristics - such as demographic structure, economic base, and social stratification - are both mediated through as well as influenced by regional and national socioeconomic factors. Therefore, it is difficult to determine empirically the exact association between the viability of their economic and social institutions and changes in farm structure.

Current Characteristics Of The Rural South

The South is an extremely interesting region for this study. Although the South has not been immune to national trends toward larger and fewer, there are distinct differences. Farms with low volume sales are concentrated in the South. For this study the South includes: Alabama, Arkansas, Delaware, Georgia, Kentucky, Louisiana, Maryland, Mississippi, North Carolina,

South Carolina, Tennessee, Virginia, and West Virginia (See Figure 1). In fact, roughly 35 percent of the nation's farms with sales under $10000 are located in the South (see Figures 2a through 2c). And while the South has roughly 27 percent of the nation's 2.24 million farms (1982 Census of Agriculture), only 17 percent of the nation's agricultural output comes from the South. Roughly 63 percent of the Southern farms had sales less than $10000 in 1982. By comparison, only 44 percent of the farms in the rest of the United States (all figures referred to as the rest of the U.S. include the remaining 35 states in the contiguous 48 states) had sales of less than $10000 in 1982. By far the largest concentration of small farms in the South is in the Appalachian states (Virginia, West Virginia, North Carolina, Kentucky, and Tennessee).

In order to emphaize the difference between the South and the rest of the nation some comparisons are appropriate. The following summary of these differences is based upon data available in Figures 2a through 2c and Table 2 (Table 1 provides a description of how the variables in Table 2 and in the later regression models were operationalized). It has already been

Figure 1: States Included in the Study of the South.

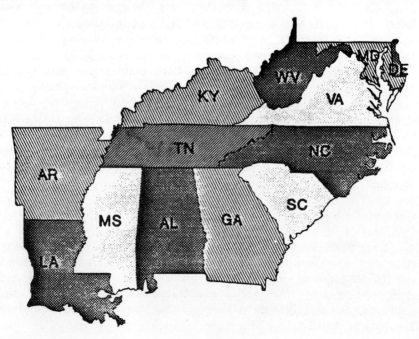

Figure 2a: Southern Farms' Sales By Sales Categories.

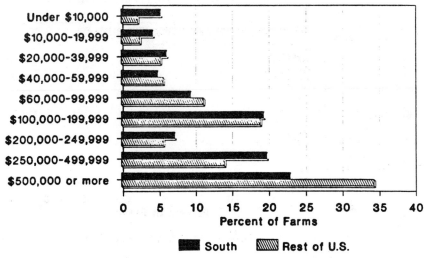

1982 Census of Agriculture

established that the South has relatively more small farms than the rest of the U.S. Farms with sales of less than $40,000 makeup 82.3 percent of the farms in the South and 67.7 percent of the farms in the rest of the U.S. Any farm with sales of less than $40,000 can be considered a small farm. Farms in the mid-size range ($40,000-100,000 in sales) account for 8.3 percent of the farms in the South and 17.3 percent of the farms in the rest of the U.S. The group with the largest sales (those with sales greater than $100,000) account of 9.3 percent of the farms in the South and 15.1 percent of other U.S. farms.

Similar differences exist between the South and the rest of the U.S. when acres in used as the measure of size. Farms with less than 180 acres makeup 73.2 percent of the total number in the South and 55.4 percent of the total number in the rest of the U.S. Farms with 180-999 acres account for 23.9 percent of the South's total and 35.8% of the total in the rest of the U.S. Finally farms of 1000 acres and greater comprise 3 percent of the South's total and 8.8 percent of the total in the rest of the U.S.

Differences according to sales figures also suggest signifi-cant variation with the rest of the U.S. Although farms with sales greater than $250,000 account for only 3 percent of the

254

Figure 2b: Comparing the South to the rest of the U.S. for Farm Size Measured by Gross Farm Sales.

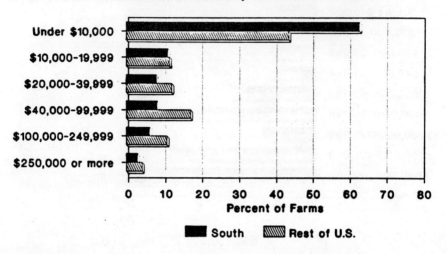

Figure 2c: Comparing the South to the rest of the U.S. for Farm Size Measured by Acres.

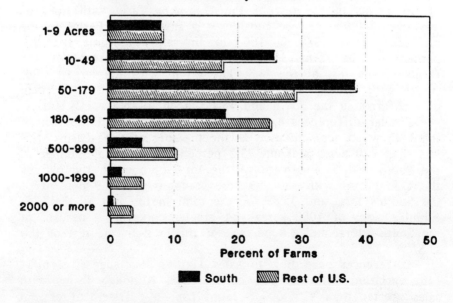

1982 Census of Agriculture

Table 1: Variables and Measures Used in Farm Structure and Community
          Well-Being Analysis

Variables: *Measurement Description*

Farm Number   Farm number was measured directly as the number of
                      farms reported by the 1969 and 1978 Censuses of
                      Agriculture.

Average Farm   Farm size was measured directly as the average gross
Size Sales   sales per farm. This was computed by dividing a
                      county's total agricultural sales by the county's
                      total number of farms.

Percent Part-   Part-time farming was measured indirectly as those
Time Farms   farm operators who stated that they worked over 99
                      days a year off of the farm. This number was then
                      divided by the total number of farms in a county.

Land-Saving Tech.   Land-saving technology expenses per farm was computed
Expenses p/fm   summing total county expenses for fertilizer and
                      other production chemicals and then dividing the sum
                      by the total number of farms in the county.

Average Value of   Average value of machinery per farm was computed by
Machinery p/fm   the Census of Agriculture.

Non-Family Labor   Non-family labor expenses per farm was computed by
Expenses p/fm   summing total expenses for hired and contract labor
                      in a county and then dividing the sum by the total
                      number of farms.

Concentration of   This is an indirect measure that uses the principle
Small Farms   of a Gini coefficient. It is the proportion of farms
                      with less than 180 acres.

Percent Full-   This variable is measured directly as those operators
Owner Operator   reporting that they own all of the farming operation.

Percent of Pop.   This variable is measured directly as those indivi-
Unemployed   duals reporting they were unemployed at the time of
                      the census enumeration.

1970 Value of   This variable is only used for the change models and
Dependent Var.   is the dependent variable's 1969 or 1970 value,
                      depending upon when the data were collected. The
                      population variables are 1970 and farm variables are
                      1969.

256

**Table 1 (continued): Variables and Measures Used in Farm Structure
and Community Well-Being Analysis**

Variables:	*Measurement Description*
Percent of Families Below Poverty	This is measured directly by the census of population and refers to all families who reported incomes below the poverty level.
Median Family Income	This variable is measured directly as the family whose income has half of all families below and half of all families above it in terms of family income.
Percent Farm of Rural Pop.	This variable is measured directly as the total number of the farm population divided by the total rural population in a county.
Percent in Manufacturing	This variable is measured directly using the industry code in the census of population. The total number of people employed in manufacturing is divided by the county's entire labor force.
Percent in Service Industries	This variable is measured directly using the industry code in the census of population. The total number of people employed in service industries is divided by the county's entire labor force.
Proximity to SMSA	This measure is based upon a county's geographical position relative to metropolitan areas of different population sizes. The measure was developed by Calvin Beale.
Percent with 12 or more years of Education	This variable reflects the percent of the county population 25 years or older who have completed at least 12 years of education.
Percent Black	This variable measures the percent of the county population who are black.
Miles Commuting	This variable is the average number of miles driven to work for residents of the county. It includes miles driven to other counties for employment.

Table 2: Comparing Basic Farm Structure Statistics in Nonmetropolitan Counties

Variable	Rest of U.S. county mean	--- South --- county mean	standard dev.
Farm Numbers	860*	849	617
	741	624	455
	(-117)	(-226)	(214)
Farm size	$48788	$24675	19605
(sales)	77140	46112	39492
	(28510)	(21357)	(23002)
Farm size	1232	205	116
(acres)	1220	232	136
	(-8.6)	(37.1)	(64)
Part-time	36.1%	44.3	10.5
farming	38.2	47.4	10.5
	(2.0)	(3.1)	(5.8)
Chemical & fert.	$2697	$2646	2994
use /farm	5713	5517	6526
	(3032)	(2872)	(3782)
Machinery value	$27584	$17023	11868
/ farm	54710	36043	27190
	(27227)	(19008)	(16261)
Hired labor	$4781	$3049	4023
/ farm	4638	3936	4386
	(-142)	(884)	(1690)
Farms below	43.4%	71.0%	13.2
180 acres	43.5	67.2	13.5
	(.1)	(-3.8)	(5.4)
% full owners	55.8%	70.6%	14.8
	38.9	38.0	10.0
	(-16.9)	(-32.6)	(13.1)
% tenant operators	13.9%	9.9%	8.4
	11.9	8.0	7.2
	(-2.0)	(-1.9)	(3.6)
% grain sales	18.4%	11.0%	16.2
	25.9	20.0	22.2
	(6.6)	(9.0)	(9.6)
% livestock sales	38.0%*	17.7%	12.4
	36.9	20.6	17.5
	(-1.4)	(3.1)	(10.5)

*1967-1970 values are listed first.
1977-1980 values are listed second.
The change between the two time periods in parentheses.

farms in the South, these farms contribute 43 percent of the total agricultural sales in the South. These same sales class accounts for 4.2 percent of the farms in the rest of the U.S. and contribute 48.5 percent of the total sales. If only farms with sales greater than $40,000 are considered, these farms contribute 84.3 percent of the total sales in the South and 90 percent of the total sales in the rest of the U.S.

The South is also undergoing change at a faster rate than Agriculture, farm numbers declined faster in the South than the rest of the U.S. The rate of decline in the South nearly double that of the rest of the U.S. The rate of increase in farm size in the South (whether size is measured by sales or acres) was greater than in the rest of the U.S.

Since farms are larger in the rest of the U.S., it is only logical that per farm expenditures on inputs would be greater in the rest of the U.S. Moreover, per farm expenditure on chemical and fertilizer and hired and contract labor are greater for the rest of the U.S. These differences are not as great as the differences in machinery value per farm (in 1978 machinery investment per farm was $34,773 in the South and $54,710 in the rest of the U.S.). Rates of change in chemical and fertilizer and machinery use were similar in the South and the rest of the U.S. The large increase in machinery investment was clearly a national trend in response to both improved agricultural prices and technological innovations in machinery.

One of the more dramatic changes in the structure of agriculture in the South involves the percent of full owners. The rate of decline was twice has great in the South (the South went from 70.6 percent full ownership in 1969 to 38.5% in 1978). The rate of change in percent of tenant operators was the same in the South and the rest of the U.S.

The concentration of grain sales within a county increased throughout the U.S. This increase was a result of market forces as the increased grain sales in international markets improved the price of grain relative to other farm alternatives. The rate of increase was greater in the South—the difference between the two points in time was 6.6 in the U.S. and 9.0 in the South.

Farm numbers declined by 8.5 percent from 1974 to 1982. Further, changes in the South are similar to the national trend—growth in number of farms is occurring in the smallest and largest sales classes. Farms in the 1-9 acre class increase 20 percent in the South. Much of the increase can probably be attributed to inflation. The largest rate of decline is for farms with between 50 and 260 acres. It should be noted for later reference that these are mid-sized operations.

The South continues to rely more on off-farm work than the rest of the U.S. Operators who work off-the-farm makeup 53 percent of the farms in the South and 45 percent of the farms in the rest of the U.S.

Six farm enterprises contribute 77.5 percent of the farm sales in the South (poultry and eggs, cash grain, tobacco, dairy, beef—except feedlots—and cotton). Using the 1982 Census of Agriculture's Standard Industrial Classifications (farms with sales of 50% or more in a specific classification fall into that class) these six classifications account for 78 percent of the farm numbers in the South.

Table 3 demonstrates the degree of concentration that exist in these six SICs. Poultry and eggs is clearly the most concentrated with 62.6 percent of the farms in this class having sales of $100,000 or more. Further, poultry and eggs account for nearly a quarter of the total agricultural sales in the South while only comprising 4 percent of the farm numbers. At the other extreme, 86 percent of the beef farms in the South have sales of less than $10,000. Although beef farms makeup 33 percent of the total farm numbers in the South, they only contribute 6.3 percent of the farm sales. Dairy and cotton farms are relatively concentrated with roughly 42 percent of the farmers in these classes having sales of greater than $100,000. Tobacco farms are predominantly small farms. While grain farms in the South are also dominated by relatively small farms.

The South produces 93.4 percent of all of the tobacco sold in the U.S. and 54.2 percent of the poultry and eggs. The South also produces a relatively large share of the cotton (37 percent of total sales). Since the South produces 17 percent of the total sales in the U.S., the other SICs (cash grain, dairy, and beef) account for a relatively small proportion of total sales in the U.S.

Moreover, these top six SICs contribute to each of the 13 Southern state's agricultural sales (see Table 4). Although there is a good deal of diversity regarding the mix of these six enterprise between states, in total, these six enterprises account for a large share of each of the states total sales (a high of 94 percent in Arkansas and a low of 64 percent in Georgia).

Table 5 provides further information on the differences between states in the South. For the most part these statistics are self-explanatory. The fact that Delaware has an average

Table 3: Top Six SIC Farms by Sales Classification

Sales	Poultry & eggs	Cash grain	Tobacco	Dairy	Beef	Cotton
more than 500000	1705	918	131	339	102	518
250000-499999	4125	2988	580	1563	217	947
100000-249999	9473	9016	4417	5992	1041	1604
40000- 99999	5135	13597	10504	5958	3331	1527
20000- 39999	1581	12091	13960	2745	7008	971
10000- 19999	659	13247	21028	1414	16455	903
less than 10000	1824	43790	72957	883	171912	1429
Total	24602	95647	123577	18894	200066	7381
% with sales greater than 100000	62.6%	13.5	4.1	41.8	.7	41.6
% with sales less than 10000	7.4%	45.8	59.0	4.7	85.9	19.0
% of total sales in the South	24.4%	21.0	11.6	9.0	6.3	5.2
% of total farms in the South	4.1%	15.9	20.5	3.1	33.2	1.2

These six Standard Industrial Classifications account for 78% of the total farms in the South and 77.5% of the total farm sales. By comparison, they account for 64% of the total U.S. farm sales.

Table 4: Top Six SIC's by Percent of Each State's Total Sales

	Poultry & eggs	Cash grain	Tobacco	Dairy	Beef	Cotton	Percent of total
Alabama	41%	13	0	5	10	7	76
Arkansas	37	43	0	4	6	4	94
Delaware	63	16	0	5	0	0	84
Georgia	35	12	5	7	4	1	64
Kentucky	1	21	29	13	8	0	72
Louisiana	10	40	0	10	6	16	82
Maryland	37	17	4	23	1	0	82
Mississippi	21	28	0	7	8	28	92
N. Carolina	26	9	33	1	2	0	71
S. Carolina	17	21	21	9	4	4	76
Tennessee	6	25	12	19	11	5	78
Virginia	19	11	12	19	11	0	72
W. Virginia	23	4	2	21	25	0	75
% of total sales in the South	24.4%	21.0	11.6	9.0	6.3	5.2	77.5
% of total sales of each SIC in the U.S. (% produced in the South)	54.2%	13.9	93.4	11.1	8.6	36.9	NA

farm size of $111,010 in farm sales can be tied to the concentration of poultry and eggs in that state. Likewise, the small average farm size in West Virginia is due to the dominance of beef. The three top states in terms of farm numbers are also major tobacco producing states.

Small farms dominate the South. Yet, in certain commodities, the South has farms that are as large as any in the U.S.—particularly in the poultry industry. Clearly, there is great diversity in farm types in the South. While 63 percent of the poultry farms in the South have sales of $100,000 or more, 86 percent of the beef farms have sales of less than $10,000. These diverse farms are located in a region that has a long history of relative rural poverty. This combination of characteristics does indeed make the South an interesting region to examine the relationship between farm structure and rural well-being.

The social and economic fabric of the rural South also varies considerably from the rest of the nations (for an excellent review see Beaulieu, 1988). Table 6 provides comparison of certain nonmetropolitan county quality of life variables. Among the more striking comparisons is the percent of families below poverty. Poverty in the South was greater than in the rest of the U.S. in both 1970 and 1980. In 1980, the average nonmetropolitan county poverty level was approximately 6 percent higher in the South than in the rest of the U.S. Average median family income values are consistent with the poverty measures. Family income in the South is lower than the rest of the U.S. in both 1970 and 1980. These inflation adjusted numbers also reveal the general economic growth that occurred in the South in the 1970's (i.e., there was a larger increase in family income in the South between 1970 and 1980). The South's unwillingness to tax property is also apparent from Table 6. Property taxes per capita (adjusted for inflation) are considerably higher in the rest of the U.S. Unemployment numbers are slightly higher in the South and the incidence of Southern unemployment appears to have increased faster in the 1970's. The proportion of farm to rural population is considerably higher in the rest of the U.S. than in the South. This suggest that Southern nonmetropolitan counties might be somewhat less dependent on farm population than similar counties in the rest of the U.S. Employment in manufacturing is notably higher in the South. Finally, employment in service industries has grown in the rest of the U.S. at a faster rate than in the South.

Table 5: Farm Characteristics by State

State	Farm Numbers	(rank)	Value of Agr. Products sold ($1000)	(rank)	Average farm size (by sales)
Alabama	48448	(7)	$1704160	(6)	$35180
Arkansas	50525	(15)	2826497	(2)	55940
Delaware	3338	(13)	370562	(12)	111010
Georgia	49630	(6)	2767679	(3)	55770
Kentucky	101642	(1)	2376882	(4)	23380
Louisiana	31628	(9)	1406458	(9)	44470
Maryland	16183	(12)	1029244	(10)	63600
Mississippi	42415	(8)	1918486	(5)	45230
N. Carolina	72792	(3)	3500750	(1)	48090
S. Carolina	24929	(10)	968554	(11)	38850
Tennessee	90565	(2)	1683852	(7)	18590
Virginia	51859	(4)	1606915	(8)	30990
W. Virginia	18742	(11)	242127	(13)	12920

South totals 602696   22402166

U.S. totals 2241124   131810903

South as a proportion of the total U.S.   26.9% of the total farms   17.0% of the total sales

Table 6: Quality of Life Variables in Nonmetropolitan Counties

Variable	Rest of U.S. County Mean	---- South ---- County Mean	Standard Deviation
County Pop	21738*	23036	18377
	25064	26723	21960
	(3331)	(3688)	(4505)
% Families	15.0%	26.6%	9.7
Below Poverty	11.8	17.6	6.5
	(-3.2)	(-9.0)	(4.9)
Total Year	7550	7500	5799
Housing Units	9840	9907	7975
	(2293)	(2406)	(2455)
Property Taxes	$346	$103	44
per Capita	396	135	66
	(50)	(31)	(49)
Retail	247	226	177
Establishments	248	237	197
	(1)	(10)	(45.5)
Median Family	$17547	$14055	2971
Income	20860	18112	3120
	(3312)	(4057)	(1642)
% Unemployment	4.53%	4.93%	2.3
	6.5	7.8	2.7
	(2.0)	(2.9)	(2.3)
Farm / Rural	27.1%	17.5%	12.3
Population	18.8	9.1	6.8
	(-8.3)	(-8.4)	(6.9)
% Employed in	16.0%	30.4%	12.2
Manufacturing	15.8	29.3	11.4
	(-.2)	(-1.1)	(4.9)
% Employed in	7.0%	7.7%	2.8
Services	18.9	16.8	4.5
	(11.9)	(9.1)	(4.7)

*1967-1970 values are listed first.
1977-1980 values are listed second.
The change between the two time periods appear in parentheses.

Table 7: Means of Variables Used in Regression Analysis

	1970	1980	Change
---Dependent Variables---			
Unemployment	4.94%	7.79	2.86
Median Family Income	$14,054.80	18,111.65	4,056.84
Poverty	26.58%	17.57	-9.00
Farm Size	$24,674.77	46,111.76	21,356.83
Farm Numbers	849	624	226
---Independent Variables---			
Small Farms	71.10%	67.23	-3.83
Part-time Farms	44.28%	47.37	3.10
Farm/Rural Pop.	17.48%	9.02	-8.46
Manufacturing	30.32%	29.27	-1.05
Service	7.71%	16.83	9.12
SMSA (Beale)	7.06%	7.06	7.06
Black Population	22.65%	21.35	-1.31
Education	30.89%	45.84	14.94
Commuting Miles	21.60	28.55	6.95
Full Ownership	70.64%	38.00	-32.63
Land-Savings Technology	$2646.00	3617.06	958.04
Machinery Investment	$17023.26	36042.90	19008.29
Non-Family Labor	$3049.39	2758.71	-290.42

Examining Forces That Contribute
To Farm Structural Change

The current structure of U.S. farms is the product of a complex interaction between a variety of economic, political, and social forces. Depending upon particular localities and points in time, these forces have been influential for more that a century, with some having more influence under particular historical circumstances. The simple model in Figure 3 illustrates the interactive system among (1) public policy, (2) technology, (3) economies of size, and (4) resource mix, with the last two representing different diminsions of farm structure. Farms expand in size for a variety of reasons, and such expansion in the aggregate will tend to facilitate the historical movement toward larger and fewer farms. Since this analysis is primarily concerned with technology, this discussion centers on technology.

Adoption of Farm Technologies

The development and introduction of farm production technologies have often been considered as an independent cause of farm structural change. This oversimplification of the role of technology is most often referred to as "technological determinism" (c.f., Rosenberg, 1982). While technological changes clearly have been associated with farm structural changes, it is equally clear that the mere existence of new technologies neither assures their adoption nor their influence on farm structure. It is not the development of technologies that drive farmers to maximize their profits, but it is the need to maximize their profits that induces farmers to adopt technology in order to remain competitive. Consequently, while technology has facilitated considerable changes in farming, the adoption of production technologies by farmers is the result of complex economic, social, and political factors. This section briefly examines how these factors have contributed to the utilization of technology by farmers and is the basis of later assumptions about the future influence of technology on farm change.

The persistence of a farm operation is dependent upon its successful participation in a competitive market. However, the low return to capital and labor invested in farm production has made it exceedingly difficult for most farmers to compete successfully. A primary reason for these historically low returns to farm investments has been an over-allocation of resources to

Figure 3: A Simple System of the Relationship Between Public
Policy, Technology, and Farm Structure.

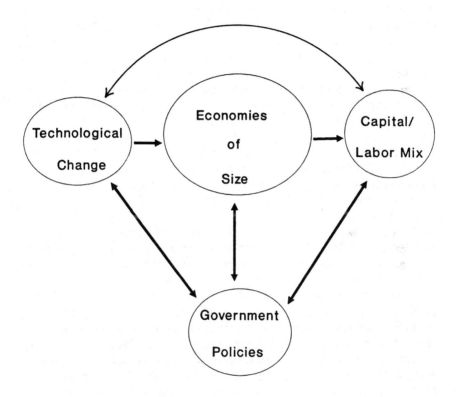

farming. Thus, there has been an historic tendency for farmers to produce more than the market can bear. That is, farms tend to overproduce for markets characterized by inelastic demand.

One way farmers have reacted to these generally unfavorable production conditions is to expand the scale of their farm operations. While such a decision appears to be rational at the individual farm level as declining profit margins make it necessary to expand in order to increase farm income, at the aggregate level such expansion contributes once again to overproduction. Since land is relatively fixed and domestic and international demand is unlikely to keep pace with technologically induced supply, those farmers who are unable to expand their scale often leave production entirely or else enter into part-time farming. Expansion of farm scale without the introduction of production technologies could have occurred with greater inputs of hired labor, which occurred in some manufacturing sectors. However, the scarcity of labor and land created a demand for the development of technologies to extend the productivity of limited resources, and both private and public research and development efforts have responded with an impressive array of resource-saving agricultural technologies. Ruttan's (1982) articulation of induced innovations provides a more detailed discussion of this process.

Technological changes have increased productivity in the production of food. What does this mean? Increases in productivity enable farmers to change resource mixes in such a fashion that they can produce more output per unit of input (or cost). Thus, since agriculture is a relatively competitive industry, profit margins per unit of output decline, and farmers are forced to expand in output (by increasing farm size) in order to receive the same income. Technology that is labor saving, land saving, and capital using has been responsible for these changes in productivity. Machinery has reduced the amount of labor necessary in many farming operations enabling one worker to farm more land or manage more livestock. Chemicals, plant breeding, and other biological technologies have increased the amount of crops or livestock that can be obtained from an acre of land. As a result, technological change has increased economies of size—per unit costs of production decline as farm size increases.

Technological innovations provided an impetus for farm expansion. Yet, other factors had to be in place in order for this expansion to occur. Adoption of new technologies only occurs if a variety of institutions are in place. Since investments in new technologies require large amounts of capital, readily available credit is necessary before farmers will adopt new technologies. Without the passage of the Federal Land Bank Act of 1916, agricultural credit would not have been as accessible, and the technological revolution in U.S. agriculture would have been slowed considerably. Since many of the new technologies of the twentieth century replaced labor, job opportunities in nonfarm activities were needed before much of the transformation in U.S. agriculture could occur. In areas of the country where off-farm job opportunities were not available, adjustments were slowed. Such is the case for much of the Appalachian region where small farms are still dominant. Although farmers in this region receive a low labor income from farming, they have relatively few off-farm activities that will give them a higher wage. Even those farmers who find off-farm employment in this region generally continue to depend upon a limited farm income.

In addition to credit policies and rural development, other government activities influence technological adoption. Adoption of most technologies necessarily means a change in the capital to labor mix. Therefore, any government policy that influences the relative costs of these inputs should also influence the adoption of new technologies. For example, federal tax laws provide a number of incentives to invest in capital-intensive technologies, espeically labor-saving technologies such as tractorsand combines. Investment tax credits, rapid depreciation, interest write-offs for borrowed money, etc., all reduce the after-tax cost of capital. On the other hand, employers are required to pay Social Security taxes for hired labor. In addition, there are other government regulations regarding hired labor. These laws increase the relative cost of labor to capital and, thus, encourage adoption of labor-saving technologies and influence the capital/labor ratio in U.S. agriculture.

There are other reasons why farmers choose capital investments over labor. Labor may be more difficult to manage than capital. Labor may be less dependable than capital. Since much farm work is seasonal, farmers may not be able to assure a hired laborer of full time work. Thus, it is difficult to maintain continuity in hired labor. Training new employees is costly. In addition, timeliness of planting and harvest can be improved with capital. This means that risk of production can be reduced with capital investments.

Another factor that influences adoption of machinery technology is the topography of a region. Many of the large machines used in modern agriculture are unsuitable for the very hilly areas in the Appalachian states (Virginia, West Virginia, North Carolina, Kentucky, and Tennessee) and parts of the Piedmont areas of the Carolinas. These regions have a large concentration of small farms. Clearly, the topography of these regions has constrained farm expansion through adoption of machinery technology.

Other barriers to the adoptions of certain types of agricultural technologies include the poor development of internal markets, particularly the absence of good roads to get produce to central markets. Furthermore, personal characteristics such as low education, a consequence of the slow social development of many areas of the rural South, reduced the readiness with which some farmers could take advantage of new information.

The continuous technological changes in farming have been associated with changes in the farm labor processes and the ability of some farms to stay in production. Cochrane (1979:393) sums up this process for American farmers in terms of a "technological treadmill":

> We know now why farmers adopt new and improved technologies and expand their output even though they complain of low product prices and rising input prices. They do so (in part) because each farmer sees the adoption of a new and improved technology as a means of either increasing his profits or reducing his losses. But in a competitive situation, with many producers, there is no way that an individual farmer can hold onto himself the short-run gains from the adoption of new and improved technology. Such income gains are lost to him in the long run through the competitive process. They are lost in a free-market situation through falling product prices. They are lost in a price-supported situation through rising prices of the fixed factors—typically land.

Thus, with each new technology, those farmers who adopt earliest are the most likely to gain the most. These farmers tend to have the best access to information or capital. They also tend to operate the largest farms. Nonadoption or late adoption does not necessarily indicate a lack of innovation, but it is often a function of limited access to capital and information, relatively small scale, or any combination of these factors. Farm numbers in the United States have been reduced by roughly four million since the end of World War II. It is safe to say that many of these farmers did not leave farming because they were bad farmers, but because they did not have the resources necessary to stay on the technological treadmill.

Influence of Government Policies on the Supply
and Demand of New Technology

Government polices also influence the development of technologies in very important ways. Besides the obvious involvement of government- supported research and development and education through the agricultural Extension service and the agricultural research complex, government policies influence the market or the demand for new technologies. When government policies provide incentives for the adoption of technologies (such as those discussed above), producers of technologies will have additional incentives. Patent laws that protect those who invent new technologies can encourage development of new technologies.

Price supports that provide protection against low prices also reduce risk and encourage investment in new technologies. On the other hand, some government policies may hamper the production of technology. Price supports that are based upon cost of production or parity reduce the need to develop new technologies that will reduce cost of production. Also, price supports that rely on supply control in order to keep price high will hamper technological innovation. In other words, if the government supports profit margins at relatively constant returns per unit of output, incentives to reduce per unit cost of production will be reduced. Government supply control and price support policies in the tobacco sector are at least partially responsible for the fact that technological development has been slow (i.e., burley tobacco production remains a highly labor intensive activity).

Government Policies that Influence
Farm Structure

There are also government policies that influence the structure of agriculture with little influence on technology. These political decisions have not been made in a sociopolitical vacuum. Rather, each of the many factions within agriculture campaign for their particular interests, which often are in conflict with other factions. The relative political power of each group mediates the degree to which final farm policies facilitate their interests. Furthermore, each succession of farm policies reflect the legacy of past attempts to reduce market uncertainty during previous periods of farm financial crisis.

The economic and political conflict over farm policies has been ubiquitous during the past century. Much of this conflict and compromise has centered upon the reduction of uncertainty and the enhancement of profits.

> Just as during the Progressive Era many industries called for order and advocated federal rules to rationalize enterprise, farmers by the end of the 1920s, after unsuccessful farm movements, cooperatives, and political lobbying, demanded that the federal government bring order to the chaos of rollercoaster prices that charted the peaks and valleys of supply and demand. The advocates of rural change reflected no more upon long-range human displacement than did the captains of industry; each wanted an efficient operation that depended more upon the regularity of machines and federal guidelines than on the whims of workers and the marketplace. (Daniel, 1985:xiii)

Perhaps the most influential among these policies were the farm programs embodied in the Agricultural Adjustment Acts of the New Deal. Among these programs, a principal policy mechanism for improving farm income was the control of overproduction through supply management.

Supply control policies that are used to increase price are usually designed in such a fashion that allotments are allocated to farmers that have been involved in the production of the particular good for a period of time. Thus, these allotments take on a monetary value that is usually reflected in land prices. Therefore, in addition to an artificially high price, farmers who own land will gain in wealth because of government action. This combination of factors can retard the exodus of small farms in some areas. On the other hand, when price supports are not tied to allotments, it can be argued that, over time, they contribute to the trend toward larger and fewer farms. To the extent that price supports are bid into asset values, they cause asset values to be overpriced for new farmers. Existing farmers use the current operation to finance purchases from exiting farmers. Thus, the trend toward larger and fewer farms is exacerbated. Also, price supports are tied to output. Therefore, larger farms receive more of the benefits than smaller farms. Yet, it can also be argued that, in the shorter run, commodity programs (price supports) slow the exodus of smaller farms that are inefficient. When prices are supported at levels that are higher than market conditions (i.e., both opportunity and real cost of production) will justify, then smaller farms are protected longer from those market conditions. Eventually, such protection must give way to the financial stress that accompanies the overvalued asset values (i.e., as producers leave farming, only those with existing assets can afford to cash flow the new purchase).

In the 1950s and 1960s, commodity programs provided a great deal of price stability. There is much disagreement regarding the implications of price stability on farm structure. Those who believe that stable prices contribute to the trend toward larger and fewer farms argue that reduced risk encourages capital investments and, thus, farm growth. Those who believe farms grow more during periods of price instability argue that farmers must seek tax shelters when they receive extraordinarily high prices. Therefore, they will chase more land and machinery than they might if they had an equal but steady long-run average income. In addition, price instability increases financial risk. As financial risk increases, odds of farm failure increase. As farms fail, existing farms are the most likely candidates to purchase them. Roughly two-thirds of the agricultural land that is sold in the U.S. is purchased by existing farmers. The current financial problems in U.S. agriculture are largely due to false price expectations on both agricultural commodities and assets that were developed during the 1970s. Farms that expanded rapidly during this period are now struggling to survive. Larger farming operations that are currently not experiencing debt problems will be the dominant beneficiaries as these farms fail. Knowledge of debt load by farm size is critical to understanding the implications of the current financial problems on future agricultural structure.

In addition to the direct government involvement in commodity programs and credit assistance programs, many macroeconomic policies influence the structure of U.S. agriculture. Tax policies have encouraged farm expansion beyond levels that a market system would have. Monetary and fiscal policies have influenced the financial environment in which farmers operate. Macroeconomic policies of the 1970s, which were directed most toward reducing unemployment, led to low real cost of interest (i.e., the difference between interest rates and inflation rates), high rates of inflation, and low value of the dollar (which expanded international trade). Negative real rates of interest and high rates of asset inflation plus a growing export market contributed to the farm expansions that occurred in the 1970s.

Macroeconomic policies of the 1980s which were directed most toward reducing inflation rates, led to high real cost of interest, lower inflation rates, and high value of the dollar. This interaction of market forces is largely responsible for the reductions in farm asset values, which have increased the cash flow and long term financial problems facing farmers. In short, once U.S. agriculture entered heavily into world trade in the early 1970s, the farming sector became extremely vulnerable to U.S. macroeconomic policy. Such policy may now be more critical to long run farm structure than traditional commodity and credit programs.

The Interaction Between Commodity Programs and Technology

In the absence of commodity programs, economic theory provides some insight into whether farmers or consumers will benefit from technological advancements. To the extent that the demand for a particular agricultural commodity is inelastic (i.e., small changes in output lead to greater changes in price), total revenue will be less when the supply curve shifts to the right due to technological advances. Therefore, if the change in total revenue is greater than the change in total cost (which occurs because of the technological change), then, in the aggregate, farmers will be harmed at the expenses of consumers. Such conditions would be more common than situations where the reduction in total costs is greater than the reduction in total revenue. Of course, farmers who are early adopters of the technology will benefit despite the fact that in the aggregate farmers would lose.

Figure 4.a illustrates the influence of technology-induced supply shifts on the total revenue of producers in the absence of price supports. Before the supply shift, the total revenue is the area in the rectangle *abco*. After the supply shift, the total revenue is the area in the rectangle *defo*. Since the area *dxco* is

Figure 4a: Influence of Technology Induced Supply Shift on Total Revenue Without Price Support

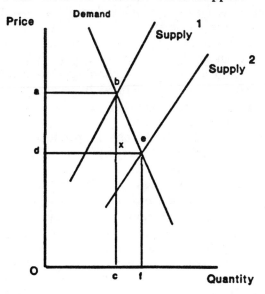

Figure 4b: Influence of Technology Induced Supply Shift on Total Revenue With Price Suppport.

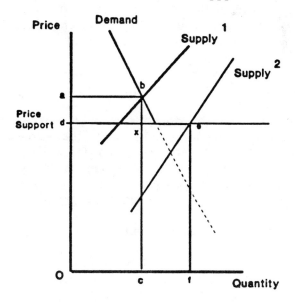

contained in both sets of revenues and it is clear that the area *abxd* is less than *cfex*, then it is also clear that total revenue (area *defo*) after the supply shift is less than total revenue (area *abco*) before the supply shift.

Figure 4.b considers the case where the government supports the price at a level that is higher than what a new market price would be after a technology-induced supply shift. The price support level is a political decision (the level for this illustration was arbitrarily chosen). In this case, the demand curve becomes perfectly elastic at the price support (i.e., government will purchase all that is produced at that price). Therefore, the total revenue is greater after the supply shift (by the same reasoning as presented above, the area *cfex* is greater than the area *abxd*). Although the likelihood that the government could sustain a price support at this level is questionable, it is clear that farmers will gain in two ways from the technology shift as long as government price supports remain above what would be a market clearing level (as presented in Figure 4.a): (1) total revenue will increase, and (2) total cost will decrease. The competitive nature of the farming sector is such that this type of increase in net income will be bid into asset values (primarily land prices). Again, it can be argued that government programs would have to adjust. Yet, lags would likely be involved with this adjustment, and as long as the adjustment is not too severe, the next technologically induced shift in the supply curve will offset the adjustment. Therefore, farmers will very likely gain in the aggregate when technology-induced supply shifts occur for price-supported commodities. And landowners will gain even more since these gains are bid into asset values.

These arguments are strengthened with further insight into likely government behavior to respond to the increase in supply. Historically, the government has been more likely to impose supply control programs rather than reduce the price support. Since most supply control programs involve some type of allotment system, such policy provides even greater gains to landowners.

The interaction between commodity programs and technological changes reinforces those who argue that government programs accelerate the trend toward larger and fewer farms over a longer period of time. Further, from a policy perspective, it provides evidence of how commodity programs have contributed to the current cash flow problems in U.S. farming, as these problems are due to the fact that asset values become overvalued in terms of what they can return. Such a cash flow problem increases the vulnerability of farmers who have used credit extensively for expansion. Therefore, although commodity programs may slow the exodus of some farmers (i.e., those unable to leverage assets and acquire additional debt), in the aggregate, *commodity programs have facilitated the dual structural distribution* by encouraging farmers with larger operations to expand and by providing profit margins suitable to maintain smaller farms that have off-farm income.

Technology, Policy And Markets:
Possible Scenarios for Southern Farms

Previous discussions have provided a foundation for assessing the role of history, technology, policy, and markets in the future of farm structure in the South. This section highlights critical technologies, policies, and market forces that will shape the six dominant types of Southern farms. Although a focus on farm types is somewhat limited in terms of a full consideration of how production patterns may change in the South, it does provide a nice tie to the emerging technologies. In the Schertz book **Another Revolution in U.S. Farming?**, McArthur (1979:303-304) summarizes the trends in Southern farms:

New patterns of structure and organization appear possible for Southern farms of the future. The emerging pattern appears to be: (1) a relatively large number of small farms (essentially part-time and part-retirement farms); (2) an increasing number of large to very large farms operated under a corporate or partnership form of organization. Small farms benefit from the growth of off-farm employment opportunities in the South. Present economic conditions and those being projected for the future enhance chances for survival of large farms, in contrast to the traditional medium-sized family farm.

In recent years, such a dual structural trend has existed. In fact, policies that would reverse the trend are extremely unlikely since, such policies would require a political movement to redistribute wealth on a scale that would dwarf the New Deal. Further, policies that would maintain the current structure would also require major political action. Therefore, this section focuses on three more likely scenarios: (1) maintaining the current trends, (2) slowing the current trends, and (3) accelerating the current trends. No attempt is made to quantify probable future farm structures for the South. Rather, qualitative assessments are developed.

Farm Change in Southern Beef Farms

Beef farms (excluding feedlots) comprise 33 percent of the total farm numbers in the South. Yet, 86 percent of the farms are extremely small (i.e., total farms sales of less than $10,000). In fact, over 28 percent of the farms in the South are beef farms with sales of less than $10,000. Therefore, in terms of farm numbers, the Southern beef sector provides the greatest potential for change. Why have Southern beef farms remained so small? It has been argued that beef farming is a consumption good. Part-time farmers enjoy the lifestyle associated with raising a few beef cattle. If this is true, then it is likely that tax laws also play a role. Beef cattle raised for breeding purposes can be counted as capital gains income. This provides a tax shelter for those who wish to raise a few beef cattle in a leisurely manner. Consequently, the repeal of capital gains tax treatment for beef producers may result in a significant loss of farms. However, it is unlikely that beef farmers exiting from farming in the South will suffer seriously from this structural adjustment, particularly if these farmers are using beef as a tax shelter for substantial off-farm income or if they farm as a hobby.

Most of the beef operations in the South are cow-calf farms depend heavily upon pasture. Therefore, emerging technologies that will increase beef cattle forage utilization obtained from grazing present potential change. Such technologies could increase the comparative advantage of beef for the Southern region versus other parts of the country. This would also potentially provide incentives for Southern beef farmers to expand their herd size. However, using the argument that the smallest farmers are slowest at adopting new technologies raises some doubt regarding how much herd expansion will occur. Further, it may be the mid-sized farms that adopt this new technology. Thus, such emerging technologies also have the potential to slow the current trends in Southern farm structure. On the other hand, embryo transplant technology will very likely be adopted by the largest beef producers.

Farm Change in Southern Tobacco Farms

Tobacco farms comprise nearly 21 percent of the farms in the South. Future government supply control and pricing policies should play a role in the future structure of these tobacco farms. Two types of tobacco dominate: (1) flue-cured tobacco in the Carolinas, and (2) burley tobacco in Kentucky and surrounding states. Both programs now allow for intra-county leasing of tobacco quota allotments. Before this program change, only owners of a quota could grow tobacco. Thus, since tobacco production has been extremely labor intensive, there was little incentive for labor-saving technologies at least among smaller operations. Flue-cured leasing occurred a decade before burley (1961 versus 1971), and labor-saving technological development in flue-cured production is probably that many years ahead of burley. Although it can be argued that other factors had a significant influence on this technological development, the leasing change was also a factor. The design of supply control programs can alter the demand for technological development.

Since flue-cured tobacco production has largely gone to labor-saving technology, the number of quota holders who grow their quota has declined dramatically (i.e., the economies of size are such that tobacco growers expand their operation by leasing quotas). The burley belt continues to have a larger share of quota holders who grow their quota (one-half versus one-quarter). Thus, one impact of elimination of the supply control provisions of the tobacco program would likely be an increased demand for labor-saving technologies. Over time, such technologies would contribute to concentration in the production of tobacco and increases in farm size. This would be more the case in the burley belt than in the flue-cured region. Yet, shifts in production of flue-cured tobacco could be expected. The topography of the Carolinas is such that the eastern sections are more suitable for machine harvest than the western regions. With the elimination of county-restricted quotas, flue-cured production may move to the eastern sections.

In short, elimination of the supply control provisions of the tobacco program would likely cause a restructuring of tobacco production as new technologies are adopted. To the extent that off-farm jobs are available, producers with small farms would be even more likely to cease tobacco production. In those regions where off-farm jobs were not available, producers with small farms would be forced to accept a lower return on their labor to compete with farmers using labor-saving technology. Thus, the two largest factors in determining how tobacco will change farm structure in the South are the tobacco program and local job opportunities.

Cash Grain Farms in the South

Three cash grains dominate: soybeans, corn, and rice. Each of these has different government programs and markets. In total, cash grain farms account for roughly 16 percent of the farms. Cash grain production in the South is generally less concentrated than in the rest of the U.S. (the notable exception is rice production, which is more heavily concentrated). In fact, 46 percent of the cash grain farms are quite small (i.e., sales of less than $10,000 in 1982).

Two emerging technologies that should influence the structure of cash grain farms are pest control and biotechnologies. Since the South is more vulnerable to pests, breakthroughs in pest control could increase the South's competitive position vis-a-vis other regions (Office of Technology Assessment). Large farms would very likely be the beneficiaries of such breakthroughs. This would also be true for any breakthroughs in biotechnology. Since there are a larger number of small grain farms in the South than in the remainder of the U.S., such technological developments have more potential to change farm structure.

Given that the outlook for grain production is highly dependent upon international markets, U.S. international trade policy and macroeconomic policy will play a major role in the future of grain production. In the unlikely event that a resurgence of world demand for grain occurs, production in the South would increase. Government programs that reduce interest rates and, thus, the value of the dollar are key elements to such a resurgence.

Finally, changes in commodity programs could also change the structure of cash grain farms. More reliance on supply control programs would facilitate maintenance of the current structural trends. Continuation of high price supports and target prices (relative to world markets) should accelerate the current trends. And elimination of or sharp reductions in price support levels would reduce the number of small farms and eventually, because of the asset value relationships, reduce the rate of concentration of the largest farms. This might mean that mid-sized farms will not disappear as fast.

Poultry Production in the South

Unlike beef and cash grain farms, poultry is already a highly concentrated industry. Rogers (1979:148-149) has summarized the poultry and egg industry as follows:

> [The] typical commercial poultry farms are large, and many exceed one-man size. Depending on the degree of mechanization and production practices, one man-year of labor is required per 20,000 to 25,000 laying hens, each 4.5 to 5 batches of 30,000 to 50,000 broilers, or each 10,000 to 30,000 turkeys per year in several batches.... Today's poultry and egg industries involve an extensive network of linkages which have developed between production units and input supplying and marketing functions.

The poultry and egg industry, then, is not only highly concentrated but it also is vertically integrated into larger agribusiness firms.

The structural characteristics of poultry and egg operations vary by region and scale of operation. However, two types appear to be dominant: (1) industrial-type farms, and (2) propertied laborer farms. Heffernan (1984) has examined the poultry operations among the delta states in some detail. He describes highly vertically integrated operations on which the operator may not be the owner and on which there is a relatively large number of hired workers. Davis (1980) describes a similarly vertically integrated operation, but it is one with a single operator. He refers to this type of farm structure as a "propertied laborer," since the operator may own the land and buildings but does not own the chicks and hens and is expected under contract to follow strict, prespecified management procedures. These farms tend to be smaller than the industrial-type farms.

The poultry and egg industry in 1982 accounted for 24.4 percent of the region's gross sales but only 4.1 percent of all farms. Approximately 62.2 percent of the farms had sales greater than $100,000, while only 7.4 percent of the farms reported sales of less than $10,000. While these figures do suggest a great deal of concentration already exists, there is still room for further decreases in farm numbers and increases in farm scale. Among farms with more than $100,000 in sales, only 11.1 percent have sales of $500,000 or more. It is conceivable, given the Office of Technology Assessment's projections for changes in poultry and other animal research, that increased efficiencies may be achieved.

It is likely that the "disappearing middle" phenomenon will continue to characterize the poultry and egg farm industry change. With such a small proportion of poultry and egg farms in the highest sales categories, it is possible that medium-sized farms ($100,000 to $499,999 in sales) will be reduced in proportion to the very large operations ($500,000 or more). However, it is also possible that the very smallest farms will find it difficult to compete with the very largest farms as well, and they may also find it increasingly difficult to arrange vertical contracts with poultry agribusiness firms. It should be noted that these are only qualitative estimates based upon past trends.

Dairy Farms in the South

Dairy farms in the South comprise approximately 3 percent of the farm numbers and account for 9 percent of the total value of agricultural products sold. The dairy farm structure is dominated by mid-sized farms. A dual structural trend is highly unlikely. Instead, the emerging technologies (bovine hormones, computer assisted management, etc.) are likely to favor the larger farms. Dairy commodity policy will play a major role as well. As program price supports are reduced, smaller farms will lose their competitive position. Therefore, most of the foreseeable changes in dairy policy will contribute to farm concentration.

Cotton Production in the South

Cotton production is primarily concentrated in the Mississippi Delta region (Tennessee, Arkansas, Mississippi, and Louisiana) though all of the South Atlantic states report some cotton sales. Since the Civil War, cotton production has tended to shift westward in order to take advantage of more fertile soils while reducing pest damage (Mann, 1984; Starbird, 1984). For the cotton-growing states in this region in 1982, 41.6 percent of the cotton farms had sales of $100,000 or more, and only 19.9 percent reported sales of less that $10,000. Throughout the region only 1.2 percent of the farms rely on cotton for at least 50 percent of their gross sales, and cotton accounts for only 5.2 percent of the South's gross agricultural sales.

As with poultry, cotton production is primarily concentrated on medium- and large-scale operations. Therefore, the trend toward a disappearing middle will apply only to the medium-sized farms. There will likely be no increase among small cotton producers. However, the potential loss of medium-sized farms is considerable. Approximately 43 percent of all cotton farms reported gross sales between $40,000 and $249,999. Emerging cotton technologies are likely to facilitate productivity, thus contributing to the continued concentration of cotton production.

Historically, government farm programs have influenced cotton prices and production (see Starbird, 1984 for an excellent short review of government cotton programs). Generally, recent participants in the cotton program have benefited, both directly from price supports and direct payments and indirectly through higher market prices. However, the "longer term effects of farm programs on the well-being of farmers and the cotton industry are still unclear" (Starbird, 1984:25).

Methods And Analysis Of Farm Structure And Community Well-Being

Variables and Models

The data analysis *first* examines how agricultural technologies are associated with farm structure and *second* how farm structure is associated with community well-being. The models of farm structure and community well-being are designed to test much of the proceeding conceptual framework.

While this research tests the general proposition of the Goldschmidt (1978) hypothesis, the unit of analysis not the *community*, per se. This is an important difference between this study and Goldschmidt's examination of Arvin and Dinuba. A county may have many different communities within it that have great differences in the degree of their dependence upon farming. Such an aggregation bias is inherent when using county as a unit of analysis. Unfortunately, there are no secondary data sources at the community level for farm structure, community well-being, and the necessary control variables. Therefore, the empirical portion of this report will examine *county* farm structure and well-being. It is important, then, that the reader keep this distinction between the study's unit of analysis and its concept of community in mind when interpreting the results and making assessments for the future. However, because the county is the smallest aggregation of data available, and since we are using it as a general indicator of community, we will, at time, use the term community when focused upon conceptual issues.

The data for this study were taken from three reliable and well-documented sources: the Census of Population, the Census of Agriculture, and the **County, City Data Book**. Twelve farm-related and nine community-related variables were employed. Table 1 lists the variables used in this report, along with their operational definitions.

Data were analyzed in two stages. First, cross-sectional linear regression models were constructed and their results analyzed for 1969/70 and 1978/80 for farm structure and community well-being. Second, the ways in which these models changed for the two points in time were analyzed. For this second stage, an additional control variable was included, the 1969/70 value of the dependent variable. This control permits the researcher to estimate the importance of uneven development while simultaneously controlling for the dependent variable's value at the first point in time. Such a control is mandatory for this type of panel analysis (Kessler and Greenberg, 1982).

It should be noted that these models utilize statistical techniques based upon the assumptions of ordinary least squares. In other words, the statistical techniques only assess linear relationships unless otherwise specified. However, by using a quadratic equation it is possible to test for MacCannell and Dolber-Smith (1985) hypothesis of an inverted "U" relationship between farm concentration and community well-being. This is accomplished statistically by including the squared value of the appropriate independent variable—in this case average farm scale. Only one of the dependent variables—percent of the labor force that is unemployed—was substantively associated with the quadratic equation of average farm scale. The use of a quadratic equation represents a test of an alternative hypothesis to that offered by Goldschmidt.

It is very important to note that none of the farm structure and community well-being models in the following analysis are fully specified. Indeed, each type is missing empirical measures of key concepts. Consequently, there are deficiencies. For example, among the farm structure models, there are no data available at the county level from the Census of Agriculture on debt-asset ratio. Clearly, the importance of this type of ratio for estimating the economic and structural viability of farming and the likelihood of major structural change are critical. Furthermore, there were no data available for farm prices and demand. In other words, the farm structure models do not contain essential information on the farm marketplace. Similarly, county data on important sociological characteristics such as class structure, level of community voluntarism, and dependence upon federal transfer payments are not included.

Another problem of specification is the absence of subregional controls. To a greater extent than other studies of this task force, the South is characterized by multiple geographical and economic regions. This region contains the traditionally poor Appalachian counties, the Piedmont of the Southeastern states, the coastal plains from North Carolina to Mississippi, and the delta region of the Mississippi River (see Figure 1). The empirical results must be interpreted as being Southern associations. Considerable internal variation can exist while being suppressed in aggregate analysis such as this. Therefore, the reader must be careful to interpret the findings as regional associations that may not be generally inferred to specific local conditions.

Table 1, presented earlier, provides a list of all the variables to be used and their operational definitions. Table 7 presents the means for each of these variables for 1970 and 1980 as well as for their change between these two points in time.

The Present Study

The purpose of this study is *first* to assess the association of selective farm variables with general measures of farm structure in order to determine the influence of past technological conditions and change on farm structure. *Second*, the association of farm structure with county well-being is examined while controlling for potential nonfarm economic and social influences. This second phase of the analysis is a general test of the Goldschmidt hypothesis since indicators of farm structure are included in three different models of county well-being. Therefore, this study includes five dependent variables: *farm structure* (1) farm size in gross sales and (2) farm numbers; and *community well-being* (1) level of unemployment, (2) median family income, and (3) percent of families below poverty.

As noted above, two cross-sectional analyses are used to determine how the independent variables are associated with the dependent variables in 1970 and 1980. The second phase of this research design not only tests the Goldschmidt hypothesis at two points in time for the South, but also permits the analysis of how change in farm structure is associated with change in county well-being, controlling for several nonfarm economic variables. Goldschmidt did not empirically examine how farm change influences community well-being over time. Furthermore, by incorporating a quadratic equation we also were able to test the MacCannell and Dolber-Smith hypothesis (see Chapter 2 by MacCannell).

Finally, we use point elasticisties which are computed from multiple regression analyses. This permits us to estimate, given measurement error, the degree to which each dependent variable is associated with each independent and control variable. A point elasticity provides for a focus on percentage changes at the mean values for all other variables. In a simple linear model where:

$y = a + bx,$

the percentage change in y with respect to x is calculated by taking the partial derivative of y with respect to x and multiplying by the ratio of the mean values:

the point elasticity = b (x/y).

The point elasticity represents the percentage response in the dependent variable as the explanatory variable is increased by one percent. All other variables are maintained at their mean values. Thus, larger point elasticities represent stronger relationships between the dependent and independent variables. Point elasticities are use because we feel this gives both the academic and lay reader a better understanding of the relative strengths of association. Each of the remaining Figures present these point elasticities as bar graphs.

Technology and Farm Structure Models

A central objective of the OTA task force is the assessment of how farm technological change influences farm structure. Farm structure is a somewhat nebulous concept. In this research it refers to various dimensions of farm economic and social organization that provide general indicators of workplace organization, factors of production such as technology and nonfamily labor, and the potential for capturing economies related to scale.

Four models are used to examine the relative influences of farm technology and farm workplace structure on farm scale and change in farm numbers. Specifically, this study examines the average gross farm sales of Southern rural counties for 1969 (see Figure 5), 1978 (see Figure 6), and change between 1969 and 1978 (see Figure 7), as well as the change in farm numbers for the same decade (see Figure 8). Each model has four independent variables representing farm technology and farm workplace structure: *farm technology* a) land-saving technologies, b) investment in machinery (labor-saving technologies); and *farm workplace* a) nonfamily labor, b) full ownership. The percent of a county's farms that are small is included as a control variable—adjusting for any skewed distribution according to acreage.

Figures 5 and 6 examine farm size for 1969 and 1978, respectively. The data suggest substantive differences for these two points in time. Both land-saving technologies and nonfamily labor were somewhat important in 1969 but not in 1978 in explaining average farm size. Moreover, while investment in machinery—land-saving technologies—were also somewhat important in 1969 both gain substantially in importance by 1978.

Each is conceptually significant. It has been asserted by land-saving technologies are not as important as they once were in facilitating the increase in farm concentration (see OTA, 1986). However, for the South between 1969 and 1978 our measure of labor-saving technology suggests an increase in importance. In 1978 (Figure 6) every increase of $1,200 in machinery was associated with approximately a one percent increase in scale. During this decade, full-ownership among Southern farms declined. This is as expected, indicating that as Southern farms have become more concentrated the number that are fully-owned has declined. An ancillary interpretation is that as concentration has increased, the financial autonomy of the owner has eroded.

Figures 7 and 8 examine which factors have been most influential in determining change in farm size and farm numbers, respectively. Figure 7 is particularly interesting because of the influence of labor-saving technologies. In all other change models the most highly associated variable is the control

288

Figure 5: Association of Farm Size with Technology Variables in 1969.

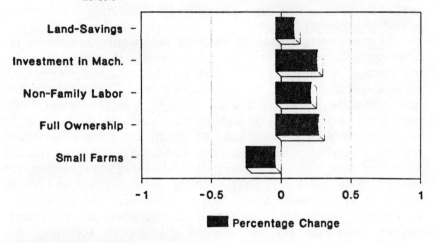

1969 Census of Agriculture
All Variables Significant at 10% Level
Explained Variance is 64% (R squared)

Figure 6: Association of Farm Size with Technological Variables in 1978.

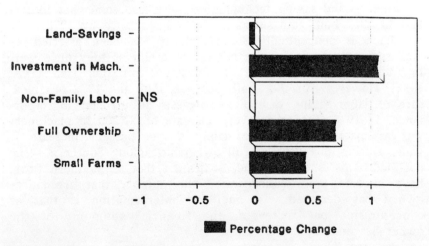

1978 Census of Agriculture
NS - Not Significant at the 10% Level
Explained Variance is 72% (R squared)

Figure 7: Association of Change in Farm Size with Changes in Technology, 1969-1978.

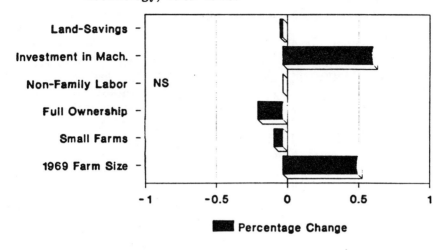

Change= 1978 - 1969 Census of Agri.
NS - Not Significant at the 10% Level
Explained Variance is 71% (R squared)

Figure 8: Association of Change in Farm Numbers with Changes in Technology, 1969-1978.

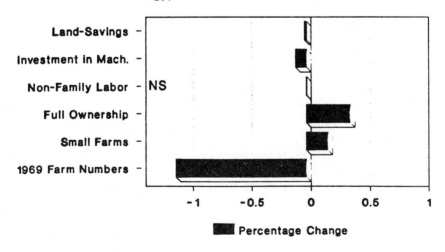

Change= 1978 - 1969 Census of Agri.
NS - Not Significant at the 10% Level
Explained Variance is 79% (R squared)

variable for the first point in time. In Figure 7 this is not the case. Labor-saving technology is the single most important factor influencing the increase in farm size between 1969 and 1978.

The model for change in farm numbers does not indicate a strong association with labor-saving technologies. Therefore, it is inaccurate to say that the farm mechanization has caused the *loss* of farm numbers for this decade. Rather, it is more accurate to state that the erosion of full-ownership that is associated with farm decline. This finding should be interpreted as the loss of family farms has also lead to a loss in farm numbers, or, more bluntly, it is the full-owner family farm in the South that is declining rapidly.

These models suggest that labor-saving, but not land-saving, technologies had a substantive influence on the trend toward larger-scale farms in the South between 1969 and 1978. Moreover, these changes were accompanied by a decline in farm numbers that was most strongly associated with a decline in full-ownership. In short, the decade of the 1970s saw Southern agriculture follow the same course of structural change as the Northeast and Midwest experienced several decades earlier.

Farm Structure and Community Well-being

The analysis of how farms and rural communities are associated with one another appear in Figures 9 through 12. These nine models represent each of the three dependent variables noted above for 1970, 1980, and change between 1970 and 1980. Each of the six cross-sectional models have the same independent variables and control variables. The three change models have these variables as well as a control variable for the dependent variables 1970 value—the initial point in time.

There are four farm structural variables, each tapping a different dimension: 1) farm size (gross sales), 2) proportion of small farms, 3) part-time farming, and 4) the proportion of the rural population that are in farming. Six nonfarm variables are used: the percent of the county's workforce employed (1) in manufacturing and (2) in service industries, (3) the county's proximity to metropolitan areas, (4) the percent of the county that is Black, (5) the percent of the county's adult population (aged 25 and over) that finished high school, and (6) the percent of the county's labor force commuting to work outside the county.

Chapter 1 of this book reviews the literature on farm and community change in some detail, so it will not be reiterated at this time. The central assumption, most articulately put forward by Walter Goldschmidt, is that farm well-being determines community well-being, *and furthermore*, that industrial agriculture will adversely affect rural communities while family farms will be beneficial. If the Goldschmidt hypothesis is correct for both cross-sectional analyses, average farm size will be positively associated with the level of unemployment and the level of poverty but negatively associated with median family income. However, the opposite association will be expected for the indicators of small farm concentration and the rural population's dependency on farming. In the case of the change models, the Goldschmidt hypothesis predicts that change in farm numbers should be positively associated with change in the median family income and negatively associated with change in the level of unemployment and poverty. Finally, the quality of life models for unemployment and poverty will have as an independent variable the level of unemployment.

Goldschmidt does not directly address the phenomenon of part-time farming. However, Swanson's (1982) study of Pennsylvania as well as the work of Bonanno (1985) suggests that part-time farming may be a function of nonfarm employment opportunities. Bonanno argues that part-time farming can represent a type of "welfare" function for rural areas and a labor pool for nonfarm industries. Swanson's work suggests that entry into part-time farming may slow the transition to a highly concentrated farm structure. Therefore, part-time farming is included for reasons other than the Goldschmidt hypothesis.

This study, then, attempts to go beyond the simple unidirectional effects of the Goldschmidt hypothesis by including indicators of regional economic conditions. By including four indicators of farm structure, we expect to give the Goldschmidt hypothesis a fair chance to be associated in a least one of several dimensions of farm structure.

It is also expected that the proportion of the county that is Black and the educational level of the county will also influence community well-being. Because of the history of apartheid in the South, counties with the greatest concentration of Blacks are expected to score poorly on indicators of county well-being. Similarly, those counties with low levels of education are most likely to score poorly on the well-being measures. Finally, the commuting measure was included as a control for employment

opportunities in nearby counties. As with the farm structure
models, only the most salient points are noted for the sake of
brevity.

We examined both the Goldschmidt and the MacCannell
and Dolber-Smith hypothesis. It should be recalled that while
Goldschmidt proposes a linear hypothesis, MacCannell and
Dolber-Smith argue for curvilinear relationship (see Chapter 1).
For two of the dependent variables—median family income and
percent of families below poverty—the use of a quadratic
equation made no substantive contribution to the analysis.
Therefore, we retained the linear assumptions of the Goldschmidt hypothesis, which assumes as average farm size
increases median family income will decrease while the percent
of families below poverty will increase. However, for the third
dependent variable—percent of the labor force unemployed—
there was a clear support for the MacCannell and Dolber-Smith
hypothesis. The quadratic equation was not used in the change
model since an inverted "U" relationship is not expected.

1970 Models

Figures 9.a through 9.c present the results for the cross-
sectional analysis for 1970. Average farm size is significantly
associated with each of the dependent variables. However, the
direction of each association is not in the direction anticipated
using the Goldschmidt hypothesis. Counties with larger average
scale farms were more likely to have higher levels of median
family income and lower percentage of families in poverty in
1970. Furthermore, in counties where the rural population was
more dependent upon farming, median family income was likely
to be lower.

In 1970 part-time farming were not associated with any of
the community well-being variables. The quadratic equation is
discussed below in the 1980 section in order to highlight their
differences. We will simply note here that the 1970 quadratic
for farm scale was highly associated with unemployment.

Counties with a higher proportion of their labor force in
manufacturing were likely to have lower levels of unemployment
and poverty, and higher levels of median family income. Service
industries were not associated with either poverty or unemployment, but it was negatively associated with median family
income—meaning that counties with higher proportion of the
labor force in service industries were more likely to have lower

Figure 9a: Association Between Poverty and the Independent Variables in 1970.

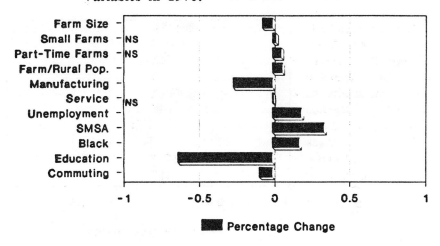

1969 for farm variables: 1970 for others
NS - Not Significant at the 10% Level
Explained Variance is 71% (R squared)

Figure 9b: Association Between Income and the Independent Variables in 1970.

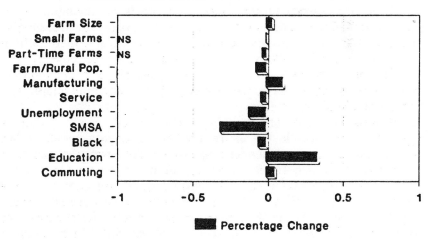

1969 for farm variables: 1970 for others
NS - Not Significant at the 10% Level
Explained Variance is 69% (R squared)

294   *THE SOUTH*

Figure 9c: Association Between Unemployment and the Independent Variables in 1970.

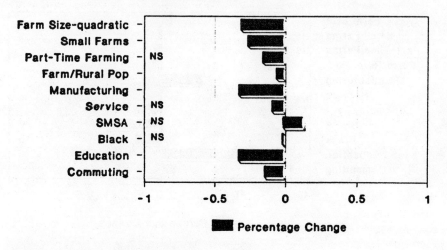

Percentage Change

1969 for farm variables: 1970 for others
NS - Not Significant at the 10% Level
Explained Variance is 29% (R squared)

levels of median family income.

Unsurprisingly, counties with high levels of unemployment, poverty is higher and income is lower. Also, unsurprisingly, counties that were at the greatest distance from metropolitan counties were more likely to have higher levels of poverty and higher unemployment. Counties with higher levels of commuters were more likely to have less poverty, lower unemployment, and higher levels of income.

It was expected that the higher the proportion of a county's population was black the more likely the county would score poorly on the three dependent variables. This was the case for poverty and median family income, but not for unemployment.

The variable that was consistently highly associated with the dependent variables was the proportion of a county's adult population that had finished high school. Indeed, it is impossible to over-emphasize its importance. Counties in which a large proportion of the adult population had not finished high school had much higher levels of poverty and unemployment and lower levels of median family income. As will be argued later, this variable offers considerable support for the notion of enhancing abilities of rural people to learn higher job skills.

1980 Models

Figures 10.a through 10.c present the results for the 1980 cross-sectional models. As with the 1970 models, the farm structure variables were either not related or only weakly related with the community well-being measures. The exception, as in 1970, was for the quadratic function of farm scale.

Figure 11 presents the curvilinear association between farm scale and unemployment for both 1970 and 1980, with the darker line representing 1970 and the lighter line 1980. While both curves were quite significant in terms of their probability, the 1970 curve is much more pronounced. Three interpretations, which are not mutually exclusive, can be made. First, for both points in time the data support the MacCannell and Dolber-Smith hypothesis of an inverted "U" association. Counties with relatively small average farm size are less likely to be associated with lower levels of unemployment than medium scale farms. Moreover, counties with very large average farm scale are likely to be associated with higher levels of unemployment, supporting the notion that large-scale farming has undesirable consequences

Figure 10a: Association Between Income and the Independent Variables for 1980.

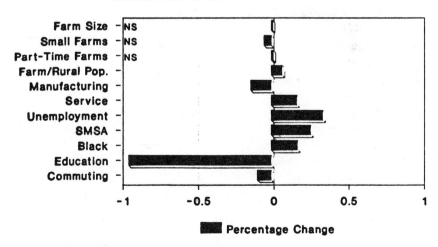

■ Percentage Change

1978 for farm variables: 1980 for others
NS - Not Significant at the 10% Level
Explained Variance is 71% (R squared)

296

Figure 10b: Association Between Income and the Independent Variables in 1980.

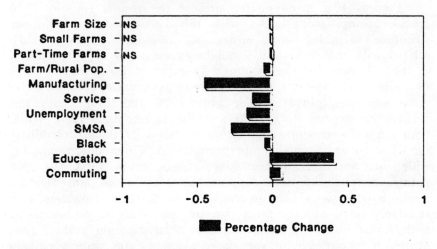

Percentage Change

1978 for farm variables: 1980 for others
NS - Not Significant at the 10% Level
Explained Variance is 61% (R squared)

Figure 10c: Association Between Unemployment and the Independent Variables in 1980.

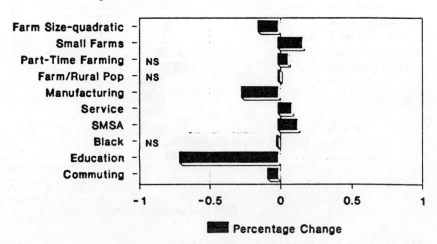

Percentage Change

1978 for farm variables: 1980 for others
NS - Not Significant at the 10% Level
Explained Variance is 29% (R squared)

Figure 11: Quadratic Relationship Between Farm Size and Unemployment for 1970 and 1980.

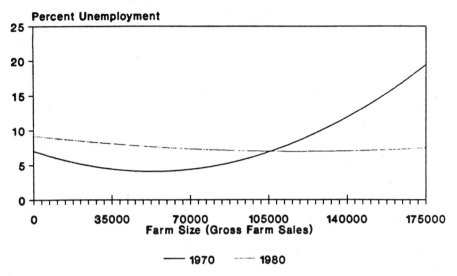

for local societies. Therefore, this finding offers some support to the argument that medium sized operations maybe the most beneficial for rural communities, even though these also may be larger-than-family operations

Second, the nadir for each point in time is different. The nadir for each line represents the average scale of farms that is most likely associated with low unemployment. In constant 1983 dollars the nadirs for 1970 and 1980 are $52,000 and $115,000, respectively. This suggests that what is a "medium-sized" farm in 1980 is considerably larger than in 1970. This finding supports the notion that the scale necessary to compete success-fully in commercial farming has been ratcheted upwards as the process of farm concentration proceeds.

Third, the seemingly weaker association for 1980 is prob-ably due to higher levels of unemployment among Southern rural counties in 1980 than in 1970. This situation creates a statistical condition in which the amount of variation in unemplyment increases the closer the region approaches full-employment. Therefore, since there was more unemployment in 1980 there was less variation. If so, then if unemployment were to decline, it is expected that the stronger association that was evident in 1970 would reemerge.

In 1980, counties with a higher proportion of their labor force in manufacturing were likely to have lower unemployment and lower poverty, but also had lower levels of median family income. This is different from 1970, and suggests that by 1980 manufacturing might keep you out of poverty but it did not promise a significantly higher standard of living. Similarly, counties with higher proportions of their labor force in service industries were likely to have lower median family incomes and higher levels of poverty and unemployment. These findings suggest that neither manufacturing nor service industries were certain keys to rural development.

In both 1970 and 1980, counties that are the farthest away from the economic sphere of influence of an SMSA were more likely to have higher levels of unemployment, lower median family income, and a higher proportion of their families in poverty. In other words, counties that are the most rural are more likely to have the lowest standard of living when these variables are used as indicators. The same patterns were found for commuting as in 1970.

As in 1970, counties with a higher percentage of Blacks had lower levels of median family income and higher levels of poverty, but was not associated with unemployment. Once again, education was the most consistent variable explaining community well-being, with the primary difference with 1970 being that the associations were *stronger*.

Change between 1970 and 1980

Figures 12a through 12c present the analysis of change between 1970 and 1980. As with the cross-sectional models, the farm structure variables do not contribute substantively to changes among the three indicators of community well-being. Change in farm numbers was only weakly associated with median family income, though this was in the expected positive direction. Farm size was associated with each of the variables, though again weakly. Counties that experienced the greatest increase in farm size were more likely to experience the greatest increase in poverty, the least in median family income, but the least in unemployment. Part-time farming was also weakly associated with each dependent variable. Counties with the greatest increase in part-time farming were more likely to have greater increase in median family income, and greater

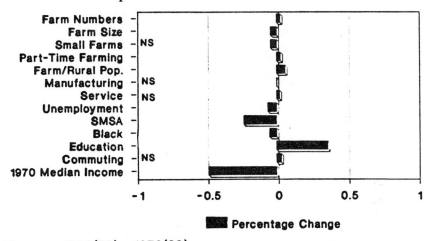

Figure 12a: Association of Income Changes with Changes in the Independent Variables.

Change = 1980(78) - 1970(69)
NS - Not Significant at the 10% Level
Explained Variance is 24% (R squared)

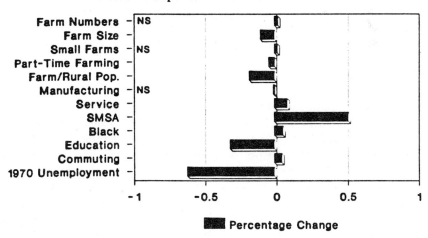

Figure 12b: Association of Unemployment Changes with Changes in the Independent Variables.

Change = 1980(78) - 1970(69)
NS - Not Significant at the 10% Level
Explained Variance is 21% (R squared)

Figure 12c: Associations of Poverty Changes with Changes in the Independent Variables.

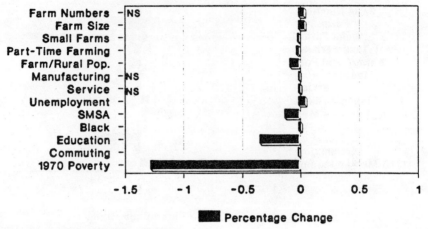

Change = 1980(78) - 1970(69)
NS - Not Significant at the 10% Level
Explained Variance is 70% (R squared)

decreases in both poverty and unemployment.

These findings, while not entirely rejecting the assumptions of the Goldschmidt hypothesis, nonetheless do not provide the type of support that was expected. The farm structural variables simply were not very important in explaining change in community well-being. Dispite the convensional wisdom that the rural South is dependent on farming, the data indicate that the influence is weak to negligible. However, the nonfarm variable did perform better.

With a single exception, change in manufacturing and service employment is not associated with change in county well-being. The exception was the association between service industries and unemployment. Counties that experienced the greatest increase in service employment were more likely to have the least improvement in unemployment. Improvements in the private sector expansion were not associated with improved indicators of community well-being, and in the case of the service sector, the association was in an undesired direction. This finding calls into question rural development efforts based simply on expanding manufacturing and service industries.

Distance from an SMSA was associated with change in all three dependent variables. The greater the distance from an

SMSA the more likely a county would experience the least improvement in poverty and median family income, while have the greatest increase in unemployment. Once again, the data suggest that those counties furthest from metropolitan areas and their regional and national markets, the more likely they are of being left further behind.

The measure of improving educational levels was also substantively associated with each indicator of community well-being. Counties that experienced the greatest increase in the proportion of their adult population graduating from high school were more likely to have the greatest decreases in poverty and unemployment *and* the greatest increases in median family income. Where changes in manufacturing and service industries make no substantial differences, improvements in education score extraordinarily well. These findings strongly underscore the necessity of community and national investment in rural education.

As expected, the control variables for 1970 were the most strongly associated with change among the dependent variables. As noted above, these findings may be interpreted as indicating the relative importance of history, that is the initial point in time, in explaining the end-point, or second point in time.

Policy Implications Of Farm Change For Community Well-Being

Farm and Community Change

The empirical results suggest that for the period 1969 through 1980 variables measuring the concentration of farm structure were differentially associated with indicators of county well-being. The strongest association of a farm variable with a measure of county well-being was the quadratic version of average farm scale and unemployment for both 1970 and 1980. This finding indicates that counties with average farm scale in the medium range were most likely to have low levels of unemployment, while counties with either relatively small or very large average scale were more likely to have high levels of unemployment. The other farm variables were weakly associated with the three dependent variables, and in some cases these weak associations were not in the direction hypothesized by Goldschmidt. Regionally, this would mean that among nonmetropolitan counties in the South, the most recent period of farm concentration did not have the degree of adverse affects on county well-being as might have been hypothesized following the Goldschmidt study. However, this may be because the degree of increased concentration during the time period was not enough to cause the effect to appear, even though the greatest decline was among family farms. However, there are indications that further concentration may indeed be associated with adverse consequences for nonmetropolitan counties.

Aside from the empirical results of this study there is other evidence to suggest that some areas of the nonmetropolitan South will experience further farm concentration, such as the coastal plains of the Atlantic Ocean and Gulf of Mexico. The five studies of this Office of Technology Assessment project suggest that industrial farms are most likely to be found when three conditions occur simultaneously. The first condition is the presence of a highly segmented agricultural labor force. This segmentation usually occurs along sexual, ethnic, and racial divisions. The presence of competing labor groups in the past has been used to keep agricultural wages for hired labors low (see Horan and Tolbert, 1984). Second, the terrain is usually very level. This condition makes it easier to piece together contiguous tracks of land that can then be operated with large labor-saving machines. Third, the economic sub-regions where industrial-type farms have occurred permit the support of large-scale operations.

Not all areas of the South appear to be capable of maintaining industrial-type farms. The mountainous Appalachian and Ozark regions presently do not have a market infrastructure that could support large-scale farming operations, and they certainly do not have the requisite terrain. While the piedmont areas may have the required market structure, the terrain presently does not appear to be suitable, though land extensive operations such as poultry do not need level land. This leaves the coastal regions along the Atlantic Ocean and the Gulf of Mexico. Historically, these regions have had large-scale farming operations, most notably during the antebellum period. Numerous large-scale operations already exist in these areas. Furthermore, this sub-region is characterized by a highly segmented nonmetropolitan labor force (Horan and Tolbert, 1984). There are signs that the present configuration of competing labor groups is expanding to include large numbers of Mexicans and immigrants from Central America. Given the relatively low number of unskilled labor opportunities in the

Southern nonfarm industries and the degree and character of labor segmentation, a portion of the current nonmetropolitan labor force may be quickly brought into an emerging industrial farm sector.

The five regional OTA studies also provide clues as to county social and economic conditions that may *reduce* the effects of industrial-type farming. At least four conditions appear to ameliorate the effects of industrial farming. First, for those areas in which welfare benefits and labor laws favor hired workers, especially in agriculture, there is less evidence that farm concentration will adversely affect measures of county well-being. Second, where nonfarm opportunities are available, part-time farming appears to act as a bridge between a marginal existence in farming and a relatively higher standard of living due to off-farm income. The availability of nonfarm employment also may drive up the wages paid by agricultural employers. Third, the skill level of the local population is relatively high in areas where farm change has not been associated with a decline in county well-being. Fourth, these areas are also characterized by relatively low ethnic and racial diversity among the unskilled labor force. However, it important to note that sexual and class segmentation continues to be prominant in all areas.

Generally, these four conditions hindering concentraton are weak among nonmetropolitan counties in the South, especially among many of the coastal and delta counties. If further concentration of farming in the South is negatively associated with county well-being and, especially, if there is a rapid industrialization of farm structure in the coastal and delta areas, the communities affected by these trends could experience the types of social and economic problems described by MacCannell and Dolber-Smith (1985) for the industrial agricultural regions in California, Arizona, Texas, and Florida. However, once again it is necessary to caution the reader that these predictions are based on three assumptions. First, the South as a region may have reached the vortex of the inverted "U" described by MacCannell and Dolber-Smith, and further concentration will adversely affect county well-being. Second, the conditions under which industrial farming now occur presently exist in the coastal areas of the South. Therefore, while there are now no strong indications of rapid industrialization, the conditions may exist for such industrialization. Third, the conditions thought to soften any adverse consequences of further farm concentration are weak in the South.

The empirical findings, then, offer some support for the notion that further concentration in the South will significantly hurt nonmetropolitan county well-being. However, there is evidence that high or increasing levels of part-time farming may be positively associated with indicators of county well-being. Furthermore, part-time farming may be a function of both hard times in farming and the availability of the nonfarm economy's influence on farm structure, i.e., levels of part-time farming.

At the regional level, these findings do not confirm the Goldschmidt hypothesis that increased farm concentration will *automatically* adversely affect county social and economic well-being. This does not, however, represent a rejection of the Goldschmidt hypothesis as much as it suggests important modifications. These would include the types of cultural, ecological, economic, and labor force conditions that are most often adversely associated with industrial farming as well as conditions that mollify the impacts of further concentration. It would also include a caveat pertaining to the association of small scale farming with community well-being. It should be recalled that Goss (1979) found the Dinuba hinterland (Goldschmidt's so-called family farm community) to be made up of medium sized farms, rather than the classic small scale family farm. Our study suggests that small scale farms are associated with higher levels of unemployment. While this finding may be unique to the South and its history of tenancy and sharecropping, nonetheless, it does provide evidence that small scale farming is not uniformly associated with positive indicators of community well-being.

Part-time farming also may have a favorable association with community well-being. While this factor was not associated for the cross-sectional models, change in part-time farming was associated with each of the community well-being measures. Counties experiencing the most rapid increase in the proportion of operators working 100 or more days off of the farm were more likely to have had a faster rate of decline in unemployment and poverty, while increasing faster in median family income.

Part-time farming requires the presence of nearby nonfarm employment opportunities. For farmers, it offers a way for many former full-time farmers to stay in farming, albeit usually on a smaller scale (see Coughenour and Swanson, 1983; Deseran, et al. 1984). For highly competitive nonfarm enterprises on the peripheral of the national economy that must constantly adjust their labor requirements in reaction to macroeconomic changes, part-time farmers represent a reliable pool of labor, since they are less likely to migrate during hard times.

Nonfarm Factors and Community Well-Being

The need for nearby nonfarm employment opportunities indicates that *the nonfarm sector can have as much, if not more, of an influence on farming than farming has on the nonfarm economy.* This observation also reinforces the conceptual framework of regional change discussed earlier, that changes in the nonfarm economy may have more demonstrable impacts on community well-being than do changes in the agricultural economy.

Indeed, the most intriguing findings are the influences of nonfarm factors upon county well-being. If the Goldschmidt hypothesis were applied to the industrialization of the nonfarm sector, then there is a considerable amount of empirical support. Of particular interest are the associations of the percent of the county's labor force in either manufacturing or service industries on measures of well-being.

Manufacturing in 1980 presents something of a Faustian dilemma for policy makers. While higher levels of manufacturing are associated with lower unemployment and poverty, it is also associated with lower median family income. This suggests that while manufacturing is beneficially in reducing poverty and unemployment, it may pay wages that keep rural workers just above poverty. Since increase manufacturing was not associated with any improvement in community well-being (the three change models), it cannot be relied upon as the principle form of rural development.

Service industries were not associate with any beneficial indicators of community well-being. Nationally, service industries are responsible for the greatest increase in jobs, yet this data suggests that for the rural South's communities, their benefits are more likely to be realized by the owners of these companies than by the communities. It is not clear whether service industries *cause* a deterioration of rural community well-being or that such industries gravitate toward depressed areas. Nonetheless, service industries may not enhance the well-being of rural Southerners, and should not be seen as a necessary component of a development strategy.

Both manufacturing and service industries have been moving into these types of counties in recent years (Bluestone and Harrison, 1982; Horan and Tolbert, 1984). The labor forces of these two types of enterprises are often low-wage and unorganized. Furthermore, nonmetropolitan counties have often made considerable financial sacrifices to attract these types of industries (Horan and Tolbert, 1984; Summers, 1979; Summers, Evans, Clemente, Beck, and Minkoff, 1976).

As with the influence of farm change, these findings for manufacturing and service industries have been considered at the regional level. Not all manufacturing and service employment will be adversely associated with either median family income or the percent of families in poverty. Furthermore, there may be considerable difference among the subregions of the nonmetropolitan South that would make these findings conditional. However, as with the farm indicators, these two nonfarm employment indicators do articulate regional associations.

A more predictable nonfarm factor is proximity to a metropolitan area. Unsurprisingly, the more isolated a county the more likely it will have higher levels of unemployment and poverty and lower levels of median family income. Furthermore, those counties farthest away are more likely to be the first hurt during the onset of an economic downturn, and they are likely to be the last to benefit from economic recovery.

The findings also point to the adverse historical conditions faced by the South's rural black population. Counties with higher proportions of Black residents were more likely to have higher poverty and lower median family incomes. Lichter (1988) argues that blacks continue to be at the bottom of the rural South's social hierarchy.

However, the most important factor explaining community well-being in the rural South is the level of education. Put simply, the lower the level of education the worse-off the rural community. Furthermore, the greatest the improvement in education for the decade of the 1970s the greater the improvement in well-being. These findings *strongly* indicate that any rural development effort must include major efforts to improve all types of education. However, as was noted earlier in the comparison of the South with the rest of the U.S., there appears to be little inclination for the South's rural areas to tax their residents more in order to pay for education, even though there may be some slack to do so.

Cautions Concerning the Empirical Results

Some of the policy implications presented here are based upon the empirical results. Several caveats noted in earlier sections are worthy of restatement.

First, it is possible for the Goldschmidt hypothesis to be useful in anticipating social dislocation or a decline in well-being of specific individuals in a community due to the increased concentration of farm structure *without* having the entire community being affected similarly. *Second*, the unit of analysis of the empirical research is the county and not a set of communities. It is very likely that communities vary considerably in their dependency on farming within a county such that some are more likely to be adversely affected by continued farm concentration than others. However, at an aggregate county level, such variation may be suppressed due to the overwhelming nonfarm character of the counties' social organizational structure. *Third*, all of the nonmetropolitan counties in the region were analyzed. As with the variation of communities within a county, so, too, the empirical results may not hold for individual counties. Given the economic, social, and geographical diversity of the region under study, such internal variation is likely.

That these cautionary statements are included is not due only to academic convention. The creation and analysis of economic and sociological models should not be considered a mystical process that produces a clear image of societal reality. Rather, they can be of great use if their inherent biases, both conceptual and methodological, are kept in mind during the interpretive process.

Conclusions

Since the early years of commercial farming, the marketplace has presented incentives for the development of agricultural technologies that would save scarce labor, land, and capital resources. This trend is not likely to end in the near future. However, the types of technologies that will facilitate further concentration may be different. Whereas the labor-saving technologies of the nineteenth and mid-twentieth century greatly contributed to farmers' ability to expand their farms' scale, these technologies may not have as decisive a role during the next twenty-five years. Instead, technologies that enhance management efficiency or resource saving technologies such as the constellation of biotechnologies that can increase production without necessarily altering the capital to labor ratio may be as important, if not more important. However, while the types of technology may be different, their utility will continue to be in helping a farm manager to improve the firm's position within the market place by expanding total production and/or reducing the cost of production.

The farm structure analysis provides considerable evidence that labor-saving technologies were important factors contributing to farm concentration in the South between 1969 and 1978. However, it is necessary to reiterated that it is not the development of technologies that drives farmers to maximize their profits, but it is the need to maximize their profits that induces farmers to adopt technology in order to remain competitive.

The new generation of agricultural technologies will be more management intensive. Given the relatively poor rural education system in the South and the lower levels of education achieved by southern farmers as compared with the rest of the country, these new technologies may not be used by a wide range of small producers. Furthermore, these new technologies may alter the farm workplace since their utility often will require a higher division of labor or greater dependency upon contract specialists. An example of the convergence of these factors with political economy of the South is the case of burley tobacco.

The Possible Case of Burley Tobacco Production

We noted earlier that tobacco dependent communities may be adversely affected by the elimination of the program. Presently, burley tobacco farming is still a small-scale family operation as a consequence of federal tobacco policy. Historically, the combination of price supports and production controls has reduced incentives for labor-saving technologies, though not for land-saving technologies. Furthermore, since the production process relies upon casual local nonfamily labor, the multiplier effect for the wealth created is not only defused among a large number of farm families but also among the nonfamily labor. Should these programs be eliminated most of the traditional barriers to larger farm scale will be eliminated as well.

The possible relationship between farm policy, farm structure, and community in this case is instructive. A mechanical tobacco harvester has been developed and continues to be modified at the University of Kentucky. This technology was initiated in *anticipation* of changes in the tobacco program, and *not* because of existing market conditons. This type of technology, the burley tobacco harvester—which can only be used on the largest burley operations—will ensure an *orderly* transition from the current federal program and toward more "free-market" conditions. The primary beneficiaries will be the tobacco companies who underwrote a significant proportion of the harvester's development. From the small farmers perspective, though, the development and existence of this harvester makes it more difficult to reject price support and quota concessions to the tobacco program for fear of losing the entire program.

If the tobacco program is removed, there will be no constraints on scale, except those that are imposed by the new market structure. This will mean new incentives to expand production while holding labor constant, that is, to adopt the labor-saving harvester. After a period of potentially very painful transition for small-scale producers, the historic national trend toward farm concentration will likely emerge as fewer family farms and less hired nonfamily local labor is used to produce burley tobacco. Should there be such a loss in the number of farm families and hired labor, it is reasonable to assume that the multiplier effect for rural communities will be considerably less than it is now. In addition, land values that were bid-up because of the federal program's production limitations will be deflated—possibly by one third. This would reduce the total sum of local government revenue derived from land taxes.

The conundrum for national policy is the continued erosion of the U.S. share of the world burley market, due to price supports well above the international markets, should the program continue. This assumes, of course, that the U.S. will continue to support the trade of a commodity that the Surgeon General has labeled as both a narcotic and carcinogen. Therefore, the tobacco program can be defended on the basis of helping small part-time farmers, local nonfamily hired labor, and the local economy, all of whom are dependent upon the income. The primary beneficiaries of the program's demise would be the larger producers and the tobacco companies.

Finally, while, the potential loss of income for individuals may be considerable at the local level, at the regional and the subregional level, these potential changes in farm structure may not record statistically significant negative associations with county well-being if there are viable alternative sources of nonfarm income for the farm families. However, given the fragility of most rural economies, any jolt such as this is likely to have regional repercussions.

Dual Farm Structure

It is difficult to imagine any scenario under present political and market conditions that will stop, much less reverse, the trend toward a more concentrated farm structure in the South, short of another great depression or massive federal intervention. Much has been said about the apparent dual structure of U.S. farming. However, some caution in interpreting this structural phenomenon is prudent. When only commercial farms (i.e., farms with a minimum of $40,000 in gross sales) are considered, the dual structure trend is less apparent. Small to medium commercial farms (approximately from $40,000 to $250,000 in gross sales) are usually the ill-fated farm group that is said to be the "disappearing middle." But when these are acknowledged to be the lower end of the commercial farm scale, their disappearance should be considered as evidence of concentration, not bifurcation.

The growth among small farms associated with the bifurcation of U.S. farming, is in actuality only a dual structure phenomenon if small part-time operations are included. Few farms in this group can subsist on income from farming alone. This observation does not trivialize the dire plight of former full-time commercial farmers who have sought off-farm jobs to support sagging farm income. Instead, the fate of middle-sized farms, and their steady attrition, should be considered evidence of the marginalization of America's smaller commercial farms.

Federal farm policies also have had important differential influences among American farms. Earlier it was proposed that price-support programs tend to encourage the concentration of farm structure among the largest farms while slowing the decline among the smallest part-time farmers. Consequently, the price support system appears to have been one of several factors facilitating the concentration process among large commercial farms while providing some limited support for small farms.

Supply control programs that establish quotas which are traded with parcels of land such as in tobacco, may contribute to the persistence of small scale farming. However, they may also contribute to a further erosion of the U.S. share of the world tobacco market.

Any estimation of how farm change will influence community well-being would have to include the potential for change in federal farm policy, especially the termination of both price-support and supply-control programs. If price supports were eliminated, that is *decoupling* farm decision-making from federal farm programs, the rate of concentration among the largest farms would be diminished: however, the loss of smaller family farms might be accelerated.

Federal farm policy will only determine the rate of concentration. Whether or not the South's farm structure continues along the present trend toward a dual structure is unclear. Commodities such as cotton, rice, sugar, and poultry are already concentrated and the smaller producers of the commodities will have a difficult time competing with the very large farms. Both beef and tobacco production are expected to move from primarily small operations into medium sized farms. This represents a break with the more general trend toward a dual farm structure. Dairy farms are expected to move from medium to large-scale operations. Only grain production is expected to move toward both smaller and larger farms, with the middle sized farms disappearing. Finally, conditions appear to exist for the further industrialization of the South's coastal areas. However, just because conditions may be favorable in terms of a macro analysis, local conditions may actually be unfavorable. Therefore, thes comments are only speculative.

Nonfarm Economy

The findings do not support the notion that further nonfarm industrialization and increased service industry employment well improve the social and economic well-being of the South's nonmetropolitan counties. However, the most recent surge in southern rural industrialization has reduced further rural counties' dependence upon the farm economy. Indeed, as a consequence of this transition a county's nonfarm employment structure may have the affect of reducing the rate at which marginal farms go out of production by offering off-farm opportunities to support limited farm incomes.

The findings underscore the continuing need for a comprehensive rural/nonmetropolitan development strategy for the
South.

Suggestions for Farm Policy

On the assumption that further concentration may cause a
decline in county economic and social well-being, farm policies
that retard concentration may provide a brief buffer during
which counties and their rural communities adjust to the
potential changes. To enhance the adjustment process, farm
policy in the short term should help the medium sized farms
(gross sales of $40,000 to $250,000) stay in production while
providing disincentives for further concentration of the very
largest farms (gross sales of $500,000 or more). Earlier, we
discussed the ways in which different farm policies either
encourage or hamper the process of farm concentration. It was
noted that price support programs tend to facilitate, indeed
encourage, concentration while at the same time helping the
smallest farms to remain in production. The elimination of the
price support system, while possibly reducing the rate of
concentration among the very largest farms, would probably
accelerate the loss of medium-sized and small farms. But, the
federal government's enormous fiscal crisis precludes the record
Commodity Credit Corporation payments of the mid-1980s—$28
Billion in 1987. Therefore, a course needs to be charted
between present price support policies and the complete elimination of price support programs.

Tobacco, cash grains, and cotton are the primary commodities that will be impacted by a transitional price support policy.
Given the current financial stress of farmers, a rapid elimination of price support programs would cause a major restructuring of farms in the South. Yet, a continuation of current
programs will likely reinforce current dual structure trends
identified in this study. This suggest two important *transitional*
program changes: 1) price support levels must be tied to world
markets, and 2) payment limitations need to be carefully
designed so as to target benefits to mid-sized farms. Previous
attempts to accomplish these objectives attest to the difficulties.
Yet, these objectives are essential to a transitional price support
policy which will allow for the least disruptive adjustment
process to Southern farm structure. Moreover, an essential
dimension of any transitional program is a comprehensive rural

development policy that fosters greater nonfarm economic viability and thereby offers off-farm opportunities for those family farms most likely to adversely affected. While this should not be seen as a panacea for the trauma of transition, it would be much more than any of the past farm policies to ease the transition to a more concentrated farm sector.

Another arena of federal policy that has influenced the dual structure distribution in farm structure is taxation. Shelters provided by capital gains taxes and inheritance taxes have encouraged an increase in outside investment, and in part have been responsible for the increase in small farms with a dependency on off-farm income. Likewise, the present tax system has inherent incentives for capital investments (including the purchase of land) which have facilitated concentration among the very largest farms. Consequently, tax policy modifications should be developed with the intent of assisting the mid-sized commercial farms without providing new incentives for non-farm investment in small farms or new incentives for the largest farms to expand.

A number of tax policy changes merit consideration. First, changes in items that are eligible for capital gains taxation may be in order. For example, investment in beef production by small farms is likely a function of the capital gains provisions which allow sale of breeding stock to be taxed at considerably lower levels. The findings suggest that such small farms do not make a strong contribution to the economic well-being of rural communities. Indeed, an argument can be made that these tax laws have caused inefficient use of southern agricultural resources. Since many of these small farms may be producing beef as a tax shelter, they are likely bidding resources away from mid-sized commercial farms. Another change that may be in order relates to inheritance laws. Wealthy individual who desire to leave a larger proportion of their wealth to their heirs are attracted to land investment by these laws. New or more rigorous laws need to be developed to guard against these types of investors. Finally, some consideration of limitations on tax write-off benefits may be in order, if there is a desire to slow the concentration of the very largest farms. For example, a limitation on interest write-offs would discourage debt financed expansion beyond certain levels. Also, a limit on the amount of farm investment tax credit could have a similar impact. Each of these taxes changes would need to be carefully designed with the broader objective of assisting mid-sized commercial farms in mind. This recommendation should not be interpreted as dismissing the importance of small part-time (usually subcommercial) farms. Rather, these farms may be better served by an aggressive rural development policy that facilitates the development of nonfarm opportunities at a livable wage.

One final policy that merits further analysis is a negative income tax, or in more polite terminology, an income maintenance tax. If the objective is to target benefits of government transfers to mid-sized farms, a negative income tax offers some distinct advantages. It would be possible to monitor farm and non-farm earnings with a negative income tax. Decision rules could be carefully designed to provide a negative income tax to only those farmers with a certain proportion of farm income. However, in order to make this policy equitable, it should be made available for all rural people who have faced generations of poverty or have recently moved into poverty. Application to metropolitan areas will also have to be considered.

The Need For A Comprehensive Rural Development Program

Nonmetropolitan counties in the South show no signs of joining in the national prosperity as full partners. The legacy of uneven development is captured in a startling statistic. In 1979 over ninety percent of the U.S. nonmetropolitan counties considered to have persistently low incomes were located in the South. There is an immediate need for a comprehensive rural development program in this region. In recent years it has been vogue to let the marketplace mediate economic development. This study provides no evidence at the regional level that such a policy will contribute to an improvement in social and economic well-being. On the contrary, this report suggests that such a laissez-faire development policy will only reinforce past patterns of underdevelopment.

The economic fortunes of the nonmetropolitan South are tied to its position in the national and international economy. Given the relatively poor position of this region in the national economy it is not reasonable to expect these areas to improve their social and economic conditions with their own resources. In a series of monographs, leading Rural Sociologists and Agricultural Economists have persuasively and forcefully argued for a comprehensive rural development program (Bradshaw and Blakely, 1983; Dillman, 1983; Wilkinson, Hobbs, and Christenson, 1983; Wilkinson, 1984). The initial premise of their arguments is that nonmetropolitan areas are presently experiencing extreme social and economic problems. Wilkinson (1984:349) has bluntly stated that "the rural economy is highly unstable today." The dire social consequences of these depressed conditions and the persistence of social inequalities include "intolerably high rates of infant mortality and homicide. . . inadequate jobs and income, inadequate services" and a decline in effective grass roots self-help initiatives (Wilkinson, 1984:350-51). While it is popular and correct to provide aid for hunger and underdevelopment abroad, it is unconscionable to ignore the consequences of underdevelopment and poverty in the United States.

There appears to be a consensus among these specialists in rural affairs concerning the character of a national rural development program. Such a program would require a "two-fold attack, one that combines federal initiatives with local initiatives—the former to increase resources, the latter to build a sense of community" (Wilkinson, 1984:351). Five general criteria are usually given. First two are foremost. There must be simultaneous programs aimed at the creation of jobs that generate a livable income, *and* a major investment in all levels of education in order to raise the technical and analytical skills of the rural population—especially in the South. "A strategy that does not start with jobs simply does not start" (Wilkinson 1984:349). The federal government must provide capital and incentives for the development of industries that are not likely to exploit rural labor. Such a package should be accompanied by labor laws that protect unorganized labor from unfair practices by industry. In particular, civil rights laws that reduce the effects of racism, that often is associated with highly segmented labor forces, need to be revised and enforced. Without such laws and their enforcement, disenfranchised segments of the unskilled and semi-skilled nonmetropolitan labor force can be played off against one another, thus forcing wages down.

It is impossible to underestimate the need of investment in our educational systems. As the world economy becomes more competitive, the wages of unskilled jobs in the rural South will be pushed downward toward world level, only be protected by the minimum wage. However, since the minimum wage will likely be higher than world wage levels for unskilled labor, products produced even at a minimum wage may not be competitive even in our domestic markets. A sound education system is a necessary condition for economic growth. In an industrial society it is both a right and an obligation. For the rural South to be vitalized it must dramatically improve its educational systems.

The Third dimension addresses the unique spatial problems of less densely populated areas. In addition to the economic problems of low income and under employment, rural service structures essential to the persistence of an industrial labor force, such as health services and education, as well as infrastructure services such as water, sewer, and electricity, tend to be more expensive on a per capita basis (Wilkinson, (1984)

The fourth dimension of a rural development program is the recognition that under these poor social and economic conditions, not all rural people have access to even these limited services. As with the proposed strengthening and enforcement of labor laws, a rural development strategy must include programs that aid all rural citizens to take advantage of local services necessary for the minimum levels of decency expected in the U.S. The rural South is characterized by several ethnic and racial groups that historically have been left behind in national development.

The fifth dimension addresses the need for local participation in any type of rural development program. The problems of inadequate jobs and income, inadequate services, and inequality pose a crisis of community in rural America (Wilkinson, 1984). These three conditions tend to discourage a shared sense of identity in rural communities, and consequently reduce the occurrence of volunteer efforts and the development and maintenance of self-help networks. By improving the employment opportunities and service structure of the South's nonmetropolitan counties while at the same time removing the legal barriers to equal access of the benefits offered by our society, the conditions that presently suppress grass-roots efforts can be overcome.

Such local initiatives are necessary for rural development efforts to garner the scarce human and economic resources necessary for a better life. Rural areas cannot handle the task of economic development on their own. Federal, state, and local initiatives are necessary. The first step must occur at the federal level, and it must be directed at job creation, service structure support, and the enforcement of civil rights and labor laws.

Rural development is an opportunity for the Land Grant Universities and the United States Department of Agriculture to renew their historic commitment to America's rural population. As the farm population has dwindled and farm structure become more concentrated and industrial in character, and as the externalities of agricultural production have threatened the environment, these two important institutions have found much of the good-well of the nonfarm public has been eroded. This study strongly suggests that it is the viability of the nonfarm economy, and thereby its ability to provide off-farm jobs, that will stabilize what is left of the family farm. Moreover, a rural development program will greatly expand the clientele and therefore the political base for both the Land Grants and USDA. Presently, USDA is charged with the responsibility for rural development, it should take this Congressional charge seriously for its own sake as well as for the sake of rural America.

REFERENCES

Bender, Thomas
  1978 *Community and Social Change in America.* New Brunswick, New Jersey: Rutgers University Press.
Billings, Dwight B.
  1979 *Planters and the Making of a New South.* Chapel Hill, North Carolina: University of North Carolina Press.
Bluestone, Barry and Bennett Harrison
  1982 *The Deindustrialization of America.*New York: Basic Books, Inc.
Bonnano, Alessandro
  1985 The Persistence of Small Farms in Advanced Western Societies. Unpublished Ph.D. Dissertation, University of Kentucky.
Bradshaw, Ted K., and Edward J. Blakely
  1983 "National, state, and local roles in rural policy development." *The Rural Sociologist* Vol 3(4):212-219.
Christaller, Walter
  1966 *Central Places in Germany.* Englewood Cliffs, NJ: Prentice-Hall.

Cochrane, Willard
  1979 *The Development of American Agriculture.*
        Minneapolis: University of Minnesota Press.
Coughenour, C. Milton, and Louis Swanson
  1983 "Work statuses and occupations of men and women in
        farm families and the structure of farms." *Rural
        Sociology* 48(1):23-43.
Daniel, Peter
  1985 *Breaking The Land.* Champaign, Illinois:
        University of Illinois Press.
Davis, John E.
  1980 "Capitalist agricultural development and the
        exploitation of the propertied laborer." Pp. 133-
        153 in Frederick Buttel and Howard Newby (eds.) *The
        Rural Sociology of Advanced Societies.* Montclair.
        N.J.: Allanheld, Osmun.
Deseran, Forrest A., William W. Falk, and Pamela Jenkins
  1984 "Determinants of earnings of farm families in the U.S."
        Rural Sociology 49(2):210-229.
Dillan, Don A.
  1983 "How a national rural policy can help resolve rural
        problems." *The Rural Sociologist* Vol. 3(6):379-383.
Forsht, R. Gar, and Dean Jansmd
  1975 Economic and Population Growth in Smaller Place
        Areas of Pennsylvania. Washington, DC., United States
        Department of Agriculture, Agricultural Economic
        Report No. 310.
Genovese, Eugene D.
  1965 *The Political Economy of Slavery: Studies in the
        Economy and Society of the Slave South.* New York:
        Vintage Books.
Goss, Kevin F.
  1979 "Goldschmidt. As You Sow: Three Studies in the
        Social   Consequences   of   Agribusiness."   *Rural
        Sociology* 44(4):802-805.
Hahn, Steven
  1983 *The Roots of Southern Populism: Yeoman Farmers and
        the Transformation of the Georgia Upcountry, 1850-
        1890.* New York: Oxford University Press.
Heffernan, William
  1984 "The structure of poultry farms." In Harry
        Schwartzweller (ed.), *Annual Review of Rural
        Sociology and Development New York: JAI Press.*

Henretta, James A.
1978 "Families and Farms: Mentalite in Preindustrial
       America." *William and Mary Quarterly* 35(1):3-32.
Horan, Patrick M., and Charles M. Tolbert II
1984 *The Organization of Work in Rural and Urban Labor
       Markets.* Boulder, Co.: Westview Press.
Kessler, Ronald C. and David F. Greenberg
1982 *Linear Panel Analysis: Models of Quantitative Change.*
       New York: Academic Press.
Kirby, Jack Temple
1983 "The Transformation of Southern Plantations, 1920-
       1960." *Agricultural History* 57(3):257-76.
Lichter, Daniel T.
1988 "Race and unemployment: black employment hardship
       in the rural South." In L. Beaulieu *The Rural South
       In Crisis. Boulder, Colorado: Westview Press.*
McArthur, W.C.
1979 "The South." Pp. 303-334 in Lyle P. Schertz,
       Another Revolution in U.S. Farming? Washington,
       D.C.: U. S. Department of Agriculture.
MacCannell, Dean, and Edward Dolber-Smith
1985 "Report on the structure of agriculture and impacts
       of new technologies on rural communities in
       Arizona, California, Florida and Texas." Paper
       prepared for the Office of Technology Assessment,
       U. S. Congress.
Mandle, Jay R.
1978 *The Roots of Black Poverty: The Southern Plantation*
       Economy After The Civil War. *Durham, NC: Duke*
       University Press.
Mann, Charles K.
1975 *Tobacco: The Ants and the Elephants.* Salt Lake City:
       Olympus Publishing Co.
Mann, Susan
1984 "Sharecropping in the Cotton South: A Case of
       Uneven Development of Agriculture." *Rural
       Sociology 49(3):412-29.*
Office of Technology Assessment
1986 *Technology, Public Policy, and the Changing Structure*
       of American Agriculture. *Washington, D.C.: U.S.*
       Government Printing Office.
Pryor, Frederick L.
1982 "The Plantation Economy as an Economic System."

Journal of Comparative Economics 6(September):
288-317.
Rogers, George B.
1979 "Poultry and eggs." Pp. 148-189 in Lyle P.
Schertz, *Another Revolution in American*
Agriculture. *Washington, D.C.: U.S.D.A.*
Rosenberg, Nathan
1982 *Inside The Black Box: Technology and Economics.*
New York: Cambridge University Press.
Ruttan, Vernon W.
1982 *Agricultural Research Policy.* Minneapolis: University of
Minnesota Press.
Sargen, Nicholas P.
1979 *Tractorization in the United States and Its*
Relevance for the Developing Countries. *New York:*
Garland Press.
Shlomowitz, Ralph
1984 "Plantations and Small Holdings: Comparative
Perspectives From the World Cotton and Sugar Cane
Economies, 1865-1939," *Agricultural History* 58(1):
1-16.
Starbird, Irving R. and Keith J. Collins
1983 *What Does the Future Hold?* Memphis: Meister
Publishing Company.
Summers, Gene F.
1979 "Manufacturing and Rural Development: Thoughts on
a Research Program." In Eldon D. Smith (ed.),
Rural Industrialization: A Monograph. Mississippi
State: Southern Rural Development Center.
Summers, Gene F., Sharon D. Evans, Frank Clemente, E. M.
Beck, and Jon Minkoff
1976 *Industrial Invasion of Nonmetropolitan American.*
New York: Praeger Publishers.
Swanson, Louis E., Jr.
1982 Farm and Trade Center Transition in an Industrial
Society: Pennsylvania, 1930-1960. Unpublished
Dissertation, University Park: Pennsylvania
State University.
Vandiver, Joseph S.
1978 "The Changing Realm of King Cotton." Pp. 242-246
in Rodefeld, Richard, Jan Flora, Donald Voth, Isao
Fujinuoto, Jim Converse (eds.), *Change in Rural
America: Causes, Consequences, and Alternatives.*

St. Louis, MO: The C. V. Mosby Company.
Warren, Roland
  1973   *The Community in America (3rd Edition).*   New York:
          Rand McNally and Company.
Weber, Max
  1947   *The Theory of Social and Economic Organization.*
          New York: Knoff.
Whiting, Edward (ed.)
  1974   *Communities Left Behind: Alternatives for
          Development.* Ames, Iowa: Iowa State University
          Press.
Wilkinson, Kenneth P.
  1984   "Implementing & National Strategy of Rural
          Development." *The Rural Sociologist* Vol. 4, (5):
          348-353.
Wilkinson, Kenneth P., Daryl J. Hobbs, and James A.
          Christenson
  1983   An Analysis of the National Rural Development
          Strategy." *The Rural Sociologist* Vol. 3, (6):
          384-389.

CATF Appendixes

Appendix A

Table 1. Arizona

Indicators	U.S.A.	Arizona State Tract Total	Maricopa County County Total	Maricopa County Tract 0608	Maricopa County Tract 0609	Yuma County County Total	Yuma County Tract 0110	Yuma County Tract 0116	Pinal County County Total	Pinal County Tract 0020	Pinal County Tract 0019
Population size x 1000	226,505.0	2700	15.1	3.7	4.3	90.5	1.4	1.9	N.A.	4.7	2.3
Rural population	59,500.0										
% with Spanish surname	6.4	44.4	20.0	2.7	3.4	29.5	0.5	1.7	26.8	56.0	55.0
Quality of Housing											
% without plumbing	2.2	2.6	0.8	3.8	10.3	1.0	5.0	3.0	3.0	4.0	8.0
All families: % living in house with >1-5 persons/room	1.2	2.5	1.1	13.6	17.8	5.0	9.0	30.0	11.6	11.25	11.0
Spanish surname families: % living in house with >1-5 persons/room	N.A.	6.0	10.0	18.8	22.5	15.0	2.7	39.0	8.3	11.25	20.0
All families: Median value of owner-occupied units x $1000	N.A.	54.8	59.2	22.4	23.4	40.4	50.1	28.7	38.2	25.2	18.8
Spanish surname: Median value of owner-occupied units	N.A.	37.3	40.5	22.7	22.6	31.2	30.0	28.7	26.5	27.7	13.2
Poverty											
All families: % At or below federal poverty level	12.2	9.5	7.5	33.5	25.6	12.3	18.9	22.4	14.3	26.5	39.9
% At or below 125% poverty level	16.7	13.6	10.8	47.9	41.6	24.2	34.1	34.0	24.4	40.1	58.9
Spanish surname families: % At or below federal poverty level	27.2	18.2	19.0	39.6	24.9	21.9	27.6	27.6	18.3	32.6	45.0
% At or below 125% poverty level	N.A.	25.8	26.6	52.4	42.8	36.2	57.0	39.2	28.2	48.6	56.1

	U.S.A.	Arizona State Total	Maricopa County			Yuma County			Pinal County		
			County Total	Tract 0608	Tract 0609	County Total	Tract 0110	Tract 0116	County Total	Tract 0020	Tract 0019
All:											
% of unrelated individuals for whom poverty status is determined	12.4	25.5	22.9	44.6	70.8	16.0	17.9	21.5	34.3	50.0	62.7
Spanish surname: % of unrelated individuals for whom poverty status is determined	23.5	40.4	38.2	11.1	72.5	17.4	22.2	25.1	50.8	65.8	59.4
Income											
All families:											
Mean income x $1000	25.8	22.1	23.8	12.3	13.6	18.0	19.4	14.4	16.7	14.9	10.3
Median income x $1000	23.4	19.0	20.5	10.5	12.3	15.0	16.7	14.1	14.5	14.0	7.9
Spanish surname families:											
Mean income x $1000	18.4	17.2	17.4	11.9	13.6	16.4	12.3	11.5	16.3	1.3	10.5
Median income x $1000	16.2	15.5	15.6	10.0	12.1	14.1	10.3	12.9	15.4	11.8	8.9
All families:											
% income > $10,000	83.2	71.2	74.7	50.9	55.5	65.0	65.0	66.0	65.0	57.0	43.0
Spanish surname families:											
% income > $10,000	66.6	65.9	67.0	51.9	58.2	63.0	57.0	57.0	69.0	N.A.	N.A.
Labor Force											
All families:											
% of labor force employed	90.0	93.8	93.4	89.0	90.0	92.0	86.0	71.0	92.0	N.A.	82.0
Spanish surname families:											
% of labor force employed	86.0	91.2	91.6	90.9	89.9	85.0	76.0	82.0	88.0	N.A.	88.0
All families:											
% in farming/forestry/fishing	9.2	2.7	2.2	24.0	21.0	13.0	30.0	58.0	72.0	16.0	28.0
Spanish surname families:											
% in farming/forestry/fishing	N.A.	7.4	7.4	30.2	23.8	29.0	65.0	60.0	13.3	25.0	39.0

N.A. = Not Available

Appendix A

Table 2. California

Indicators	U.S.A.	California State Total	Fresno County			Imperial County			
			County Total	Firebaugh Tract	Mendota Tract	County Total	0101	Tract 0102	0119
Indicators									
Population size x 1000	226,505	23,668	514.6	3.9	4.0	92.1	2.5	1.3	2.6
Rural population	59,500								
% with Spanish surname	6.4	19.0	29.1	48.0	71.0	58.0	19.1	18.8	24.0
Quality of Housing									
% without plumbing	2.2	0.2	2.0	19.3	N.A.	4.0	1.0	0.3	0.3
All families: % living in house with > 1-5 persons/room	1.2	0.5	1.0	12.3	16.3	4.0	N.A.	N.A.	N.A.
Spanish surname families: % living in house with > 1-5 persons/room	N.A.	4.0	4.0	18.4	23.0	N.A.	N.A.	N.A.	N.A.
All families: Median value of owner-occupied units x $1000	19.8	84.5	60.9	20.0	22.8	47.9	42.4	61.5	61.5
Spanish surname: Median value	N.A.	78.1	46.9	N.A.	N.A.	51.3	N.A.	N.A.	N.A.
Poverty									
All families: % At or below federal poverty level	12.2	8.7	11.4	28.9	26.3	12.7	12.9	14.1	6.7
% At or below 125% poverty level	16.7	12.2	16.2	48.6	49.7	31.1	24.2	25.0	40.2
Spanish surname families: % At or below federal poverty level	27.2	16.8	22.2	53.7	29.7	19.1	19.4	18.8	23.7

328

	U.S.A.	California State Total	Fresno County County Total	Fresno County Firebaugh Tract	Fresno County Mendoua Tract	Imperial County County Total	Imperial County Tract 0101	Imperial County Tract 0102	Imperial County Tract 0119
Poverty (cont'd)									
% At or below 125% poverty level	N.A.	23.7	31.3	83.8	56.0	30.0	29.2	55.9	12.4
All:									
% of unrelated individuals for whom poverty status is determined	12.4	19.7	34.0	N.A.	N.A.	22.1	34.2	33.3	15.4
Spanish surname:									
% of unrelated individuals for whom poverty status is determined	23.5	30.8	48.9	N.A.	N.A.	30.5	34.2	33.3	41.9
Income									
All families:									
Mean income x $1000	25.8	25.5	22.3	N.A.	N.A.	18.8	13.9	16.4	19.7
Median income x $1000	23.4	21.5	18.4	12.9	12.3	14.7	11.2	13.9	13.5
Spanish surname families:									
Mean income x $1000	18.4	18.6	15.5	N.A.	N.A.	16.0	13.4	15.6	18.2
Median income x $1000	16.2	16.1	13.1	11.7	11.6	14.8	11.6	13.6	13.0
All families:									
% income > $10,000	83.2	82.0	77.0	N.A.	N.A.	67.0	57.0	70.0	69.0
Spanish surname families:									
% income > $10,000	66.6	72.0	65.0	N.A.	N.A.	64.0	63.0	91.0	70.0
Labor Force									
All families:									
% of labor force employed	90.0	93.0	91.0	77.3	91.2	90.0	89.0	90.0	86.0
Spanish surname families:									
% of labor force employed	86.0	90.0	81.0	89.1	89.0	88.0	83.0	92.0	77.0
All families:									
% in farming/forestry/fishing	9.2	3.0	10.0	57.5	50.6	10.0	N.A.	N.A.	N.A.

329

	U.S.A.	California State Total	Fresno County County Total	Firebaugh Tract	Mendota Tract	Imperial County County Total	Tract 0101	Tract 0102	Tract 0119
Labor Force (cont'd)									
Spanish surname families: % in farming/forestry/fishing	N.A.	7.0	23.0	75.3	55.0	21.0	42.0	50.0	29.0

N.A. = Not available

Appendix A

Table 3. Florida

Indicators	U.S.A.	FLORIDA State Total	MADISON County Total	BROWARD County Total	DADE County Total	IMMOKALEE County Total	HARDEE County Total	MARION County Total
Population size x 1000	226,505	9,746	18.9	10.2	9.7	11.0	19.4	122.5
Rural population	59,500							
% Black	N.A.	14.0	34.0	11.0	17.0	4.8	3.2	2.4
Quality of Housing								
% without plumbing	2.2	1.2	4.0	.2	1.4	18.6	1.0	2.3
All families: % living in house with >1-5 persons/room	1.2	2.0	2.0	.9	4.2	12.2	2.4	.9
Black families: % living in house with >1-5 persons/room	N.A.	11.0	5.0	4.3	4.0	19.2	15.2	2.7
All families: Median value of owner-occupied units x $1000	19.8	55.5	21.8	66.5	61.3	28.7	25.9	36.0
Black families: Median value	N.A.	37.9	16.3	37.9	37.4	24.1	21.6	39.0
Poverty								
All families: % At or below federal poverty level	12.2	9.9	26.4	6.3	11.9	38.0	19.3	14.0
% At or below 125% poverty level	16.7	14.2	35.6	9.0	16.2	55.2	26.1	20.4
Black families: % At or below federal poverty level	N.A.	31.2	N.A.	27.0	26.4	46.8	43.1	19.2
% At or below 125% poverty level	N.A.	39.9	N.A.	34.3	34.1	63.0	59.2	31.3

	U.S.A.	FLORIDA State Total	MADISON County Total	BROWARD County Total	DADE County Total	IMMOKALEE County Total	HARDEE County Total	MARION County Total
All:								
% of unrelated individuals for whom poverty status is determined	12.4	34.6	55.9	26.3	16.2	48.3	42.4	34.5
Black:								
% of unrelated individuals for whom poverty status is determined	N.A.	55.0	59.9	47.5	47.0	40.4	49.3	48.7
Income								
All families:								
Mean income x $1000	25.8	21.3	14.2	23.9	23.5	12.3	17.3	17.0
Median income x $1000	23.4	17.3	11.9	19.6	18.6	8.4	13.7	13.4
Black families:								
Mean income x $1000	N.A.	13.7	N.A.	14.5	14.9	9.3	11.9	14.8
Median income x $1000	N.A.	10.8	N.A.	11.4	12.1	7.3	10.3	9.9
All families:								
% income > $10,000	83.2	76.0	59.0	81.0	76.0	31.9	58.7	58.7
Black families:								
% income > $10,000	N.A.	53.0	N.A.	59.0	55.0	28.9	50.1	49.6
Labor Force								
All families:								
% of labor force employed	90.0	95.0	93.0	95.0	94.0	92.6	91.7	93.4
Black families:								
% of labor force employed	N.A.	91.0	86.0	93.0	93.0	89.8	79.3	92.5
All families:								
% in farming/forestry/fishing	9.2	3.0	14.0	2.0	2.0	39.3	22.3	6.3
Black families:								
% in farming/forestry/fishing	N.A.	7.0	15.0	5.0	3.0	54.9	61.0	11.1

N.A. = Not available

Table 4. Texas

Indicators	U.S.A.	Texas State Total	Cameron Tree County Total	Hidalgo County Total	Bell County			Harris	Brownsville		
					224	225	226	233	102.01	102.02	103
Indicators											
Population size x 1000	226,505	14,000	209.7	283.3	5.8	5.8	3.9	3.1	1.4	3.5	6.0
Rural population	59,500	3,000	161.7	230.3	5.4	5.6	3.5	0.2	1.1	2.2	4.3
% with Spanish surname	6.4										
Quality of Housing											
% without plumbing	2.2	2.58	7.4	7.9	11.4	6.9	8.8	25.0	16.1	41.0	14.1
% Rural without plumbing	5.4										
All families: % living in house with >1-5 persons/room	1.2	1.59	8.3	9.9	17.6	17.5	21.0	19.0	4.5	8.5	10.4
Spanish surname families: % living in house with >1-5 persons/room	N.A.		12.3	14.0	19.9	19.9	21.3	20.1	16.6	17.1	16.1
Rural	0.4	7.68									
All families: Median value of owner-occupied units x $1000	19.8	39.1	24.6	23.9	15.5	18.8	14.5	10.0	16.9	25.2	15.1
Spanish surname: Median value	N.A.	N.A.	13.8	19.8	15.1	18.4	14.5	10.0	14.6	20.6	12.3
Poverty											
All families: % At or below federal poverty level	12.2	11.1	26.0	29.0	44.1	47.1	46.1	44.0	27.1	24.9	30.3
% At or below 125% poverty level	16.7	15.1	34.5	38.0	57.3	70.3	N.A.	59.6	36.9	45.4	47.1

	U.S.A.	Texas State Total	Cameron Tree County Total	Hidalgo County Total	Bell County 224	Bell County 225	Bell County 226	Harris 233	Brownsville 102.01	Brownsville 102.02	Brownsville 103
Poverty, (cont'd)											
Spanish surname families:											
% At or below federal poverty level	27.2	24.7	33.7	36.6	46.1	49.0	46.3	46.4	33.6	40.1	43.5
% At or below 125% poverty level	N.A.	33.3	44.0	47.3	59.6	71.8	53.3	61.6	47.4	61.4	39.4
All:											
% of unrelated individuals for whom poverty status is determined	12.4	27.2	41.3	43.8	59.7	55.4	71.7	78.0	46.7	60.1	47.2
Spanish surname:											
% of unrelated individuals for whom poverty status is determined	23.5	42.7	58.9	61.8	79.5	72.7	71.7	78.0	80.0	56.3	89.7
Income											
All families:											
Mean income x $1000	25.8	23.2	16.5	15.9	11.4	10.2	10.7	1.2	16.0	20.5	12.8
Median income x $1000	23.4	19.6	12.9	12.1	9.3	8.2	7.8	0.7	15.2	22.6	10.3
Spanish surname families:											
Mean income x $1000	18.4	15.7	13.4	13.1	10.9	9.9	10.7	1.0	13.2	14.3	10.4
Median income x $1000	16.2	13.3	11.0	10.4	8.9	8.2	7.7	0.9	11.2	8.8	8.5
All families:											
% income > $10,000	83.2	70.5	56.7	55.2	44.2	33.6	35.2	39.0	56.0	54.0	50.0
Spanish surname families:											
% income > $10,000	66.6	59.8	50.5	48.6	41.7	33.2	35.3	35.0	51.0	53.0	38.3
Labor Force											
All families:											
% of labor force employed	90.0	96.0	92.2	91.5	91.7	85.2	89.5	83.0	56.0	50.0	49.0

334

Labor Force, (cont'd)

	U.S.A.	Texas State Total	Cameron Tree County Total	Hidalgo County Total	Bell County			Harris	Brownsville		
					224	225	226	233	102.01	102.02	103
Spanish surname families:											
% of labor force employed	86.0	93.6	90.7	90.2	90.9	84.3	83.9	81.0	53.4	50.0	44.0
All families:											
% in farming/forestry/fishing	9.2	2.85	5.1	10.0	18.2	22.4	13.2	22.0	13.6	6.0	13.2
Spanish surname families:											
% in farming/forestry/fishing	N.A.	4.23	5.7	12.4	19.0	23.1	13.3	22.0	16.7	8.3	14.8

N.A. = Not Available

Table 1. Percent Urban Population 1980

Analysis of Variance

Source	DF	Sum of Squares	Mean Square	F Value	Prob > F
Model	2	15665.48	7832.741	10.574	0.0001
Error	93	68891.6	740.7699		
C Total	95	84557.08			

Root MSE	27.21709	R-Square 0.1853
Dep Mean	46.29662	ADJ R-Sq 0.1677
C.V.	58.78851	

Parameter Estimates

Variable	DF	Parameter Estimate	Standard Error	T for HO: Parameter = 0	Prob> ITI	Standardized Estimate	Tolerance
Intercep	1	44.40223	3.590305	12.367	0.0001	0	
V10	1	-0.00150725	0.000713309	-2.101	0.0383	-0.199259	0.9741552
V1208	1	0.00315346	0.0008523916	3.700	0.0004	0.3508332	0.9741552

Variable	DF	Variable Label
Intercep	1	Intercept
V10	1	1978 Avg. Size of Farms (Acres)
V1208	1	1978 No. Hired Workers, 150 days or more

Appendix B

Table 2. Rural Population as Percent of Total Population: 1980

Analysis of Variance

Source	DF	Sum of Squares	Mean Square	F Value	Prob > F
Model	2	1.566548	0.7832741	10.574	0.0001
Error	93	6.88916	0.07407699		
C Total	95	8.455708			

Root MSE	0.2721709	R–Square	0.1853
Dep Mean	0.5370338	ADJ R–Sq	0.1677
C.V.	50.6804		

Parameter Estimates

Variable	DF	Parameter Estimate	Standard Error	T for HO: Parameter = 0	Prob> ITI	Standardized Estimate	Tolerance
Intercep	1	0.5559777	0.03590305	15.486	0.0001	0	
V10	1	0.00001507252	.00000717331	2.101	0.0383	0.1992594	0.9741552
V1208	1	−.0000315346	.00000852392	−3.700	0.0004	−0.350833	0.9741552

Variable	DF	Variable Label
Intercept	1	Intercept
V10	1	1978 Avg Size of Farms (Acres)
V1208	1	1978 No. Hired Workers, 150 days or more

Appendix B

Table 3. Farm Population as Percent of Total Population: 1980

Analysis of Variance

Source	DF	Sum of Squares	Mean Square	F Value	Prob > F
Model	1	0.1554859	0.1554859	10.574	0.0001
Error	94	0.5336837	0.005677486		
C Total	95	0.6891696			

Root MSE	0.07534909	R-Square	0.2256
Dep Mean	0.1074828	ADJ R-Sq	0.2174
C.V.	70.10342		

Parameter Estimates

Variable	DF	Parameter Estimate	Standard Error	T for HO: Parameter = 0	Prob> |T|	Standardized Estimate	Tolerance
Intercep	1	0.1472296	0.01080864	13.621	0.0001	0	
V751P	1	-0.00873475	0.001669103	-5.233	0.0001	-0.474988	1

Variable	DF	Variable Label
Intercep	1	Intercept
V751P	1	Percent of farms corporately owned: 1980

Appendix B

Table 4. Non-Farm Population as Percent of Total Population: 1980

Analysis of Variance

Source	DF	Sum of Squares	Mean Square	F Value	Prob > F
Model	2	4701.28	2350.64	27.023	0.0001
Error	93	8089.644	86.98542		
C Total	95	12790.92			

Root MSE	9.326598	R-Square	0.3675
Dep Mean	79.93025	ADJ R-Sq	0.3539
C.V.	11.66842		

Parameter Estimates

Variable	DF	Parameter Estimate	Standard Error	T for HO: Parameter = 0	Prob> |T|	Standardized Estimate	Tolerance
Intercep	1	78.73689	2.078667	37.879	0.0001	0	
V751P	1	1.699475	0.2312148	7.350	0.0001	−0.6783576	0.7984091
V1069	1	−0.000127158	.0004011687	−3.170	0.0021	−0.292534	0.7984091

Variable	DF	Variable Label
Intercep	1	Intercept
V751P	1	Percent of farms corporately owned: 1980
V1069	1	1978 Avg. Value Machincs, Equip/Farm ($)

Appendix B

Table 5. Median Family Income 1979

Analysis of Variance

Source	DF	Sum of Squares	Mean Square	F Value	Prob > F
Model	2	90282105	45141053	6.740	0.00018
Error	93	622901880	6697870		
C Total	95	713183985			

Root MSE	2588.024		R-Square	0.1266
Dep Mean	15817.43		ADJ R-Sq	0.1078
C.V.	16.35185			

Parameter Estimates

Variable	DF	Parameter Estimate	Standard Error	T for HO: Parameter = 0	Prob> |T|	Standardized Estimate	Tolerance
Intercep	1	15737.63	341.3956	46.098	0.0001	0	
V10	1	-0.132168	0.06820971	-1.938	0.0557	-0.190255	0.9741552
V1208	1	0.2242205	0.0810524	2.766	0.0068	0.2716208	0.9741552

Variable	DF	Variable Label
Intercep	1	Intercept
V10	1	1978 Avg. Size of Farms (Acres)
V1208	1	1978 No. Hired Workers, 150 Days or More

Table 6. Percent Unemployed 1980

Analysis of Variance

Source	DF	Sum of Squares	Mean Square	F Value	Prob > F
Model	4	312.4484	78.1121	11.589	0.0001
Error	91	613.37	6.74033		
C Total	95	925.8184			

Root MSE	2.596214	R-Square	0.3375
Dep Mean	4.706846	ADJ R-Sq	0.3084
C.V.	55.15826		

Parameter Estimates

Variable	DF	Parameter Estimate	Standard Error	T for HO: Parameter = 0	Prob> ITI	Standardized Estimate	Tolerance
Intercep	1	4.186181	0.6284856	6.661	0.0001	0	
V10	1	-0.000259542	0.0000799102	-3.248	0.0016	-0.327909	0.714267
V1208	1	0.0003644622	0.000088926	4.098	0.0001	0.3875057	0.814417
V297P	1	0.1381821	0/04501746	3.070	0.0028	-0.347193	0.3058669
V1069	1	-.0000406023	.00001804226	-2.250	0.0268	-0.347195	0.3058669

Variable	DF	Variable Label
Intercep	1	Intercept
V10	1	1978 Avg. Size of Farms (Acres)
V1208	1	1978 No. Hired Workers, 150 Days or More
V297P	1	Percent of farms w/$100K in annual sales: 1980
V1069	1	1978 Avg. Value Machines, Equip/Farm ($)

Appendix B

Table 7. Percent Below Poverty 1980

Analysis of Variance

Source	DF	Sum of Squares	Mean Square	F Value	Prob > F
Model	2	424.4869	212.2435	6.573	0.0021
Error	93	3002.922	32.28949		
C Total	95	3427.409			

Root MSE	5.682384	R-Square	0.1239
Dep Mean	14.86446	ADJ R-Sq	0.1050
C.V.	38.228		

Parameter Estimates

Variable	DF	Parameter Estimate	Standard Error	T for HO: Parameter = 0	Prob> ITI	Standardized Estimate	Tolerance
Intercep	1	14.64889	0.749538	19.543	0.0001	0	
V10	1	0.0003827215	0.0001497643	2.555	0.0122	0.2513089	0.9741552
V1208	1	-0.000378673	0.0001779623	-2.128	0.0360	-0.209252	0.9741552

Variable	DF	Variable Label
Intercep	1	Intercept
V10	1	1978 Avg. Size of Farms (Acres)
V1208	1	1978 No. Hired Workers, 150 Days or More

Appendix B

Table 8. Unrelated Individuals in Poverty 1980

Analysis of Variance

Source	DF	Sum of Squares	Mean Square	F Value	Prob > F
Model	2	537.664	268.832	8.569	0.0004
Error	93	2917.796	31.37415		
C Total	95	3455.46			

Root MSE	5.601263	R–Square	0.1556
Dep Mean	14.65104	ADJ R–Sq	0.1374
C.V.	38.23116		

Parameter Estimates

Variable	DF	Parameter Estimate	Standard Error	T for HO: Parameter = 0	Prob> |T|	Standardized Estimate	Tolerance
Intercep	1	15.0952	0.8375829	18.022	0.0001	0	
V10	1	0.0005128827	0.0001474362	3.479	0.0008	0.3354078	0.976669
V751	1	-0.345152	0.1255502	-2.749	0.0072	-0.265063	0.976669

Variable	DF	Variable Label
Intercep	1	Intercept
V10	1	1978 Avg. Size of Farms (Acres)
V751	1	Percent of farms corporately owned: 1980

Appendix B

Table 9. Total Local Government Taxes ($1000) 1977

Analysis of Variance

Source	DF	Sum of Squares	Mean Square	F Value	Prob > F
Model	2	14334092350	7167046175	310.836	0.0001
Error	93	21443296569	230573081		
C Total	95	16478421918			

Root MSE	1518.63	R–Square	0.8699
Dep Mean	18481.07	ADJ R–Sq	0.8671
C.V.	82.16316		

Parameter Estimates

Variable	DF	Parameter Estimate	Standard Error	T for HO: Parameter = 0	Prob> |T|	Standardized Estimate	Tolerance
Intercep	1	2676.573	2083.126	1.285	0.2020	0	
V1208	1	12.56815	0.5702139	22.041	0.0001	1.001618	0.6775732
V786	1	-966.876	331.0163	-2.921	0.0044	-0.132736	0.6775732

Variable	DF	Variable Label
Intercep	1	Intercept
V1208	1	1978 No. Hired Workers, 150 Days or more
V876F	1	Per farm expenditure on Fertilizer: 1980

Appendix B

Table 10. Local Government Expenditures per Capita 1977

Analysis of Variance

Source	DF	Sum of Squares	Mean Square	F Value	Prob > F
Model	1	762933.6	762933.6	8.139	0.0053
Error	94	8811212	93736.3		
C Total	95	9574146			

Root MSE	306.1638	R-Square	0.0797
Dep Mean	774.5208	ADJ R-Sq	0.0699
C.V.	39.52945		

Parameter Estimates

Variable	DF	Parameter Estimate	Standard Error	T for HO: Parameter = 0	Prob> |T|	Standardized Estimate	Tolerance
Intercep	1	729.9588	34.9342	20.895	0.0001	0	
V1208	1	0.02699945	0.009463799	2.853	0.0053	0.2822886	1

Variable	DF	Variable Label
Intercep	1	Intercept
V1208	1	1978 No. Hired Workers, 150 Days or more

Appendix B

Table 11. Retail Sales per 1000 Persons: 1980

Analysis of Variance

Source	DF	Sum of Squares	Mean Square	F Value	Prob > F
Model	5	10115187	2023037	85.943	0.0001
Error	90	2118531	23539.23		
C Total	95	9574146			

Root MSE	153.425	R-Square	0.8268
Dep Mean	168.8594	ADJ R-Sq	0.8172
C.V.	90.85962		

Parameter Estimates

Variable	DF	Parameter Estimate	Standard Error	T for HO: Parameter = 0	Prob> |T|	Standardized Estimate	Tolerance
Intercep	1	55.57176	33.14854	1.677	0.0971	0	
V1208	1	0.1037574	0.007908685	13.119	0.0001	0.9596837	0.3595894
V751P	1	15.80906	6.107101	2.589	0.0112	0.204043	0.3096936
V892F	1	-6.81463	2.100437	-2.864	0.0052	-0.314066	0.1599522
V297P	1	-5.02268	1.85083	-2.714	0.0080	-0.152653	0.6080838
V900F	1	12.37264	6.357296	1.946	0.0547	0.1735298	0.2420277

Variable	DF	Variable Label
Intercep	1	Intercept
V1208	1	1978 No. Hired Workers, 150 Days or more
V751P	1	Percent of farms corporately owned: 1980
V892F	1	Per Farm expenditure on Hired Labor: 1980
V297P	1	Percent of farms w/$1000K in annual sales: 1980
V900F	1	Per Farm expenditure on Contract Labor: 1980

346

Appendix B

Table 12. Percent Employed in Services: 1980

Analysis of Variance

Source	DF	Sum of Squares	Mean Square	F Value	Prob > F
Model	2	181.1819	90.59096	6.754	0.0018
Error	93	1247.324	13.41209		
C Total	95	1428.506			

Root MSE	3.662251	R-Square	0.1268
Dep Mean	17.85015	ADJ R-Sq	0.1081
C.V.	20.51664		

Parameter Estimates

Variable	DF	Parameter Estimate	Standard Error	T for HO: Parameter = 0	Prob> |T|	Standardized Estimate	Tolerance
Intercep	1	18.05275	0.4831008	37.368	0.0001	0	
V10	1	-0.000283629	.0009652193	-2.731	0.0075	-0.268139	0.9741552
V1208	1	0.0002280582	0.0001146953	1.988	0.0497	0.195206	0.9741552

Variable	DF	Variable Label
Intercep	1	Intercept
V10	1	1978 Avg. Size of Farms (Acres)
V1208	1	1978 No. Hired Workers, 150 Days or More

Table 13. Percent Employed in Manufacture: 1980

Analysis of Variance

Source	DF	Sum of Squares	Mean Square	F Value	Prob > F
Model	1	332.2057	332.2057	12.726	0.0006
Error	94	2453.827	26.10455		
C Total	95	2786.033			

Root MSE	6.109261	R-Square	0.1192
Dep Mean	9.085417	ADJ R-Sq	0.1099
C.V.	56.23584		

Parameter Estimates

Variable	DF	Parameter Estimate	Standard Error	T for HO: Parameter = 0	Prob> |T|	Standardized Estimate	Tolerance
Intercep	1	10.12673	0.5976024	16.946	0.0001	0	
V10	1	-0.000474126	0.0001329077	-3.567	0.0006	-0.345311	1

Variable	DF	Variable Label
Intercep	1	Intercept
V10	1	1978 Avg. Size of Farms (Acres)

Appendix C

Table 1. 1970–1980 Changes in Farm Population

Analysis of Variance

Source	DF	Sum of Squares	Mean Square	F Value	Prob > F
Model	9	1.204787	0.1338653	1.900	0.0642
Error	76	5.35424	0.07045053		
C Total	85	6.559028			

Root MSE	0.2654252	R–Square	0.1837
Dep Mean	-0.232316	ADJ R–Sq	0.0870
C.V.	-114.252		

Parameter Estimates

Variable	DF	Parameter Estimate	Standard Error	T for HO: Parameter = 0	Prob> |T|	Standardized Estimate	Tolerance
Intercep	1	-0.252311	0.09230104	-2.734	0.0078	0	
SizeLoHi	1	-0.159977	0.0809501	-1.976	0.0518	-0.256403	0.6380864
SizeHiHi	1	-0.205285	0.08940327	-2.296	0.0244	-0.324331	0.5383606
SizeHiLo	1	0.01872932	0.08947653	0.209	0.8348	0.02758949	0.6182769
ChemLoHi	1	0.09227513	0.08976509	1.028	0.3072	0.1534539	0.4819957
ChemHiHi	1	0.234498	0.1139504	2.058	0.0430	0.3222117	0.4381286
ChemHiLo	1	0.1378575	0.09616897	1.433	0.1558	0.2379118	0.3899451
MachLoHi	1	0.08714001	0.08802689	0.990	0.3254	0.1283629	0.6388084
MachHiHi	1	-0.0536858	0.08352056	-0.643	0.5223	-0.0892797	0.5567642
MachHiLo	1	-0.0380494	0.1049734	-0.362	0.7180	-0.0548691	0.4687339

Variable	DF	Variable Label
Intercep	1	Intercept
V10	1	1978 Avg. Size of Farms (Acres)

Appendix C

Table 2. 1970–1980 Change in Median Family Income

Analysis of Variance

Source	DF	Sum of Squares	Mean Square	F Value	Prob > F
Model	9	12.88083	1.431203	4.961	0.0001
Error	76	21.92353	0.288467		
C Total	85	34.80435			

Root MSE	0.5370917	R–Square	0.3701	
Dep Mean	4.293918	ADJ R–Sq	0.2955	
C.V.	12.5082			

Parameter Estimates

Variable	DF	Parameter Estimate	Standard Error	T for HO: Parameter = 0	Prob> ITI	Standardized Estimate	Tolerance
Intercep	1	4.949415	0.1867725	26.494	0.0001	0	
SizeLoHi	1	0.142011	0.1638037	0.867	0.3887	0.09880756	0.6380864
SizeHiHi	1	0.1173236	0.1809088	0.649	0.5186	0.08046755	0.5383606
SizeHiLo	1	0.1168935	0.1810571	0.646	0.5205	0.07475067	0.6182769
ChemLoHi	1	-0.29744	0.181641	-1.639	0.1053	-0.214951	0.4819957
ChemHiHi	1	-0.571222	0.2305802	-2.477	0.0155	-0.340733	0.4381286
ChemHiLo	1	-0.550889	0.1945993	-2.831	0.0059	-0.412717	0.3899451
MachLoHi	1	-0.406032	0.1781237	-2.279	0.0254	-0.259648	0.6388084
MachHiHi	1	-0.478721	0.1690051	-2.833	0.0059	-0.34604	0.5567642
MachHiLo	1	-0.68509	0.2124151	-3.225	0.0019	-0.428875	0.4687339

Appendix C

Table 3. Percent Unemployed in 1980

Analysis of Variance

Source	DF	Sum of Squares	Mean Square	F Value	Prob > F
Model	9	331.77	36.86334	5.775	0.0001
Error	76	485.1062	6.382977		
C Total	85	816.8762			

Root MSE	2.526455	R-Square	0.4061
Dep Mean	4.895975	ADJ R-Sq	0.3358
C.V.	51.6027		

Parameter Estimates

Variable	DF	Parameter Estimate	Standard Error	T for HO: Parameter = 0	Prob> |T|	Standardized Estimate	Tolerance
Intercep	1	4.405794	0.8785695	5.015	0.0001	0	
SizeLoHi	1	-2.25525	0.7705253	-2.927	0.0045	-0.323892	0.6380864
SizeHiHi	1	-1.95554	0.850987	-2.298	0.0243	-0.276847	0.5383606
SizeHiLo	1	-1.11102	0.8516843	-1.305	0.1960	-0.146652	0.6182769
ChemLoHi	1	0.07815207	0.854431	0.091	0.9274	0.01164596	0.4819957
ChemHiHi	1	3.675764	1.084639	3.392	0.0011	0.452949	0.4381286
ChemHiLo	1	3.73867	0.1945993	-2.831	0.0059	-0.412717	0.3899451
MachLoHi	1	0.6477781	0.8378858	0.773	0.4419	0.08550463	0.6388084
MachHiHi	1	-0.561466	0.7949923	-0.706	0.4822	-0.0836678	0.5567642
MachHiLo	1	-0.552286	0.9991913	-0.553	0.5821	-0.0713651	0.4687339

Variable	DF	Variable Label
Intercep	1	Intercept
V10	1	1978 Avg. Size of Farms (Acres)

352

Appendix C

Table 4. 1970–1980 Change in Percent of Families Below Poverty

Analysis of Variance

Source	DF	Sum of Squares	Mean Square	F Value	Prob > F
Model	9	0.6206672	0.06896304	2.713	0.0086
Error	76	1.931825	0.02541876		
C Total	85	2.552493			

Root MSE	0.1594326	R–Square	0.2432
Dep Mean	-0.184118	ADJ R–Sq	0.1535
C.V.	-86.5928		

Parameter Estimates

Variable	DF	Parameter Estimate	Standard Error	T for HO: Parameter = 0	Prob> ITI	Standardized Estimate	Tolerance
Intercep	1	-0.3903	0.05544325	-7.040	0.0001	0	
SizeLoHi	1	0.03607772	0.0486242	0.742	0.4604	0.09269191	0.6380864
SizeHiHi	1	0.1056988	0.05370175	1.968	0.0527	0.2676947	0.5383606
SizeHiLo	1	0.06737564	0.05374575	1.254	0.2138	0.1590971	0.6182769
ChemLoHi	1	0.08613006	0.05391908	1.597	0.1143	0.2296072	0.4819957
ChemHiHi	1	0.1370836	0.06844642	2.003	0.0488	0.3019457	0.4381286
ChemHiLo	1	0.1422494	0.05776569	2.463	0.0161	0.3935262	0.3899451
MachLoHi	1	0.03538969	0.052875	0.669	0.5053	0.08356722	0.6388084
MachHiHi	1	0.110486	0.05016819	2.202	0.0307	0.2945357	0.5567642
MachHiLo	1	0.07593959	0.06305422	1.204	0.2322	0.1755439	0.4687339

Variable	DF	Variable Label
Intercep	1	Intercept
V10	1	1978 Avg. Size of Farms (Acres)

Table 5. Unrelated Individuals in Poverty in 1980

Analysis of Variance

Source	DF	Sum of Squares	Mean Square	F Value	Prob > F
Model	9	533.744	59.30489	1.791	0.0834
Error	76	2517.228	33.12142		
C Total	85	3050.972			

Root MSE	5.755121	R-Square	0.1749
Dep Mean	14.64419	ADJ R-Sq	0.0772
C.V.	39.2997		

Parameter Estimates

Variable	DF	Parameter Estimate	Standard Error	T for HO: Parameter = 0	Prob> |T|	Standardized Estimate	Tolerance
Intercep	1	11.90532	2.001331	5.949	0.0001	0	
SizeLoHi	1	3.477419	1.755213	1.981	0.0512	0.2584181	0.6380864
SizeHiHi	1	4.959341	1.9385	2.558	0.0125	0.363293	0.5383606
SizeHiLo	1	4.560217	1.940088	2.351	0.0213	0.311464	0.6182769
ChemLoHi	1	-0.490045	1.946345	-0.252	0.8019	-0.0377859	0.4819957
ChemHiHi	1	0.8277767	2.470746	0.335	0.7385	0.05273752	0.4381286
ChemHiLo	1	4.129687	2.085198	1.980	0.0513	0.3304482	0.3899451
MachLoHi	1	-0.380831	1.908656	-0.200	0.8424	-0.0260108	0.6388084
MachHiHi	1	-2.94061	1.810947	-1.624	0.1086	-0.226741	0.5567642
MachHiLo	1	-4.46371	2.276101	-1.961	0.0535	-0.298453	0.4687339

Variable	DF	Variable Label
Intercep	1	Intercept
V10	1	1978 Avg. Size of Farms (Acres)

Table 6. 1970–1980 Change in Retail Establishments

Analysis of Variance

Source	DF	Sum of Squares	Mean Square	F Value	Prob > F
Model	9	1.573895	0.1748773	4.327	0.0002
Error	76	3.071372	0.04041279		
C Total	85	4.645267			

Root MSE	0.2010293	R-Square	0.3388
Dep Mean	-0.0849802	ADJ R-Sq	0.2605
C.V.	-236.56		

Parameter Estimates

Variable	DF	Parameter Estimate	Standard Error	T for HO: Parameter = 0	Prob> |T|	Standardized Estimate	Tolerance
Intercep	1	-0.0259542	0.06990752	-0.371	0.7115	0	
SizeLoHi	1	-0.150092	0.06131047	-2.448	0.0167	-0.285849	0.6380864
SizeHiHi	1	-0.167292	0.06771278	-2.471	0.0157	-0.314067	0.5383606
SizeHiLo	1	0.1048696	0.06776827	1.547	0.1259	0.1835632	0.6182769
ChemLoHi	1	-0.669197	0.06798682	-0.984	0.3281	-0.13224	0.4819957
ChemHiHi	1	0.0596876	0.08630442	0.692	0.4913	0.09745538	0.4381286
ChemHiLo	1	0.03970031	0.07283703	0.545	0.5873	0.08141305	0.3899451
MachLoHi	1	0.02071585	0.06667033	0.311	0.7569	0.03626092	0.6388084
MachHiHi	1	-0.647526	0.0632573	-1.024	0.3093	-0.127957	0.5567642
MachHiLo	1	0.06664273	0.07950536	0.838	0.4045	0.114195	0.4687339

Variable	DF	Variable Label
Intercep	1	Intercept
V10	1	1978 Avg. Size of Farms (Acres)

Appendix C

Table 7. 1970–1980 Change in Retail Sales Volume

Analysis of Variance

Source	DF	Sum of Squares	Mean Square	F Value	Prob > F
Model	9	81.39561	9.043957	3.839	0.0005
Error	76	179.0396	2.355784		
C Total	85	260.4352			

Root MSE	1.534856	R-Square	0.3125
Dep Mean	3.781324	ADJ R-Sq	0.2311
C.V.	40.59045		

Parameter Estimates

Variable	DF	Parameter Estimate	Standard Error	T for HO: Parameter = 0	Prob> |T|	Standardized Estimate	Tolerance
Intercep	1	4.804703	0.533743	0.002	0.0001	0	
SizeLoHi	1	-1.05531	0.4681047	-2.254	0.0271	-0.268419	0.6380864
SizeHiHi	1	-0.777816	0.5169863	-1.505	0.1366	-0.19502	0.5383606
SizeHiLo	1	1.204823	0.5174099	2.329	0.0225	0.2816534	0.6182769
ChemLoHi	1	-1.11936	0.5190786	-2.156	0.342	-0.295421	0.4819957
ChemHiHi	1	-0.189603	0.6589332	-0.288	0.7743	-0.0413449	0.4381286
ChemHiLo	1	-0.365245	0.6589332	-0.657	0.5133	-0.100032	0.3899451
MachLoHi	1	-0.20509	0.5090272	-0.403	0.6881	-0.0479443	0.6388084
MachHiHi	1	-0.586039	0.4829688	-1.213	0.2287	-0.154664	0.5567642
MachHiLo	1	-0.391146	0.6070225	-0.628	0.5320	-0.087225	0.4687339

Variable	DF	Variable Label
Intercep	1	Intercept
V10	1	1978 Avg. Size of Farms (Acres)